INVEST IN YOUR FINANCIAL LITERACY

INVEST IN YOUR FINANCIAL LITERACY

A GUIDE FOR FINANCIAL DECISION-MAKING

FIRST EDITION

J. Ian Norris And Nancy Sowers

Berea College

cognella

SAN DIEGO

Bassim Hamadeh, CEO and Publisher
Jennifer Codner, Senior Field Acquisitions Editor
Carrie Baarns, Manager, Revisions and Author Care
Anne Jones, Project Editor
Susana Christie, Senior Developmental Editor
Celeste Paed, Associate Production Editor
Jess Estrella, Senior Graphic Designer
JoHannah McDonald, Licensing Coordinator
Stephanie Adams, Senior Marketing Program Manager
Natalie Piccotti, Director of Marketing
Kassie Graves, Senior Vice President, Editorial
Jamie Giganti, Director of Academic Publishing

Printed in the United States of America.

CONTENTS

PREFACE

What do Oprah Winfrey and Warren Buffet have in common? Not much, it would seem. One of them is a well-known celebrity who built a multimedia television and print empire from humble beginnings as a TV news anchor. And the other? Well, you might not even know him. He lives in Omaha, Nebraska, a long way from Hollywood, in a modest but tasteful house he purchased in 1958. While Oprah Winfrey is interviewing the most popular and influential people in the country and attending star-studded parties, Buffet is reading the *Wall Street Journal* and attending stuffy company board meetings with people who are quite likely a lot less interesting.

What do Curt Schilling and MC Hammer have in common? Perhaps a bit more, it would seem. Both of them achieved top celebrity status in the 1990s in their respective arenas—Schilling as a cutthroat fastballer and MVP with the Boston Red Sox, and Hammer as the reigning king of popular hip-hop for a brief but glorious time. Both graced the covers of popular magazines, such as *Sports Illustrated* and *Rolling Stone*. Both were loved by their many fans around the world. And both of them made a great deal of money.

Perhaps what makes them even more similar, though, is that they lost it all even more quickly. Schilling lost nearly all of the $115 million he earned over his playing career in a video game company built on a shaky business model and a get-rich-quick strategy. The company filed for bankruptcy in 2012. Hammer spent every penny he earned between 1991 and 1996—somewhere around $50 million—on luxury automobiles, racehorses, a California mansion, and a 200-person entourage. By 1996 he was $13 million in debt and filing for bankruptcy.

Schilling and Hammer join the storied ranks of those whose stars burn bright but fade fast. They are not alone—unfortunately, such tales of financial misfortune are too common among celebrities, athletes, entertainers, and business owners who make great sums of money in short periods of time. Curt Schilling and MC Hammer prove the point that, while you have to make money to have money, making money is not enough to keep it. What you do with it matters more. And while there are a ton of ways to lose money, this book will teach you that there is only one real way to make it: through a long-term focus on sustainable saving, spending, and investment habits.

Back to Oprah and Warren. Today, Oprah Winfrey is worth $2.7 billion. Oprah began earning this fortune in the early 1990s, around the same time that Schilling and Hammer did. Unlike them, however, she planned carefully for the future, slowly adding a magazine and a television network to her media portfolio, while balancing the risk and reward of these investments.

Warren Buffet is worth about thirty-five times that, around $100 billion. Like many in the finance industry, he is extraordinarily wealthy. In fact, he is one of the richest people in the world. Like Oprah Winfrey, he has planned for the future, spent wisely, and carefully balanced the risk and reward of his investments. While this is not the only reason for his extraordinary wealth, his company, Berkshire Hathaway, is currently worth $660 billion. A single share of their stock costs $433,000. In 1990, a single share was worth about $6,000, which is about a 7,100 percent increase in value over thirty years. Had Schilling and Hammer invested just *half* of what they earned in the prime of their careers with Berkshire, their investments would be worth about $2.4 billion and $1 billion today, respectively. Instead, each is reported to have a net worth of about $1 million.

That is no small sum, to be sure. But you don't need to be a star pitcher or famous musical artist to make a million dollars. In fact, you will learn in this book that any working stiff like you or me who is making a middle-class salary can expect to accrue a net worth of at least $1 million, and probably much more, by planning for the future, spending wisely, and carefully balancing the risk and reward of your investments.

This probably sounds like a lot of money. It probably sounds like it will take a long time. You may only be able to save $50 a month right now, or $100 when you take your first job. It probably seems as though you will never get there. But because you are reading this book, you have an enormous advantage over all the other working stiffs out there, like me, who didn't start saving money until they actually decided they needed to learn something about money, which wasn't soon enough.

Warren Buffet is wealthy because he has planned carefully, spent wisely, and balanced the risk and reward of his investments. He is extraordinarily wealthy because he happens to be a particularly good investor. He is one of the richest people in the world, though, because he has an extra advantage. And while you may not care to ever become an expert investor yourself, Buffet's greatest advantage of all is one that you also have on your side.

Warren Buffet is very, very old. And he started saving and investing when he was very, very young.

You have time on your side. If you follow the advice in this book, plan for the future, spend wisely, and balance the risk and reward of your investments, time will take care of everything else.

This book is not exclusively about investment in the financial sense. It is about investing in your financial future, from the time you graduate college and land your first paying gig to the time you retire and beyond. Ultimately, it's less about investing in stocks and bonds than it is about investing in yourself—your hobbies, your interests, and the security of your family.

Investment begins with saving, and saving begins with smart spending and borrowing. Spending begins with earning, and earning begins with smart choices about what to study, where to live, and how to work. This is where we start: from the beginning. Long-term sustainable investments are built on a solid foundation, and because this is your financial future, that solid foundation is you—your skills, goals, values, and good financial habits.

A personal note from Ian. This book does not assume you know much about finance. I know what it is like to be a young college graduate staring into the financial void with trepidation. This book also doesn't assume you already have good financial habits or know how to create them. Like many young people, I made nearly all of the mistakes that I have written about in this book to help keep others from repeating them. I took out too many student loans, without paying much attention to interest rates or repayment terms. I studied psychology, a field I love dearly, but without paying much attention to what my career options might be with the degree, or to which other areas of study might best supplement my value on the job market. I obtained a PhD and decided to become an academic, knowing almost nothing about the competitiveness of the academic market or the typical salaries of college professors. While in graduate school, I racked up a good deal of credit card debt and nearly quit school as a result. Much of this debt went to the local beer store and to Whataburger, like it does for many students, as a result of poor budgeting and personal care habits.

When I got my first academic job at twenty-nine, I sat down in bewilderment with Human Resources to talk about health insurance and retirement plans and realized just how inadequately prepared I was to make these seemingly monumental decisions. At this age, many of my peers had already been working for seven to ten years or so, having amassed some savings and bought a home. Meanwhile, I was sitting on a $1,000 credit card bill for my U-Haul trip from Texas and no savings in the bank. The 400-page retirement guide in my hands may as well have been written in another language. I couldn't tell the difference between a high-deductible health insurance plan and a high-dividend-yield ETF. Then I got my first paycheck. And paid my first student loan bill.

At that moment, I decided I needed to learn something about finance. Being an academic, I didn't go to AskJeeves.com—a good thing, considering our internet search options in those days. I didn't go to the local bookstore either, which was ***not*** named Amazon and was actually made of bricks. I enrolled in Economics and Accounting 101 at my university. As a brand-new assistant professor of psychology, I spent my nights sitting side-by-side with the same freshmen I taught during the day, learning things I should have learned when I was their age, if not sooner. This new knowledge was intoxicating. It was empowering. Learning takes on a whole new dimension when you are personally invested, so to speak. So I kept taking courses. Five years later, I had an MBA (and tenure!).

I now teach marketing at Berea College and help oversee the financial literacy program. I cowrote this book with my colleague in finance, Nancy Sowers, so you don't have to wait until you are twenty-nine to figure out what I should have learned sooner. I wrote this book so that perhaps you will make better financial choices and develop good financial habits without making some of the all-too-common mistakes that I made. And I wrote this book so that you do not have to obtain an MBA to learn how to read your paycheck stub or diversify your retirement portfolio.

A personal note from Nancy. The kernel of this book came from Ian's early experiences as a smart guy without the financial academic background in finance to make the best, personal financial choices. He calls his choices "mistakes," but let's face it, the choices are so complicated nowadays! There is almost too much information out there now, and it is often very difficult to distinguish between good advice and what is really an advertisement for a "get-rich-quick" scheme. I came to this book from a much more circumspect place. Ian asked me to write this book with him, to lend my expertise on the more financial aspects that needed to be covered, but in my own personal financial decisions, I operated with a hesitancy that marked every important decision. I was almost paralyzed with the typical choices in front of me. I was always so careful with my money and closely considered every financial decision I made with a ton of research and long conversations with my father. Decisions took me ages to make as I tried to figure out what was best.

Growing up, financial choices were a regular topic of discussion at the dinner table in my family. I remember my dad pulling out his three-ring notebooks of the investment research he did for investing in mutual funds. He would show me what he looked for when choosing his investments and he would repeatedly tell me, "No one looks after your money like you do." I am not certain the detail of these lessons really registered with me at the time, but they must have left an indelible impression because I majored in economics and went on to pursue a PhD in it. I remember that friends and family would ask me about the stock market, but my field was economic history, and I had no idea about the ways that investing worked in the stock market. On my first academic job teaching economics, the chair of the department knew my dissertation, about railroad organizations at the turn of the century, taught me a lot about financial statements and the manipulations a firm might do to hide bad financial results. He needed someone to teach the finance course in the business program and I agreed. I loved it! Soon my research revolved around corporate finance issues, and I dove into earning a charter in the Chartered Financial Analyst (CFA) program. I was hooked and have never looked back at the more traditional economic questions I used to ask.

Through my work as the other half of the academic team in the Personal Finance course at Berea College, I quickly realized that not everyone had the foundation in personal finance that my parents cultivated so actively with me and my little brother. When I was in college, no one taught personal finance; it was assumed that a good college degree would provide the critical thinking skills necessary for making good, personal financial decisions. But this presumption does not hold water anymore because the evidence is in and too many people do not make good financial choices without some dedicated exposure to the content. Further, how can you be expected to make good choices in this area if you never saw good decisions being made yourself? Not everyone has a detail-oriented, research scientist as a father! And, if we are being totally honest, you should not have to major in finance to understand the basics for making good financial choices. This book was born out of this belief.

We make a pretty good team for writing this kind of book. One of us is a consumer psychologist who has published research on decision-making, materialism, and consumer values. The other is an economist who teaches finance and has published research on the impact of corporate governance models on firm returns and the increased volatility of the stock markets in recent years. On the one hand, there are plenty of books out there about cool research findings in consumer psychology, but few that tell you what this means for your personal financial decision-making. On the other hand, there are lots of personal finance books out there, but most of them are more finance than personal. They bury you in finance terms and lists of options that can feel overwhelming for the young adult striving to make sense of it all. Our partnership allows us to write a book based on sound financial decision-making principles, but with lots of references to consumer research and the more psychological—and practical—aspects of saving, spending, and making decisions about money.

One final note about the structure and format of the book. You will notice that we use first-person "I" in our stories throughout the book. This makes the textbook style a little less formal and more relatable. We decided that trying to acknowledge whose story was whose was just too distracting for the reader. Thus, sometimes the "I" is Nancy, and sometimes it is Ian. The point is to learn from the stories and understand how to apply the situation to your own financial circumstances. Know that though each of us led the writing on different chapters, we both contributed extensively to all the chapters. We look forward to sharing our experiences and our expertise with you.

INTRODUCTION

This book follows the narrative journey of your financial life: from the decisions you will make about earning an income to the decisions you will make about retirement. The book is organized this way because each set of financial decisions will have an important impact on future decisions. For instance, the earning decisions you make now—with respect to what you choose to study in college, what kinds of jobs you hope to get, and what kinds of retirement benefits those jobs provide—will have an important impact on how much you decide to save, both for short-term purposes and for longer-term retirement goals. In turn, how much you are able to save will have an impact on how much you can budget for spending and what kinds of spending decisions you will make.

An important theme running through the book is that each of these decisions represents an *investment* of sorts. An investment is something that provides a greater return than it costs you to make. Too often, we think about money in a zero-sum sort of way—that is, money comes in, money goes out. The size of the money pie is static under this treatment. Earning represents a positive change in our financial worth, and spending represents a negative change in our financial worth. But the more you can think about earning and spending as financial investments, the more successful you will be at increasing the size of your wealth through the choices made. For instance, if you make good earning decisions, you will earn enough to save more later, which will allow you to realize a greater return on these savings. Your financial decisions make the money pie bigger. If you spend in a way that maximizes your happiness while maintaining your financial security, then you have decided to invest in your well-being, and that makes the money pie bigger. And so on. A bigger money pie means more personal financial wealth.

The book assumes that you are either a high school student thinking about college or a college student thinking about starting your career. It is equally well suited to any young working adult with or without a college degree, although you may wish to skip the small sections on college majors and areas of study if they are not relevant to you. The book is guided by a philosophy of long-term, sustainable saving, spending, and investing: there is no get-rich-quick scheme here. Get rich quick means go broke fast. If you are starting young, you don't need to get rich quick. You already have the greatest asset for long-term financial success at your disposal—time.

The first chapter of the book, "The Decision to Be Financially Literate," is about the decision you have made to take charge of your financial life and develop financial literacy. It will introduce you to some basic financial terms and concepts that will help you understand later topics, such as saving and investing. Most important among these is the *time value of money* concept. Time is money, and money is time. Understand this now, and everything else will fall into place. And don't worry, math and jargon will be kept to a minimum. This book is about creating good financial habits, not about finance in the academic sense. Creating good financial habits, and creating them early on, is as much about psychology as finance, and psychologists have learned a great deal of interesting things about the way people behave with money. Because this book is organized around the important financial decisions you will make over the course of your life, it is important to understand how we think and make decisions about money more generally, in order to understand how to make good financial decisions in particular.

The next chapter, "The Decision to Earn," is about how to make money and how to understand the money that you are making. Not in the stock market or your million-dollar bedroom startup company, but just in the practice of working for a living. A key point of this chapter is that it doesn't really matter what your college major is or how much money you make. Although some college majors clearly prepare graduates for higher-paying jobs than others, many jobs that pay somewhat lower salaries, such as those in public service professions, provide excellent benefits that should be thought of as part of your overall compensation. Furthermore, where and how you choose to live matter nearly as much as how much money you make. Forty-thousand dollars in Waco, Texas, is not the same thing as $40,000 in Miami, Florida—or even $60,000 in Miami, for that matter.

Having begun to earn, you will now begin to consider "The Decision to Save." In this chapter, you will learn how to make saving a lifelong habit that is as natural as spending on groceries and rent. You will learn how to think about saving broadly, rather than thinking of a pile of money sitting somewhere in a savings account. This, in fact, is not a terribly effective way to save. Saving can come in the form of tax benefits for health care spending and investing for retirement, and there are many different vehicles that can be used for this purpose. In this chapter, you will learn how to compare savings vehicles to each other, differentiating a 401(k) from a CD and a stock from a bond.

Now you can make "The Decision to Spend." That's right—by the philosophy of this book, only after making money and establishing a habit of saving should you think about spending any money at all. This chapter will cover basic household budgeting. It will also provide some data on what kinds of expenditures tend to get people into trouble and why. It will provide you with tips on how to spend less, and, more importantly, how to save more. Perhaps most importantly, you will learn that much, if not most, of what we spend has little to do with our material security needs, such as housing, clothing, and food. Rather, it has more to do with our emotional and psychological needs. Understanding the motives that drive your own spending habits will help you make better spending decisions that maximize your happiness and well-being.

Unfortunately, some of the greatest investments that you will make in your life might have to be leveraged—that is, purchased with borrowed money. Houses, cars, and college degrees don't come cheap, and if you were only to purchase them after saving to pay for them in full, you would likely never reap the benefits of obtaining them. In "The Decision to Owe," you will learn that there is nothing inherently wrong with debt. Borrowing money for things that will provide a return on your investment is sound financial planning. A college degree, for instance, should be an investment in your financial future. In this chapter, you will learn about how mortgages are structured and how credit cards work, among other topics. You will also learn that credit card usage, while not to be avoided, is best thought of as a *spending* decision, not a method for borrowing.

Few people will retire comfortably without taking advantage of the financial power of the stock market. The good news, though, is that you do not have to be an expert investor in order to benefit from strong and stable market returns. In the chapter "The Decision to Own Shares," you will learn about various investment strategies, including some simple ways that you can invest in the stock market in a relatively safe way, even if you are not particularly interested in developing a great deal of investing expertise or following markets closely. Nevertheless, this book assumes that investing is for everyone. You will learn the basic language and tools that you will need to evaluate stocks, should you be interested in taking the next step as an active investor. Perhaps most importantly, in this chapter you will learn about how to adjust your investment strategy over the course of your lifetime and how to account for your own risk tolerance.

The last chapter, "The Decision to Retire," is about drawing on the various investments you have made over the course of your life to achieve financial independence. While it likely seems very far off, making good financial decisions now will make retirement decisions forty years from now much, much easier, and knowing a little about finances in retirement will help you make those decisions now.

You will likely want to achieve financial independence so that you can have and do the things you love when you finally have few constraints on your time and few other financial responsibilities, such as a mortgage or college tuition, to pay. But you will also want to achieve financial independence so you can leave something of value behind—financial or otherwise. Not even Carnegie, Vanderbilt, or Bill Gates, for that matter, could/can take their massive fortunes with them. Luckily for us, today we have access to libraries, universities, or foundations in their names. While it would be nice to see your name gracing a gleaming new performance hall one day, it is never too early to think about your financial impact on the world. Many of you will leave children or partners behind. You will be members of churches and community organizations. You will be alumni of college and graduate institutions. You will have a love of the arts or of nature, or a strong desire to provide for the disadvantaged. In this way, developing a sustainable, long-term savings strategy can be a critical component of living a life that is consistent with your value system.

Ideally, the ultimate return on your investments is one that allows you to give back. If you know and understand your value system now, you can make the kinds of financial decisions that will allow you to give even more than you have received over the course of your financial journey. Maybe it is hard to imagine having enough money to give back to society, when you are a college student living on frozen pizza or a young adult trying to save for a down payment on your first house or a young parent paying for childcare. That's a good thing. That means you have time on your side. The more distant this goal seems, the more likely it is that you will get there.

Financial literacy is about making good financial decisions. You have already made the most important decision in getting this book. Congratulations on making the choice to take charge of your financial future.

CHAPTER 1

The Decision to Be Financially Literate

Invest in Your Education

Imagine...

After you win a bet over a recent sports game, your friend owes you $100. Just before handing over the cash, your friend makes a desperate last-minute attempt to get out of it, offering you double or nothing. You get to call a coin toss, and if you win, you will get $200. But if you lose—nothing. Your friend keeps the money.

Would you take this bet?

As you consider the offer, imagine that the tables are turned. You lost the bet, and you owe your friend $100. Would you make the same desperate, last-minute offer to hang on to your precious, hard-earned cash—with a 50 percent chance to erase the debt—or lose $200?

Whatever your tolerance for risk, if you are like most people, you feel a bit differently about each of these scenarios. In fact, even if you are a risk-taker, you might feel a little more hesitant to gamble in the first case, when you are up $100. And even if you are more conservative, you might feel a little more tempted when you are down $100. This discovery, by the Nobel Prize-winning psychologists Danny Kahneman and economist Amos Tversky,[1] has revolutionized the understanding of how people think about money. The next few pages will share these and other insights with you and demonstrate just how important it is ***to understand how we think about money to make financially literate decisions.***

Introduction

Making smart financial choices **is not** hard, but thinking about money **is**.

1. Daniel Kahneman and Amos Tversky, "Prospect Theory: An Analysis of Decision under Risk," *Econometrica* 47, no. 2 (1979): 263–92.

The internet is filled with headlines suggesting that Americans are ***not financially literate***—they do not demonstrate the knowledge or skills needed for achieving financial goals like home ownership and stable retirement. *Forbes* tells us that "Financial Literacy Is More Essential Than Ever,"[2] and *Market Watch* argues that "Financial Literacy Skills Have Taken a Nose Dive since the Great Recession."[3] The lack of financial wellness can be blamed on financial behaviors, our own and those we see from our family members. Our habits are established early by what we see around us and, without any education in personal finance, they can become ingrained. If that were not enough, economic volatility and the costs of things like education and healthcare have consistently outpaced our wages. This makes money management more challenging for young people as they move toward adulthood.

Perhaps beyond knowledge, skills, and the questions of basic financial decisions, however, two bigger issues loom for all of us. The first is the widening gap between the haves and the have-nots. A Charles Schwab survey found that respondents ranked financial literacy education as more needed in our schools than health education, college planning, career development, and so on.[4] Much of the literature on financial literacy shows that underserved communities and women in general struggle with financial decision basics. Financial illiteracy perpetuates social inequalities among households today. This must be fixed.

The second issue raised in assessing Americans' financial literacy is confidence and motivation issues around financial decision-making. So much about making basic financial decisions involves having the confidence to do so. A practical, decision-driven financial education can fix this. Understanding the ways that the psychology of money and traditional financial behaviors undermine good decision-making is the first step towards the financial literacy we all deserve.

Chapter Objectives

After reading this chapter, you will be able to:

- Understand basic principles of judgment and decision-making—with respect to risk, probability, and mathematical thinking—that can thwart financial literacy.
- Apply these insights in financial behavior and habits to sound financial decision-making.

2. Mayra Rodriguez Valladares, "Financial Literacy Is More Essential Than Ever," *Forbes*, December 15, 2020, https://www.forbes.com/sites/mayrarodriguezvalladares/2020/12/15/financial-literacy-is-more-essential-than-ever/?sh=cfc5b796304f.
3. Andrew Keshner, "Financial Literacy Skills Have Taken a Nose Dive since the Great Recession," Market Watch, June 27, 2019, https://www.marketwatch.com/story/americans-financial-literacy-skills-have-plummeted-since-the-great-recession-2019-06-26.
4. Carrie Schwab-Pemerantz, "Americans Want Financial Literacy ... Now!" Charles Schwab, September 2, 2020, https://www.schwab.com/resource-center/insights/content/americans-want-financial-literacy-now.

OK, Why Is It So Hard to Think about Money? I Think about Money All the Time!

A bat and ball cost $1.10 together. The bat costs $1.00 more than the ball. How much does the ball cost?

If you are like most people, you immediately thought $.10. Think again. If the bat costs $1.00 more than $.10, it must cost $1.10. This would mean they cost $1.20 together.

To solve the problem, you must take the remaining difference—the $.10 difference—and split it evenly between the bat and the ball. That makes the bat $1.05, and the ball $.05. However, this is not obvious, and it is certainly not intuitive.

Let's try another one. It takes forty-eight days for a lake to be completely covered in lily pads. Every day, the number of lily pads doubles. In how many days will the lake be halfway covered in lily pads?

If you said twenty-four days, you are wrong. The answer is forty-seven days, only one day less than the total number of days to fill the space of the lake—on the last day, the number of lily pads will double, ensuring full coverage on day forty-eight. The problem in this case is linear thinking. We can't simply halve the number of days because doubling is an exponential function. The gut reaction we had, to choose twenty-four days, is critical to understanding how we think about money. When you save money—earning some rate of return, expressed as a percentage—your savings will grow exponentially, as you will see in multiple ways over the next few chapters.

These example puzzles come from a psychological measure known as the Cognitive Reflection Test.[5] The test demonstrates that our quick, intuitive judgments are often wrong, even for problems that seem relatively simple. Now, in retrospect, the correct answers are surely obvious—and congratulations if you got them right the first time! These two items from the test were chosen because they do a good job of illustrating that we are not particularly good at thinking about money. Our brains are remarkable machines; however, they are specialized for survival, not algebra. But just as the answers are obvious with a little reflection, ***anyone*** can learn how to approach financial decisions better, with some key insights in place.

The link between emotion and money is very strong. As Kahneman and Tversky have shown in a number of different contexts, one important driver for people is a phenomenon known as *loss aversion*.[6] Simply put, losses hurt more than gains—about twice as much, in fact. Another way of saying this is that it would take a gain of $200 to compensate us adequately for the pain of losing $100. Most of us do not like risk very much; we are ***averse to risk***.

This observation means we think very differently about gains and losses. When we stand to gain something, we prefer a sure thing. We don't want to roll the dice and risk losing out, because losses hurt more than equivalent gains cause pleasure. In many ways, this is highly adaptive. It keeps most of us from making risky decisions like leaving a secure job every time a new opportunity comes along or gambling away our life savings at the horse track. But such loss aversion can be costly as well. For instance, it might explain

5. Shane Frederick, "Cognitive Reflection and Decision Making," *Journal of Economic Perspectives* 19, no. 4 (2005): 25–42.
6. For a very accessible version of the ideas here, see Daniel Kahneman, Thinking, Fast and Slow (New York: Macmillan, 2011). See also Amos Tversky and Daniel Kahneman, "Loss Aversion in Riskless Choice: A Reference-Dependent Model," *The Quarterly Journal of Economics* 106, no. 4 (1991): 1039–61.

why many people keep their savings in bank accounts that offer low interest rates instead of investing their money in the stock market, which is riskier, especially over the short run, but can provide much higher returns in the long run.

In fact, the cases in which we are likely to be a little more tolerant of risk are specifically those situations in which risky strategies can be the most damaging. The pain of loss can be so great that once its initial shock is felt, we can be numb to the pain of additional losses. In the example above, for instance, the difference between losing nothing and losing $100 is much greater than the difference between losing $100 and losing $200. As a result, people are often more motivated to erase the initial loss than to avoid the additional one. This can lead to the kind of behavior known in gambling circles as "going for broke." One reason that gambling is so addictive is that the impulse to continue placing larger and increasingly risky bets gets stronger when you are in the hole. Gamblers want to win, no doubt. But even more so, they want to ***not lose***. And to our brains, winning and losing are not opposites—they are two different things.

Clearly, loss aversion has a number of important implications for how we think about saving and investing, which this book will explore more specifically in chapter 3, "The Decision to Save," and chapter 6, "The Decision to Own Shares." Loss aversion also has a number of important implications for spending, as discussed in chapter 4, "The Decision to Spend." Findings from gambling scenarios such as the one above, for instance, demonstrate that the way we think about money is relative—it depends on the context. It depends on the alternative outcome in question (double or nothing?) and on the reference point (gain or loss?).

Consider a different scenario: how would you feel about winning $10? Seems obvious, right? Most of us would feel pretty good about such an outcome. But what if the alternative was winning $25? What if you expected to win $25 but only won $10? Would you feel the same? Would it feel the same as expecting to *lose* $25 but only losing $10?

Like the gambling scenario, this one can be run in reverse. Losing $10 would be no fun, especially if you expected to win $25. But what if you expected to lose $25? Would it be so bad then? In fact, some research evidence suggests that losing $10 in this case might actually be a mildly pleasant experience for some people, perhaps even more pleasant than *winning* $10 (!) when you could have won even more.[7] Psychologically, if you expect to lose $25, losing only $10 may even make you feel like you "won" $15.

Once again, such scenarios illustrate the fact that our thinking about money is highly *context-sensitive*. Marketers capitalize on this. Would you spend $40 on a new pair of Levi's? You would probably find it a lot easier to do so if they were on sale, and if they typically cost $50. That would be almost like getting $10! On the other hand, you probably would *not* spring for a $40 pair of Levi's if you learned that they are usually only $30.

The takeaway point is that although money has a clear *objective* value, we don't always compute this value *subjectively* in a way that corresponds to its objective value. In some ways, this can be adaptive; it might make us feel better when bad things happen to us, if we are able to see how they could have been worse. The key idea for understanding your financial literacy is that our natural tendencies to think in this way won't often lead to better financial decision-making and longer-term financial security.

7. Barbara Mellers and Peter A. McGraw, "Anticipated Emotions as Guides to Choice," *Current Directions in Psychological Science* 10 (2001): 210–15.

Longer-Term Financial Security? I Want It All, and I Want It Now!

We have seen that our emotions play a pretty big role when we are making financial choices. Sometimes our initial reaction will allow our hearts to rule our minds. We react quickly because our bodies are made to *survive*, but we now live in a world where we want to do more than survive; we want to *thrive*. Further, we want to *thrive over the long run*. To do this, our mind must balance out the pull of the heart. Consider the following scenarios in the textbox below.

DO YOU FOLLOW YOUR HEAD OR YOUR HEART?

- A child asks for a piece of candy from the Easter basket. The parents give their child a choice between having one piece now, but no more for the rest of the day, or eating dinner first and then having two pieces of candy from the basket.
- A good friend is turning twenty-one tonight. You know that many of your classmates will be at the party. Unfortunately, you have a statistics exam at 8 a.m. the next morning. You currently have a C in the class, and this exam could make the difference between a D or a B in your final grade.
- You just finished paying the final $200 on your six-year-old Toyota Corolla car payment. Of course, you've been driving it for six years now, and you make a few hundred more per month than you did when you purchased it on your initial salary right out of college. Your boss drives a Lexus and is not that much older than you. Should you upgrade a bit? Maybe not to a Lexus, but to a Camry at least? Of course, if you were to invest the $200 and keep driving the Corolla for free for a few more years, perhaps you could easily afford the Lexus with the down payment you would be able to make from capital gains on the investment.

These typical scenarios at various stages of the lifespan all illustrate the same eternal conflict. It is the conflict we face between the head and the heart—our struggle to delay gratification in the service of some greater goal. Just as our brain is specialized to hold on to what we have and avoid the pain of loss, it is equally well-specialized for prizing *now* over *later*.

Imagine you are given an offer: $100 today or $110 a year from now?

If you are like most people, you will prefer the $100 now. Or, at least, it will prove very hard to resist! You probably know exactly what you would do with that $100 now. Perhaps there is a new video game you have been waiting to buy, or a new pair of boots you have had your eye on. Perhaps you even have an overdue bill to pay, or desperately need to replace your front brakes.

What will you need a year from now? That is much harder to envision. Perhaps you can convince yourself that your need is greater now than it will be then. That should be easy to do, particularly if you really do have pressing money concerns. But the *now* preference is selected because contemplating the ways the money might be used now makes it real, tangible, and *emotional*. In the distance, what can be done with the money *later* is an abstraction. A concept that exists in theory, but not in reality.

Of course, you might recognize this offer as essentially a 10 percent return on investment, which, by the way, is excellent—particularly when combined with a 100 percent rate of certainty! A 10 percent annual return on a stock investment is highly desirable to a typical investor. Expert investors can and do receive much higher rates of return, but they also risk losing (and sometimes do lose) a lot in the process.

The bias built into the system is easily identified when we shift the time frame a bit. Imagine you were offered a choice between $100 one month from now or $110 thirteen months from now. Perhaps it would be a little bit easier to take the second option. Contemplating receiving that amount a month from now makes it just abstract enough that we can think a bit more rationally, without the rush of positive energy that comes from thinking about what we would do if we had that money *now*.

This phenomenon, known in economics as *temporal discounting* (valuing things less when they are far from us in time), is perhaps the single greatest barrier to your personal financial security. Nobody gets rich quick—at least, not without taking on a level of risk that is too great for most people on middle-class incomes with an eye toward retirement to consider. Getting wealthy will take commitment to delayed gratification, and this means the need for time. A long time. To delay the money now often means asserting the head over the heart and not getting lost in the math of compounding.

Some of you might recognize the Halloween candy scenario from the text above as what has become known in psychology as the marshmallow test. In the 1960s, psychologist Walter Mischel brought children into the laboratory and put a marshmallow on a plate in front of them. They were told they could eat it then, or they could wait and receive two instead. The researcher then left the room.[8]

Mischel tracked the participants in his study years later. Remarkably, children who were able to delay gratification to receive the greater reward had higher grades, better test scores, and jobs with higher incomes, among other things. Apparently, the ability to resist temptation is highly adaptive, and it comes along with the potential to pursue any number of greater, long-term goals.

There is a bit of an update to the story. It is often assumed that such self-control is largely biological. Some people have it, and others don't—dooming them to a cycle of ineffective diets, poor fitness habits, and empty savings accounts. More recent research suggests, though, that this might not be the case. In a replication of the original marshmallow study, researchers introduced a condition in which the researcher was unreliable. The children were made a promise that the researcher did not fulfill. In this situation, many more children chose immediate gratification.[9] Perhaps they did not trust the researcher to return with the two marshmallows, so they made the adaptive decision to consume now. After all, there might not be more later.

The lesson is this: we have all seen successful people who seem like they have had it made their whole lives. They coast through school, get into great colleges, and land high-paying jobs. Then they marry people just like them and have kids who do the same thing.

8. Walter Mischel, *The Marshmallow Test: Understanding Self-Control and How to Master It* (New York: Little, Brown, 2014).

9. Celeste Kidd, Holly Palmeri, and Richard N. Aslin, "Rational Snacking: Young Children's Decision-Making on the Marshmallow Task is Moderated by Beliefs about Environmental Reliability," Cognition 126, no. 1 (2013): 109–14.

If this person doesn't seem like you, or you don't think it could be, then you might feel like the odds are stacked against you. You may feel like the efforts to delay gratification are not worth it, because the future is uncertain. But this research should make you question that assumption. It shows that uncertainty in the environment can affect our sense of self-control, *for perfectly sensible reasons*. But more importantly, it shows that we are not slaves to our genetic destiny either. Those people who seem to have it easy may have the great advantage of growing up in predictable, secure environments. Their brains have been trained in such a way that it is beneficial to delay gratification, because the future rewards are great, and they are attainable. If you come from a family that had some financial insecurity or experienced any kind of uncertainty or unpredictably growing up, your brain may have been trained differently. You are not stuck though, because:

Financial illiteracy is not inherently biological ...

Anyone can learn the same habits that help financially successful people achieve their financial goals.

One major key to making financial success is to recognize that ***time is inextricably linked to money***. You may not have much of one, but you may have a lot of the other. Making use of what you do have is all you need to do to set the path towards financial security.

Wait ... I Am a College Student! What If I Don't Have Time *or* Money?

Fair point. College students are busy, in addition to often being broke! When it comes to money, however, time is on your side. Smart financial decision-making recognizes this and uses time to its best advantage.

Think back to that offer for $100. Do you want it now, or are you willing to wait a year for $110? We often talk about temporal discounting in the context of conflicts between the head and the heart. If reason prevails, you will wait for the greater return. If you give into temptation—if your feelings prevail—you will take the money now.

It is undoubtedly true that feelings matter for financial decision-making. In fact, we will talk extensively about the role of emotions throughout the book. That said, *it is not necessarily irrational* to take the $100 now. The fact is, with all else held constant, money now is worth more than money later. There are a few reasons why we temporally discount the future. The future is uncertain. Will we really get the promised return? Will the promised return tomorrow buy more than the lower amount buys us today? Let's explore this a bit.

One reason why money now is worth more than money later is that it loses value due to *inflation*. One dollar today will buy less than it did twenty years ago; likewise, it will buy more today than it will twenty years from now. In 1950, an average home cost about $15,000; a Ford automobile, $1,500; a gallon of gas, $.20. A dollar in 2020 was worth the equivalent of $10.85 in 1950. While many other things affect the cost of goods and services, simply because of inflation, we would expect homes, cars, and gasoline to cost at least ten times more in 2021 than they did in 1950.[10]

10. To get a feeling for all that this involves, go to the following CPI Inflation Calculator website: https://www.in2013dollars.com/us/inflation/1950. Ian Webster, "Value of 1950 Dollars Today--Inflation Calculator," February 10, 2021.

The average annual rate of inflation since 1950 is about 3.5 percent, for a total rate of about 1,000 percent, which is why things cost about ten times more in 2020 than they did back then. Inflation fluctuates over time and is influenced by a number of factors, including the global economy and government monetary policies. Inflation was extraordinarily high in the 1970s, for instance, but averaged less than 2 percent from 2010–2020.[11]

Inflation tends to be higher during periods of economic growth, so it is not necessarily a bad thing, just a necessary consequence of heightened economic productivity. As the economy in the United States has matured, most economists expect that inflation will be a bit lower over the coming decades—perhaps around 2–2.5 percent. Over the long term, however, it is almost guaranteed to occur.

Effectively, this means that each year, in very small amounts—even each day—your money is worth less than it was worth before. At a 2 percent rate of inflation, for instance, $10 will only be worth the equivalent of $9.80 the following year, largely as a function of the increasing costs of goods and services.

So, once again, in a very real sense, temporal discounting is adaptive. Your money *is* worth more to you now than later. How much more, though, we are not particularly good at determining. To forgo $110 a year from now is to forgo an interest rate of 10 percent, which is still an 8 percent return even after accounting for the 2 percent loss of value due to inflation.

Money now is worth more than money later, which is the first reason that *time and money* are so intimately connected. But this is as true for businesses, governments, banks, and investors as it is for you. These institutions need money to fund their operations to provide goods and services, and they can get this money from savers like you. To convince you to give up money now, they must compensate you in a way that offsets the value you lose by setting your money aside instead of spending it. Traditionally, this might come in the form of an interest payment, a dividend, or growth in the value of an investment. And most of the time, the longer you save, the higher the return you will make; this is the second reason that *time and money* are inseparable.

Historically, it has not been difficult to achieve a rate of return on your savings that is greater than the rate of inflation. Figure 1.1 below shows a dollar's growth over time in stocks, corporate bonds, and government Treasury bonds, against inflation.

11. World Bank, Inflation, consumer prices for the United States [FPCPITOTLZGUSA], FRED, Federal Reserve Bank of St. Louis. 2010-2021. https://fred.stlouisfed.org/series/FPCPITOTLZGUSA.

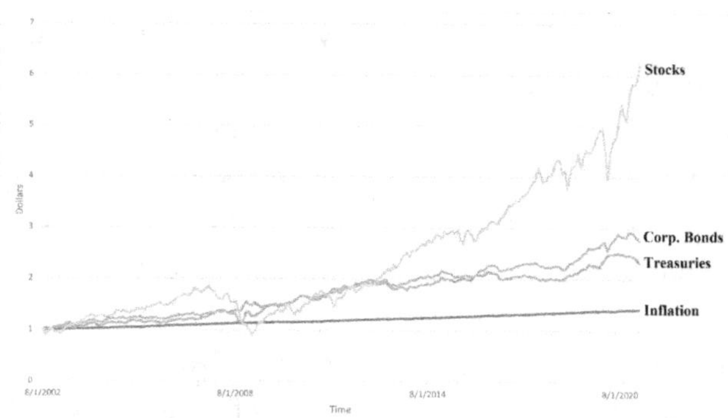

FIGURE 1.1 The Growth of $1 Invested/Saved across Time

There are a couple things to notice in the figure above. First, investing in stocks means that you do a lot better than inflation over time. Second, Treasuries and corporate bonds beat inflation, too. This is crucial because our investments/savings have to beat inflation. Notice, though, how much more the stock line moves around. You can see the huge drop the market took in 2020 when we first encountered the pandemic. That was a very bad day for investors in stock! If you panicked and sold your investments, you might have missed the rebound and felt a lot of regret. One major implication is that not all savings vehicles are the same, but time can take care of a lot of the risk you face due to the uncertainty of returns.

Finding the right savings vehicles or investments is thus the easy part. Admittedly, the delaying gratification part might be a bit harder. You will need to set money aside, and the sooner you start, the better. But if you start early, you might be surprised by just how much you can save over the long term. The key point:

If you have a long time before you retire, you don't need to put back as much money.

Who Wants to Be a Millionaire?

The average person likely needs $1.75 million to retire comfortably. Did your head just explode? Did I get your attention? Try not to run from the idea at this point because in your heart you know it sounds like a ridiculous amount of money. Stop. Breathe. Use your head. Typically, retirees will want to have 70–90 percent of preretirement income to live on for thirty years in retirement. We will explore what you, specifically, will need more carefully in chapter 3, "The Decision to Save," and chapter 7, "The Decision to Retire." But for right now, assume you will want over $1 million. The question becomes, how much do you think you would need to save, every month, to have a million dollars in forty years, after your working career?

When this question is asked in a classroom, the answers are as varied as you can imagine. Oftentimes, the responses are in the $2,000 range. Of course, if you think you have to save $2,000 a month for forty years to have a million dollars, you probably find the task laughably impossible. After all, that's $24,000 a year—half a typical college graduate's starting salary, before taxes.

In fact, $2,000 is roughly the amount you would need to save per month *if you were **not** considering the time value of money*. That is, saving $24,000 a year for forty years would leave you with $960,000 *at an* *interest rate of zero.* But if interest rates were zero, you would be better off spending your money, because setting it aside would mean steadily losing its value to inflation.

Now, many students understand that they will receive a return on their investment and try to take that into consideration when they answer the question about the amount of savings needed. Because of this, many responses tend to group together in the $500–$1,000 range. While this is closer to actuality, these amounts probably still sound extraordinarily high to someone anticipating take-home net pay of around $2,500 per month early in their career.

Relying on historical data, you could have saved *less than $200 per month* over the last forty years and had a million dollars today. Notice that this is only 10 percent of what you would need to save if you received *no return on your savings at all* ($2,000 per month)!

How is this possible? What this means is that most of that million dollars is not coming from the actual amount you are setting aside, or the *principal* amount. It is coming from investment returns, and, more importantly, *returns* on those *returns*. The process for earning interest on that principal is called ***compounding***, and it is the most important reason of all that *time and money are connected so integrally.*

Here is how it works. Imagine that you put $1,000 into an account that earns 5 percent annual interest. You probably determined right away that at the end of the year, you will receive a $50 interest payment, leaving you with $1,050. But how much will you have after two years? $1,100? Actually, you will have $1,102.50, or $2.50 more than that. Why this amount? In year one, you will receive 5 percent interest on the $1,000 principal. In year two, however, you will receive 5 percent on the $1,000 principal—another $50 on the original $1,000, but also 5 percent of the $50 interest payment. Look at the math:

$$\$1{,}000 \times 1.05 = \$1{,}050 \text{ at the end of year 1,}$$
$$\$1{,}050 \times 1.05 = \$1{,}102.50 \text{ at the end of year 2, or}$$
$$\$1{,}000 \times (1.05)^2 = \$1{,}102.50$$

An extra $2.50 may not seem like much. But over time, interest on interest can really accumulate. After nine years, your savings will be worth over $1,500. In fifteen years, it will have doubled to over $2,000. After forty years, your $1,000 will be worth over $7,000, all without adding a single dollar to the account, at a rate of return that, by historical standards, is pretty low. And the longer the period, the greater the rate of growth. Notice that it took nine years to increase by 50 percent to $1,500, but only another six years to increase by another $500 to over $2,000. Notice that the calculation in this example is very simple. Most people will save on a monthly basis, for instance, but time and money will interact in a similar way.

When you consider the fact that you will probably make continual monthly additions to your retirement savings, and quite likely achieve a higher rate of return than 5 percent per year, perhaps that million-dollar goal doesn't sound so unreasonable. Let's say that once you are working, you can save $200 from your paycheck each month. If we grow that $200 contribution at a range of returns, from 5 percent to 10 percent, you can compare likely savings outcomes. At 5 percent, savings will grow to $305,204, which is a lot more than the previous example suggested after forty years. The difference is regular and continuous contributions to your savings. But at 10 percent, savings accumulate to $1,264,815, which is over $1 million. Becoming a millionaire may not be so crazy after all!

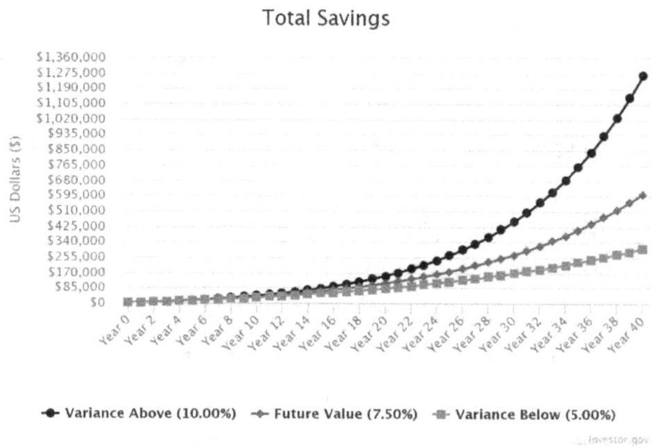

FIGURE 1.2 The Power of Compounding: $200 per Month, Forty Years, 5–10 Percent APR (Compounded Monthly)

The skeptic in you is now asking, "Is 10 percent a reasonable expectation though?" Over the last ninety years, the stock market has averaged near a 10 percent rate of return,[12] enough to turn $200 a month into over $1 million after forty years—a principal savings of just $96,000, without accounting for the time value of money. That is, over $1.1 million of the $1.2 million dollars will have come from interest compounding. It all starts with just $200 per month.

Now that I have convinced you that you can become a millionaire, a quick reality check is in order. The stock market does not provide returns in the form of steady, reliable interest payments. That 10 percent represents the average increase in market value over time. Of course, stocks are not guaranteed to increase in value, so you do take on some risk when investing in the stock market. As you will learn, however, this risk can be nearly completely mitigated by creating a long-term savings strategy. While individual company stocks can decrease significantly in value over short time frames, over the long term, the stock market as a whole—including the gains and losses in the stock values of thousands of companies—has only gained in value, on average, over time.

That said, a 10 percent rate of growth may be higher than anticipated in the future. For one thing, you will likely not save all your money in the stock market. Particularly as you get older, it will become prudent to adjust your savings strategy to invest in vehicles that are less risky but also provide lower returns. Additionally, for a variety of reasons, many economists do not believe that the stock market will perform quite as well over the next few decades as it has over the last few decades.[13]

12. The market is being measured here using the S&P 500 Index. See James Royal and Arielle O'Shea, "What Is the Average Stock Market Return?" NerdWallet, April 26, 2021, https://www.nerdwallet.com/article/investing/average-stock-market-return.

13. For one thing, the stock market has experienced a boom since about 2009 that lasted for eleven years, and though there was a sizeable market correction in 2020, the market bounced back quickly. Most financial economists lower their expected stock return forecast after significant market rises. See Ivo Welch, "Views of Financial Economists on the Equity Premium and on Professional Controversies," *The Journal of Business* 73, no. 4 (2000): 501–37.

For those of you who have a higher risk tolerance and plan to be aggressive in the stock market, perhaps 7.5 percent is a reasonable target. For those with less risk tolerance, 5 percent is an even more conservative target. With lower expected rates of return, you would have to save a bit more, of course. At an 7.5 percent rate of return, you would need to save approximately $330 per month instead of $200 to get your savings to $1 million dollars in forty years.

But you don't necessarily need to start at that amount of savings per month. If you were to start at $100 per month for four years and increase your savings by $100 per month every four years, you would easily achieve the same goal. The more money you can save earlier, the better, but time is the more critical factor. Smaller amounts of savings early on will be more than compensated for by the longer amount of time those savings have to grow.

To illustrate, imagine that you don't start saving right away. You may have $100 to save, but this hardly seems like enough to amount to much of anything, so you decide to wait until you make more money. Well, you will make more money. But you will also spend more money. Plan on buying a house? Better save for a down payment. Getting married? Will you need two cars? Might need to set aside $400 a month for a car payment. Having children? Will your partner be working? Count on $500–$1,000 per month for childcare for each child. Now they are in school; you'd better put that amount into their college fund. You may quickly find yourself forty and midcareer—making a good salary, yes, but no longer able to put off thinking about retirement.

How much will you need to save now to have a million dollars? You only have twenty years.

When I ask students this question before they understand compounding, they often take the $200 amount and double it. Half the amount of time means twice the amount of principal, right?

Wrong. Saving $400 a month for twenty years at a 10 percent annual percentage rate (but compounding monthly) will leave you with around $300,000—less than 30 percent of what you could have had if you had saved half that amount monthly but for twice as long. The difference is illustrated in figure 1.3.

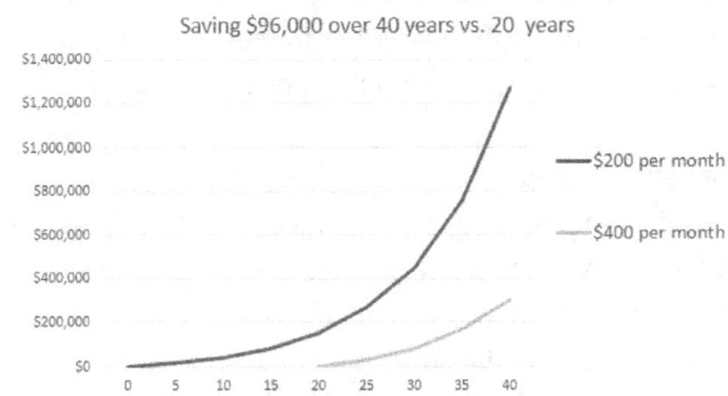

FIGURE 1.3 Saving $200 a Month for Forty Years Compared to $400 a Month Twenty Years Later

Of course, the amount of principal you saved hasn't changed. It is exactly the same amount in both cases: $96,000. So, this can't be the difference. The only difference is the amount of time that your returns have in which to *compound*. That extra twenty years on the front end matters much more than the amount of the monthly contribution.

The amount you would need to save if you only had twenty years is not even *double* the amount of principal ($800 monthly). It's *more than triple* the amount of principal, at about $1,400 per month. That's about $1,000 per month *more* than the equivalent amount in principal—$400 per month—over a twenty-year period.

Remember, this is compared to saving less than $200 per month, but for forty years, at a 10 percent rate of return. At an 8 percent rate of return, which requires a $300 monthly savings rate for forty years, the difference is even starker. To reach $1 million at an 8 percent rate, you would need to save about $1,750 per month for twenty years, or $1,150 more than the equivalent amount of principal ($600 for twenty years instead of $300 for forty years). The rate of return has an outsized impact on gains over longer periods of time.

To make things even more challenging, the longer you wait to save for retirement, the more likely you are to receive lower returns. Following the logic of a typical retirement savings diversification strategy, you can tolerate higher-risk, higher-return investments early in your career. Later on, most experts recommend shifting savings to safer investments that offer lower returns. You no longer have as much time for the market to bounce back after a downturn. This is yet one more reason why time is linked to money: having a longer period of time in which to save allows you to tolerate a higher-risk strategy, which provides the opportunity for higher returns.

Time is money is a circular argument. Time is what you have to give up in order to make money. But you can put your money to work for you by taking advantage of time. These are critical and related concepts. After all, it can't be an accident that Pink Floyd wrote songs about both of these things for the album *Dark Side of the Moon*. (If you got this reference, I guess you have very cool ... grandparents?) In fact, someone who started working right out of college the year this album came out, in 1973, would by 2020 have reached the age of seventy, which is the maximum age before you must take money out of tax-deferred savings. That's right—this album came out a long time ago! But to really drive home the point of just how valuable time can be for money, every dollar invested in the stock market in 1973 would be worth approximately $150 today. If our hypothetical Pink-Floyd-loving retiree invested $100 a month their first year working, the money invested *that year alone* would now be worth approximately $180,000!

So, if you don't have a lot of time, you need to save more money—a lot more money. But if you don't have a lot of money, that's okay. You are even better off if you have time. It's like the lily pad puzzle which took forty-seven days just to cover half the lake but only needs one more day to cover the entire lake (this is just an analogy; don't expect 100 percent returns—doubling—on your investments!).

Of course, you have to make money in order to save money. Now that you know you can become a millionaire by starting out saving just $100 per month for the first few years of your working life, in the next chapter we turn to chapter 2, "The Decision to Earn."

Key Takeaways

Directions: Review the following list of key takeaways to help you remember what you learned in this chapter:

- We are not particularly good at thinking about money because we are not particularly good at thinking about numbers in general.

- Money has objective value. But our financial decisions are more easily influenced by the *subjective*, psychological value that money represents to us. This value is fluid and highly context sensitive.
- Financial illiteracy is not hereditary. Anyone can learn the principles behind smart financial decisions to create stable wealth under most economic circumstances.
- Our emotions influence our financial decisions. We are more sensitive to losses than gains, and we find it hard to delay gratification.
- Time and money are inextricably linked to each other. You may not have a lot of money, but if you are young, you have a great deal of time. Time is very valuable in the creation of wealth. Time makes a BIG difference as you move towards sound financial habits.
- Money today loses value over time due to inflation. But you are more than compensated for that loss of value through investment returns over long periods of time.

Application Opportunity: Do This Now!

Directions: Complete the activities below to apply what you have learned in this chapter.

Activity 1

Using a compound interest calculator, play around with different amounts of money over different time frames at different rates of return (say, between 6 percent and 12 percent). You can find several just by searching for "compound interest calculator" online. Try to get a sense for how your total savings is differentially affected by these three factors. Which ones seem most influential over the long run—the amount you save annually, the rate of return, or the length of time?

Activity 2

On the time-value-of-money calculator of your choice, see how much more you have to save each month/year as the rate of return goes down and as the length of time decreases. Remember: the longer you wait to save, the more you will have to save.

Bibliography

Compound Interest Calculator. Investor.Gov. Accessed July 17, 2022. https://www.investor.gov/financial-tools-calculators/calculators/compound-interest-calculator

Frederick, Shane. "Cognitive Reflection and Decision Making." *Journal of Economic Perspectives* 19, no. 4 (2005): 25–42.

iShares iBoxx $ Investment Grade Corporate Bond ETF (LQD). *Yahoo Finance.* https://finance.yahoo.com/quote/LQD?p=LQD&.tsrc=fin-srch

iShares 7-10 Year Treasury Bond ETF (IEF). *Yahoo Finance.* https://finance.yahoo.com/quote/IEF?p=IEF&.tsrc=fin-srch

Kahneman, Daniel. *Thinking, Fast and Slow.* New York: Macmillan, 2011.

Kahneman, Daniel, and Amos Tversky. "Prospect Theory: An Analysis of Decision under Risk." *Econometrica* 47, no. 2 (1979): 263–92.

Keshner, Andrew. "Financial Literacy Skills Have Taken a Nose Dive since the Great Recession." Market Watch, June 27, 2019. https://www.marketwatch.com/story/americans-financial-literacy-skills-have-plummeted-since-the-great-recession-2019-06-26.

Kidd, Celeste, Holly Palmeri, and Richard N. Aslin. "Rational Snacking: Young Children's Decision-Making on the Marshmallow Task Is Moderated by Beliefs about Environmental Reliability." *Cognition* 126, no. 1 (2013): 109–14.

Lin, Judy T., Christopher Bumcrot, Tippy Ulicny, Gary Mottola, Gerri Walsh, Robert Ganem, Christine Kieffer, and Annamaria Lusardi. *The State of U.S. Financial Capability: The 2018 National Financial Capability Study.* FINRA Investor Education Foundation, June 2019. https://www.usfinancialcapability.org/downloads/NFCS_2018_Report_Natl_Findings.pdf.

Mellers, Barbara, and Peter A. McGraw. "Anticipated Emotions as Guides to Choice." *Current Directions in Psychological Science* 10 (2001): 210–15.
Mischel, Walter. *The Marshmallow Test: Understanding Self-Control and How to Master It.* New York: Little, Brown, 2014.
Rodriguez Valladares, Mayra. "Financial Literacy Is More Essential Than Ever." *Forbes*, December 15, 2020. https://www.forbes.com/sites/mayrarodriguezvalladares/2020/12/15/financial-literacy-is-more-essential-than-ever/?sh=cfc5b796304f.
Royal, James, and Arielle O'Shea. "What Is the Average Stock Market Return?" NerdWallet, April 26, 2021. https://www.nerdwallet.com/article/investing/average-stock-market-return.
Schwab-Pemerantz, Carrie. "Americans Want Financial Literacy ... Now!" Charles Schwab, September 2, 2020. https://www.schwab.com/resource-center/insights/content/americans-want-financial-literacy-now.
SPDR S&P 500 ETF Trust (SPY) *Yahoo Finance.* https://finance.yahoo.com/quote/SPY?p=SPY&.tsrc=fin-srch
Tversky, Amos, and Daniel Kahneman. "Loss Aversion in Riskless Choice: A Reference-Dependent Model." *The Quarterly Journal of Economics* 106, no. 4 (1991): 1039–61.
U.S. Bureau of Labor Statistics, Consumer Price Index for All Urban Consumers: All Items Less Food and Energy in U.S. City Average [CPILFESL], retrieved from FRED, Federal Reserve Bank of St. Louis; https://fred.stlouisfed.org/series/CPILFESL
Webster, Ian. "Value of 1950 Dollars Today—Inflation Calculator." February 10, 2021. https://www.in2013dollars.com/us/inflation/1950.
Welch, Ivo. "Views of Financial Economists on the Equity Premium and on Professional Controversies." *The Journal of Business* 73, no. 4 (2000): 501–37.
World Bank, Inflation, Consumer Prices for the United States 2010-2021 [FPCPITOTLZGUSA], FRED, Federal Reserve Bank of St. Louis. June 27, 2021. https://fred.stlouisfed.org/series/FPCPITOTLZGUSA.

Figure Credits

Fig. 1.1: Data source: https://fred.stlouisfed.org/series/CPILFESL.
Fig. 1.2: Source: https://www.investor.gov/financial-tools-calculators/calculators/compound-interest-calculator.

CHAPTER 2

The Decision to Earn

Invest in Your Vocation

Imagine...

You are a college senior. Looking back over the previous years, you have had successes and failures. But you have made it this far, and you should be proud. Only about one-third of American adults have at least a bachelor's degree.[1] You are bittersweet about the thought of leaving friends and the relative stability and security of college life behind. But you are excited about the career prospects that lie ahead and the opportunity to finally strike out on your own.

Your excitement quickly turns to anxiety as you come face-to-face with the complexity of the job market and the magnitude of the decisions that must be made. Where to live? What kind of job can you get with your degree? How much will those jobs pay?

Once you have a job, you still have some decisions to make. How to choose a healthcare plan? Where to put retirement savings?

Introduction

In this chapter, you will learn about the financial decisions that go along with accepting a new position, possibly in a new city. You will learn, for instance, that there are important relationships between what you study and what kind of job you can get, but often the relationship between the two can be surprising. You will learn, critically, that salary alone should not be the driving factor in deciding to accept a job offer. Healthcare and retirement benefits also represent important sources of financial compensation. Another essential consideration is where you will live. The amount of your salary that will go to living expenses—rent, in particular—can make you worse off financially in the long run. This means

1. Camille L. Ryan and Kurt Bauman, "Educational Attainment in the United States: 2015," US Census Bureau, March 2016, https://www.census.gov/content/dam/Census/library/publications/2016/demo/p20-578.pdf.

that what seemed like a great salary at first glance may not be high enough to justify the increased costs of living. Perhaps most importantly, the work that you do will have an impact on your well-being over and above your financial security. You have to be able to meet your financial obligations, yes, but after working so hard to get through college, you deserve to love your career. It is worthwhile to get yourself to a financial place where you can do that. At the end of the day, your career should maximize your overall well-being. Financial well-being is a critical aspect of this, but you will have to choose whether you want to *live to work* or *work to live*.

Chapter Objectives

After reading this chapter, you will be able to:

- Access and interpret data relevant to employment decisions, including career choices, job locations and cost-of-living considerations, and employment outlook.
- Understand employee and employer contributions to retirement funds, retirement savings vehicles, and paycheck withholdings (FICA, HSA and FSA, etc.).
- Think about total compensation, including salary, cost-of-living considerations, and retirement benefits, when making employment decisions.

Why Does the First Job Search Feel So Stressful?

Looking for a job while you are trying to maintain your grades in your final year of college can feel very overwhelming. You have spent four years in a major, and you dream of that perfect career that matches your interests and your skill set. *Where* you look for your job is a critical factor to finding a great job match.[2] The pressure is real. Companies seem to be looking to fill positions earlier and earlier. They have turned the process of recruiting into such a high-stress situation, calling three-day interviewing schedules "super interviews" and handing you a case-study scenario with only one hour to prepare. They say you don't need a PowerPoint, but really, you know they expect a polished presentation. The competition feels fierce, and all you have energy for is getting the offer. Once the offer is in place, surely that is all you need to worry about, right? Actually, this is where a different round of research should begin. Your objective is to figure out the *job and place* where you will be happy, yes, but you also need a combination that will set you on the path for financial stability. There can be great happiness in financial stability.

Cost of Living and Salary Are Inseparable Considerations

There are a lot of factors to consider as you determine where to live. Realize that the cost of living varies greatly across areas of the country, so the decision of where to move should be based on more than personal

2. Jaison R. Abel and Richard Deitz, "Agglomeration and Job Matching among College Graduates," *Regional Science and Urban Economics* 51 (March 2015): 14–24.

preference. If you decide that New York City or Los Angeles is perfect for you, just be sure that the salary you earn compensates you for the cost of living there. Or make sure that the future prospects of advancement in that job mean that you will eventually be able to afford it.

Consider the following two job offers:

- $70,000 per year in Washington, DC.
- $50,000 per year in Lexington, Kentucky.

If you are trying to maximize income, the offer in Washington looks pretty good. It is 40 percent more in base salary than the offer in Lexington. But of course, there is a catch. It is much more expensive to live in the DC metro area than it is to live in Lexington—about 77 percent more expensive, in fact.[3] This, being larger than the difference in salary, effectively means that you can have a higher standard of living on the lower salary in Lexington. The difference in rent alone eats up most of the additional salary, as housing in D.C. is 234 percent more on average—a typical one-bedroom in DC might go for $2,000 a month compared to $953 in Lexington. That represents over $12,000 of the extra $20,000 in salary.

The point is, if you are trying to maximize income, you cannot consider the salary in isolation from the cost of living in wherever it is you are working. Of course, maximizing income may not be your only goal. Perhaps you value excitement, interaction with international cultures, and the arts. These are important aspects of your job-seeking utility that you should factor into the decision. Perhaps you would prefer to live with a roommate, which could absorb a good deal of the differential in rent costs in Washington. If you think you might want to own a home in a few years, though, or you look forward to a lower-key, family-oriented life, Lexington might be additionally attractive for these reasons. Balancing these considerations is crucial for good financial decision-making. After all, you can decide that the aesthetic factors are worth the difference in the standard of living, but it is good to know what you are getting before you commit.

Two general rules are true about cost of living in the United States. Bigger cities tend to be more expensive, and coastal cities tend to be more expensive. Cities that qualify on both counts—Seattle, San Francisco, New York—are particularly expensive. But they are also locales with low unemployment, strong job growth, and excellent career opportunities. So, it is simply not possible, or even advisable, to ignore larger metropolitan areas on account of cost of living alone.

There are, of course, large cities outside of California and New York that have affordable housing, provide great employment opportunities, and offer reasonably high salaries. Many cities in Texas make this list, as well as places like Atlanta, Minneapolis, and Pittsburgh. The Southeast in particular offers a low cost of living and several midsize cities with strong labor markets, such as Nashville, Tennessee, and Charlotte, North Carolina. Many smaller cities these days, such as Greenville, South Carolina; Boise, Idaho; and Omaha, Nebraska, have a surprisingly high quality of life as well, with redeveloped downtown districts, arts, entertainment, and shopping. Being open to these places may provide many benefits worth considering.

If you really want to get a feel for this, try a cost-of-living calculator. You will find many of these with a quick online search, and different calculators will give you cost comparisons in different ways. One might

3. The difference was determined using CNN Money's cost-of-living calculator. CNN Money, "Cost of Living: How Far Will My Salary Go in Another City?" accessed January 15, 2020, https://money.cnn.com/calculator/pf/cost-of-living/index.html.

calculate the expected cost-of-living change and the expected salary change for you, so that you can decide if a move is worth it to you. Another might allow you to input your actual expenses for housing and food and then estimate the same expenses for where you want to go. By trying a few different calculators, you can get information from different perspectives. The calculators are so easy to play with that the time spent is really minor. Consider the text box below.

COMPARING CHICAGO WITH A FEW COST-OF-LIVING CALCULATIONS

As an example, consider Chicago, the nation's third-largest city, with a population of nearly nine million people. A city of this size has, of course, many excellent job opportunities, in industries such as aviation, agriculture, and IT. Chicago is also home to a number of Fortune 500 companies, such as United Airlines and Conagra Foods. Chicago makes a great comparison case. On the one hand, it is a large city with lots of job opportunities, and it is reasonably expensive—much more so than a lot of smaller cities. On the other hand, given its location in the Midwest and its flat landscape, which is conducive to expansive growth, it is considerably cheaper than a lot of cities, particularly those on the coast.

Let's say you have an offer for $60,000 in Chicago. How will this compare to other places where you are thinking about living? Houston, Texas, is the nation's fourth-largest city, with a metro population of nearly seven million. However, you will only need to make about $47,000 to have the same standard of living in Houston.[4] In that case, if you are comparing a $60,000 offer in Chicago to a $50,000 offer in Houston, in theory, your $50,000 in Houston will buy more for you than the $60,000 in Chicago will. Of course, this will depend on a number of factors—such as how far from the city you are willing to live and how far you are willing to commute (both cities have awful traffic). It will also depend on whether you find bitter cold and winds or sweltering heat and humidity more unpleasant!

If you were instead comparing this offer to one in Boston, you would need to make $73,000. Seattle? $78,000. San Francisco? $100,000. The differences are starker when you compare low-cost-of-living cities, such as Columbus, Ohio. $60,000 in Columbus is equivalent to $120,000 in New York—and that's if you live in Brooklyn!

Beyond considering the cost of living in a particular locale, keep in mind that your starting salary may not be informative for your career or earning potential. If you are working in the technology industry or for a nonprofit with key input on issues of public policy, you might choose to be in Silicon Valley or Washington,

4. These figures were determined using the CNN Money cost-of-living calculator. See CNN Money, "Cost of Living: How Far Will My Salary Go in Another City?"

DC, and tolerate the high cost of living for greater career mobility and future earning potential. If you are an aspiring television writer or theater performer, Los Angeles and New York may be inevitable.

Of course, starting salary is not the only thing to consider. You are looking to maximize your overall quality of life. A good climate, a reasonable commute, access to arts and entertainment, the outdoors—all these things matter in different ways to different people. But financial stability and security are a critical component of this, perhaps more than young people realize, as financial obligations tend to increase with age. If you are making career decisions with an eye toward your long-term financial security, it is essential to take cost of living into account. In general, it is true that you will get paid higher salaries in cities that are more expensive. But be forewarned: these salaries are often not high enough to compensate for that difference.

Your Job Choice May Not Be as Limited as You Initially Think

If you are like many college students, you may already feel destined for a certain income bracket, based on your chosen area of study. It is true that certain majors have higher starting salaries than others. You will probably not be surprised to learn that computer science majors lead the pack, with an average starting salary around $77,000 among 2018 graduates.[5] This is approximately 50 percent higher than the overall average starting salary of graduates, which is around $50,000. Didn't study computer science? The good news is that the average starting salary should be more than enough in compensation to set yourself up for long-term financial success, assuming you budget carefully and establish long-term savings goals.

Some majors pay starting salaries well below the average, of course, and it is important to be realistic about your area of study and expected earnings. Humanities and social science majors are earning a little below the average; business majors are earning a little more. Outside of a few specific areas—engineering, computer science, and information systems—the differences are not as great as might be expected.

Area of study is not the only factor that affects compensation. Graduates of more prestigious colleges attain higher salaries, and graduates located in more expensive areas, such as the East and West coasts, also attain higher salaries. The average starting salary for a college graduate in the Southeastern United States is around $48,000.[6] Of course, such geographical differences in compensation are commensurate with differences in cost of living—to some degree, at least.

While it is important to be realistic, it is also important to understand what such numbers can and cannot tell you. The averages are not necessarily informative regarding the range of salaries that graduates obtain or the lifetime earning potential of a particular college major. For instance, 25 percent of psychology majors obtain graduate degrees. Many jobs in psychology require graduate training, so the average starting salary of a psychology major at the undergraduate level may tell you little about the lifetime earning potential of a psychology degree.

5. US Bureau of Labor Statistics, "Occupational Outlook Handbook," accessed February 19, 2021, https://www.bls.gov/ooh/management/home.htm.
6. NACE Staff. "First Destinations for the College Class of 2018," National Association of Colleges and Employers, accessed March 15, 2019, https://www.naceweb.org/job-market/graduate-outcomes/first-destination/class-of-2018/interactive-dashboard/.

Perhaps an even more critical point is that your area of study does not necessarily confine you to a limited set of job options. A *New York Federal Reserve Bank* study reports that only 27.3 percent of college graduates work in careers that are linked to their major in college.[7] It is true that gender studies majors will likely not land jobs in computer science. But it is not true that only business majors land jobs in business-related fields. The humanities in general provide an excellent skill set for work in business, particularly for management-related jobs that require interpersonal and critical thinking skills and marketing-related jobs that require creativity and problem-solving abilities. Salary data tends to be distorted by the fact that people major in the humanities because they are not necessarily interested in working in business-related settings, whereas business majors are. But businesses regularly hire liberal arts majors, and, indeed, national survey data repeatedly indicate that the top skills employers require are those that liberal arts degrees provide.[8]

In fact, some of the nation's most successful entrepreneurs and business leaders have degrees in the traditional liberal arts disciplines. Reid Hoffman, founder of Netflix, and John Mackey, CEO of Whole Foods, both studied philosophy. Denise Morrison, former CEO of Campbell's soup, studied psychology. Indra Nooyi, CEO of Pepsi, studied chemistry, and Meg Whitman, former CEO of eBay and Hewlett Packard, studied math and switched to economics. In fact, fully one-third of all Fortune 500 CEOs have liberal arts backgrounds.[9] Considering that liberal arts majors are perhaps less likely to go into business than, say, business, computer science, or engineering majors, this number may still underestimate the true value of a liberal arts degree.

If you are a humanities major and you are seeking employment in a traditional business setting, you can make yourself more attractive to businesses by trying to do some coursework in applied or technical areas. Minor in marketing or graphic design, for instance. Take statistics or computer science classes. Pairing a psychology major with a sociology major is unlikely to yield any additional career payoff, but pairing a psychology major with a marketing minor, or an English major with a computer science minor, could be very powerful.

This logic cuts both ways. Computer scientists and business majors can attain a major job market advantage by balancing their technical training with liberal arts coursework. Computer science and philosophy is a powerful combination, as is business and foreign language, or engineering and psychology.

If it is too late to change course, or if you are a recent college graduate, consider the fact that many of the technical skills that could supplement a liberal arts or humanities degree can be developed without formal coursework. A recent study by *Burning Glass Technologies* finds that developing one of eight specific skills can increase a graduate's starting salary by an average of $6,000, enough to equate a humanities major with a science major.[10] These skills include marketing, social media, graphic design, and data analysis. There are many online platforms offering certificates in these skills, some of them for free. For instance, Google

7. Jaison R. Abel and Richard Deitz, "Do Big Cities Help College Graduates Find Better Jobs?" Liberty Street Economics, Federal Reserve Bank of New York, May 20, 2013, https://libertystreeteconomics.newyorkfed.org/2013/05/do-big-cities-help-college-graduates-find-better-jobs.html.
8. Lynn Pasquerella, "Yes, Employers Do Value Liberal Arts Degrees," *Harvard Business Review*, September 19, 2019, https://hbr.org/2019/09/yes-employers-do-value-liberal-arts-degrees.
9. Sanjeev Verma, "Career Guide: A Third of Fortune 500 CEOs Have This Degree," *Friday Magazine*, December 7, 2020, https://fridaymagazine.ae/life-culture/ask-the-experts/career-guide-a-third-of-fortune-500-ceos-have-this-degree-1.2310482.
10. Burning Glass Technologies, "What Can You Do with a Liberal Arts Degree? Plenty, with the Right Skills," February 20, 2018, https://www.burning-glass.com/category/liberal-arts/.

offers a free certification in Google Ads, their online advertising platform, and in Google Analytics, their internet usage research platform.

In fact, recent research demonstrates that the fastest job growth is in fields in which liberal arts majors should flourish—those that require interpersonal skill, emotional intelligence, and careful judgment.[11] This is because artificial intelligence and automation are continually replacing routinized and quantitatively oriented jobs at an ever-increasing rate.

Liking Our Jobs

Our job satisfaction may not depend solely on how happy we are with what we do and how much we make. One research study asked people whether they would prefer a job in which they made $50,000 and everyone else made $25,000, or a job in which they made $100,000 but everyone else made $200,000.[12] A surprising number actually chose the first option—that is, they chose to make half as much as they could have otherwise. Those individuals have an intuitive understanding of the phenomenon of social comparison. For some things, it is hard to know how we should feel about ourselves without comparing ourselves to others. This is particularly true for something like money. How much is enough? Oftentimes, the answer might depend on our standard of comparison. Will an amount that feels like enough when you first start working start to feel like less than enough once your friends start landing higher-paying jobs and your coworkers receive promotions? A great deal of research demonstrates that the impact of money on our well-being is inherently relative in this way. Psychologically speaking, more is not always better. You may not be happy making $100,000 if you *feel* poor because you know everyone is making more money than you. Consider the example in the text box below.

EVALUATING A JOB OFFER

Imagine you have the following two job offers:

- $35,000 a year in Knoxville, Tennessee, working for a nonprofit
- $50,000 a year in Lubbock, Texas, working for a marketing agency

Both Knoxville and Lubbock are similar in terms of cost of living, making it possible to compare salaries more directly. If your goal is to maximize income, you should take the job in Lubbock. $15,000 more per year translates into roughly $1,000 per month extra, after taxes. But there are important differences between the two jobs that are worth considering.

11. Aaron Smith and Janna Anderson, "AI, Robotics, and the Future of Jobs," Pew Research Center, August 6, 2014. https://www.pewresearch.org/internet/2014/08/06/future-of-jobs/.
12. David Card, Alexandre Mas, Enrico Moretti, and Emmanuel Saez, "Inequality at Work: The Effect of Peer Salaries on Job Satisfaction," *American Economic Review* 102, no. 6 (2012): 2981–3003.

If the nonprofit is a cause you truly believe in, this provides extra utility that you cannot translate into income. If you don't think you would be happy in a business setting, the extra money may not compensate you for that dissatisfaction.

The point is that money isn't everything when it comes to your career. But you need to have a job that will provide the standard of living that you desire; this is unavoidably true. You can take the $35,000-a-year nonprofit job in a place with a low cost of living like Knoxville, Tennessee. But you will really have to make difficult choices and sacrifices to take a salary like that in Austin, Texas, or Madison, Wisconsin, great college towns with a much higher cost of living.

You need to consider more than the salary you are being paid. You need to consider your goals, values, and objectives in life. You need to consider your own well-being and what will most greatly contribute to it. Money is a means to an end. We have already seen that you can start your path to financial security for a relatively low monthly savings amount. If you have made a commitment to saving, your salary should provide you with the lifestyle that you want to achieve for yourself and your family. And if you want to enjoy it, it will help to have a job that you find meaningful, fulfilling, and consistent with your values.

Another study asked people whether they would prefer a job in which they received two weeks of vacation and everyone else received one week or a job in which they received four weeks of vacation and everyone else received six weeks. What would you choose? If you are like most people, you will take the four weeks of vacation. The impact of money on our well-being may be relative, but the impact of vacation is not. More is always better when it comes to some aspects of job satisfaction. While income may have relative effects on happiness, leisure time does not.

How you balance your income needs with your broader needs for meaning, fulfillment, and well-being in life is something only you can determine. But you do need to be realistic about your ability to meet your financial goals. Most people intuitively understand the importance of meaning and fulfillment in work. But a lot less attention gets paid to the stress of financial insecurity. Having a meaningful job will not provide a great deal of psychological comfort if you are struggling to meet your monthly expenses. And the thesis of this book is that you cannot afford to put off savings. When you choose a job that feeds your soul but does not compensate you accordingly, you sacrifice the time that you put into the job, when time is the most valuable resource you possess as a young person. You do deserve a career you love, but be very clear on the choices you are making as you move into this stage of your life.

Is Salary the Only Kind of Compensation?

Be sure *not* to look *only* at salary as you make your job selection. The best jobs will be more about the *package* offered to employees than about the base salary alone. Choosing the best placement means understanding the benefits for healthcare and retirement that are offered in conjunction with the salary.

Retirement Benefits Add a Lot to Financial Stability

It is important to ask questions about the perks of the job in the later stages of the interview process so that you have a full picture of the position being offered. One more scenario for you to consider follows below.

Evaluating a Job Offer with Benefits

Which job would be the better offer:

- A job that pays $65,000 a year
- A job that pays $60,000 a year, plus an additional 9 percent contribution toward a company-sponsored retirement plan

With all else held constant, you should take the second job. That 9 percent retirement contribution corresponds to an extra $5,400 in compensation, which is more than the $5,000 base difference in compensation between the two offers. The only difference is that this money is being withheld and saved on your behalf.

Now, you could of course save $5,000 of the first salary on your own, leaving you with nearly the same amount in base salary as the second offer. But if you really want those savings to better equate the two job offers, you need to save those funds in an Individual Retirement Account (IRA). In fact, if you were to do so, the first job might even become more attractive than the second job!

How could this be, when the second job pays $400 more in total compensation?

Read the textbox below to understand this question.

TAX ADVANTAGED SAVINGS VEHICLES

Understanding the implications of tax-advantaged savings takes a little research. When you contribute money to a retirement savings account, you pay less in taxes. In a traditional retirement account, this is because your contributions are made before taxes are taken out of your paycheck. This means you can put more into your savings now.

To illustrate, someone who is paid $65,000 a year will owe (roughly) 15 percent of that income to the federal government in income taxes. This comes out to $9,750. However, the individual who contributes $5,000 of their income to a retirement account will only be taxed on $60,000 of income. This is due to a *tax deduction*. Tax deductions lower the amount of income that is subject to taxes by an amount equivalent to the deduction. Every dollar saved in a qualifying retirement account decreases taxable income by that same amount.

Taxes on $60,000 come to only $9,000–$750 less than before. That $750 of tax savings is essentially income, and it is more than the additional $400 provided by the second job's company-sponsored contribution. So, the first job actually wins after all—if you are disciplined enough to take full advantage of the tax benefits of retirement savings. In the next chapter, "The Decision to Save," you will learn that taking advantage of such pretax savings is an important component of a long-term savings strategy. Understanding the tax consequences of your own saving will make it easier for you to compare the retirement benefits that various employers offer.

Now imagine that the second offer comes with *employee matching*. That is, suppose the employer will increase their retirement contributions on your behalf up to a certain amount—say, 3 percent. That is, in addition to the 9 percent they are putting into your account, they will give you an additional 1 percent for every 1 percent that you contribute of your own money. If you contribute a full 3 percent of *your own* income, they will contribute 12 percent of your salary to your retirement account.

The second job wins again. You should take this offer, and you should contribute the full 3 percent, because if you do not, you are leaving money on the table—an additional $1,800, to be exact (3 percent of $60,000).

Evaluating Retirement Plans

Now that you are starting to get a feel for this, which of the following retirement accounts is most attractive?

- Option A: Employer contributes 6 percent of salary; as long as the employee contributes 4 percent.
- Option B: Employer contributes 4 percent and matches additional contributions up to 8 percent.

The first scenario is one we haven't encountered yet, but it is not uncommon. In this retirement account, you are required to contribute a flat amount in order to receive the employer's contribution. There is nothing wrong with this requirement. You should be thankful that your employer is forcing you to save 4 percent that you don't have to motivate yourself to save on your own! And it will likely be deducted from your paycheck pretax, so it will affect your take-home pay by less than 4 percent.

Under option B, you could choose to contribute nothing, and your employer would only contribute 4 percent. This is 50 percent less than the employer contributes to plan A, but this is actually the better benefit. If you were to contribute 2 percent, the employer would match that 2 percent and contribute a total of 6 percent, making the benefit options effectively equivalent at a rate that requires 50 percent less in contribution from you. But if you were to contribute the same 4 percent that is required of you under option A, your employer would match that full 4 percent for a total 8 percent contribution, which is 2 percent more than is being offered under option A. In total, option B is a pretty good benefit. Fully 12 percent of your income is being saved—over the 10 percent target that many financial planners recommend—and two-thirds of that amount is being paid in by your employer.

Any time matching is offered, the plan is probably worth taking advantage of. For one, such plans motivate saving on the part of the employee, saving that you would benefit from doing on your own anyway. But by saving as part of a matching plan, you increase your employer's contribution as well.

This is not to say that matching plans are always better. Consider the following two plans.

- Option A: Employer contributes 5 percent.
- Option B: Employer matches contributions up to 4 percent.

In this case, option A wins. Under option B, all contributions are matching contributions. But under option A, you could save the 4 percent on your own in a tax-sheltered retirement account and still get 5 percent from your employer, earning 1 percent more than you would get by contributing the full 4 percent under option B.

Wait, Employers Should Simply *Pay* for Retirement

The kind of retirement accounts we have been comparing above are known as ***defined contribution*** plans. They often go by the name 401(k), which is basically the code that documents how they are taxed. A 401(k) retirement plan is the tax code that covers private companies, so you will likely have a 401(k) if you work at a for-profit business. Virtually identical plans go by the names of 501(c) and 403(b), which are the tax-code designations for government, nonprofit, and educational organizations. All plans have the same benefit—that is, contributions to retirement savings lower taxable income. If they are employer-provided plans, this is typically done through payroll deduction, which means that your retirement contributions are "taken out" prior to taxes. However, anyone can take advantage of the same tax benefits by using an Individual Retirement Plan (IRA). In this case, the tax deduction is taken when you complete your annual taxes.

In a defined contribution plan, savings for retirement are typically invested in the stock market, and the amount you have available at retirement depends on the investments you have selected and how well they have performed. Defined contribution plans were originally developed in the 1980s as an alternative to the more common ***defined benefit plans*** that were popular for many decades prior to that time. Defined benefit plans are also known as ***pensions,*** and this is likely the type of plan you saw your grandparents get. Most typically, they are funded entirely by the employer. However, they are called defined benefit plans because the amount you have available at retirement is predetermined, usually based on a simple formula. At one of my former employers, the pension was a percentage of your highest salary. The percentage was determined by doubling the years of service. So, if you worked for thirty-five years, you would receive 70 percent of the average of your highest three years of salary. An individual who achieved a salary of $100,000 in their last few years of employment, then, would receive a pension of $70,000 every year for the rest of their life after retiring. Often, the benefit would move to your spouse if you died but would not be passed on to grown children.

If this sounds pretty good, it is. Pensions were common in many industries throughout the twentieth century. In some industries, such as the automobile industry, they were fiercely negotiated by workers' unions. Unfortunately, pensions were very expensive for employers, and employers began to move away from them as a result of many competitive forces acting on businesses in the 1980s and 1990s. By the end of the '90s, most private employers had transitioned to defined contribution plans.

There are mixed opinions as to whether the move from defined benefit to defined contribution plans has had a positive outcome.[13] Supporters of 401(k)-style plans point to higher market returns that are not possible with public pension plans. Detractors point to the greater risk of the 401(k) compared to the attractive security of a fixed, guaranteed income. The debate might not matter for new workers in the labor force. Pensions are still popular in the public sector, particularly in government and education, where they compensate for the somewhat lower salaries you will find in these professions relative to the private sector. However, the long-term trend does not look favorable for pensions in the public sector, either. Many state governments have proposed transitioning to private retirement accounts.

If you can take a job that offers a pension, great. But do not consider it a substitute for your own long-term retirement savings plan. As you will learn in the next chapter, you can still set up and make contributions to your own personal retirement account, even if you have a pension. Back in the day when a person worked for the same firm for over twenty years, perhaps the standard pension made the best sense. Now, according to a US Bureau of Labor Statistics study published in 2019, starting in 1979, the typical worker changed positions over twelve times in their working lifetime![14] To be fair, this statistic is historical and thus applies to the baby boomers, but do you think young people today change jobs more or less frequently than their parents and grandparents? The point is that several small pensions from multiple firms where the worker has not put in the time to fully vest the benefits of a pension may not make for comfortable retirement, even when a pension is available.

By now, I hope you are convinced that your employer's retirement contribution is a critical component of total compensation that should factor into your employment decision. Over a lifetime of earnings, a 3 percent or 4 percent difference in an employer's contribution could result in a difference in retirement savings of hundreds of thousands of dollars.

Financial Well-Being Is Important ... What about My Physical Well-Being?

Another critical component of total compensation you should factor into your employment decision is the employer's healthcare plan. After housing and food, healthcare will likely be your next biggest category of spending. Perhaps early on in your career, this spending will not be as much, but once you start a family or move toward your middle career, these bills will be increasingly central to your budget.

As you are probably already aware, healthcare is complicated—particularly in the United States. But familiarity with just a few simple terms and concepts can greatly simplify the process of evaluating a healthcare plan. The text box below highlights a few terms you will need to understand.

13. For the pros and cons, see John Broadbent, Michael Palumbo, and Elizabeth Woodman, "The Shift from Defined Benefit to Defined Contribution Pension Plans–Implications for Asset Allocation and Risk Management," Reserve Bank of Australia, Board of Governors of the Federal Reserve System and Bank of Canada, December 2006, 1–54, https://www.bis.org/publ/wgpapers/cgfs27broadbent3.pdf.
14. US Bureau of Labor Statistics, "Number of Jobs, Labor Market Experience, and Earnings Growth: Results from a National Longitudinal Survey," economic news release, August 22, 2019, https://www.bls.gov/news.release/pdf/nlsoy.pdf.

HEALTH INSURANCE TERMS TO UNDERSTAND

- **Premium**. The premium is what you pay to have an insurance policy. It is usually paid monthly or bimonthly as a payroll deduction, depending on how frequently you are paid.
- **Deductible**. The deductible is the amount you must pay toward your healthcare expenses before insurance benefits apply.
- **Coinsurance**. Usually expressed as a percentage, coinsurance is the amount that you will pay toward healthcare expenses after you have paid the deductible.
- **Copayment**. Copayments are flat rates paid for basic services, such as doctor's office visits and prescriptions.
- **Maximum Out-of-Pocket.** Once your deductible plus the total coinsurance you pay hits the max, you pay no more of your health expenses. The insurance company covers the rest. There will be a maximum for individuals, and this may be doubled for families.

Perhaps the easiest way to see the differences and implications involved in choosing a healthcare plan is to consider the following two healthcare plans:

- Plan A has a $50 monthly premium and a $5,000 deductible.
- Plan B has a $200 monthly premium and a $1,000 deductible.

The *premium* is the price you pay to have insurance. You will pay this premium whether or not you utilize any healthcare services. For plan A, then, you will pay a total of $600 in premiums for the year, and for plan B, you will pay a total of $2,400 in premiums. So, plan B appears to be more expensive. This is true if you are very healthy and have no accidents for the year. Each year, you will have the chance to choose plans again. If your circumstances change, this also opens the window for choosing a different plan from the list of employer-supplied choices.

You will not pay the *deductible* until you are billed for healthcare expenses. Under plan A, you are responsible for every dollar of expenses you incur, up to $5,000. In plan B, you are only responsible for expenses up to $1,000, at which point your insurance benefits will begin to kick in more aggressively. Suddenly, plan B could be a better choice, if you experienced a significant illness or were a victim in an accident. Given how exorbitant hospital costs can be, only a few days in the hospital would make plan B look a lot better.

Imagine that you are billed for $1,000 worth of medical services. This could have come from one outpatient medical procedure or several visits to a specialist (a typical charge for one visit to an orthopedist, for instance, might be about $200, not counting any tests or additional medical services provided). Under both plans, you will have to pay all $1,000 out of pocket. When you add this to the premium expenses, you can see that plan B still appears to be more expensive.

- Plan A: $600 annual premium + $1,000 toward deductible = $1,600.
- Plan B: $2,400 annual premium + $1,000 toward deductible = $3,400.

Of course, $1,000 is not a great deal of medical billing. Imagine a situation in which you utilized a greater amount of healthcare resources, and you were billed for a total of $5,000 in medical expenses. Under plan A, you are responsible for every dollar, because you have a $5,000 deductible. So, your total medical spending for the year is $5,600=$5,000 plus the $600 in premiums.

What about plan B? Under plan B, you have met the deductible after $1,000 of billing. However, this leaves an additional $4,000 of expenses. On a typical insurance plan, this is where *coinsurance* applies. A 20 percent coinsurance rate is typical, meaning you are responsible for only 20 percent of the amount that remains after the deductible is met. This is $800, or 20 percent of the remaining $4,000 amount. Under plan B, your total spending is $4,200:

- Plan A: $600 annual premium + $5,000 toward deductible = $5,600.
- Plan B: $2,400 annual premium + $1,000 toward deductible + $800 coinsurance (20 percent × $4,000) = $4,200.

Clearly, you will be much better off with plan B in this more expensive medical case. Plan A will cost $1,400 more under this scenario.

One more thing to note is the maximum out-of-pocket you will face under each plan. Usually, the maximum you will pay is higher under the higher deductible health plan, equal to or close to the total deductible. So, you will want to be sure that you can pay the maximum should the worst happen in a given year. Once the maximum is met through deductible and coinsurance, you will no longer be responsible for any additional medical billing for the year. Your insurance company will pay all remaining expenses that are covered.

The scenario serves to illustrate an important difference in healthcare coverage options: the difference between low-premium, high-deductible plans and high-premium, low-deductible plans. Low-deductible plans used to be the standard, but high-deductible plans are becoming more common. And you will often have to make the choice for yourself. As in this exercise, a basic logic holds—high-deductible plans tend to be best when expenses are low. This is because, when there is little medical billing, you are better off minimizing the liability of the monthly premium, which you will pay no matter what. At higher levels of billing, however, this difference disappears and then reverses. If plan B has a $2,000 out-of-pocket maximum, your total liability for any given year will be $3,600 ($2,400 premium + $1,000 deductible + 20 percent of remaining $1,000 toward out-of-pocket maximum). This means that any medical expenses greater than $3,000 will make plan A more expensive ($3,000 medical billing + $600 premium).

There are some other differences between the two plans that you might need to consider as well. High-deductible plans don't always have a separate out-of-pocket maximum or coinsurance rate, meaning that once the deductible is met, there is no remaining liability—no more expenses will be billed to you. High-deductible plans do not typically offer copayments for services, though, which can be a benefit of a lower-deductible plan. A copayment is a flat amount that is paid for a specific service—say, $25 for a doctor's office visit or $20 for a prescription. Copayments made under low-deductible plans, however, do not typically count toward the deductible. Once a deductible is met, as in the scenario we utilized above, you will still need to pay the $20 or $25 copayment for office visits, though you will not be billed for any services.

On a high-deductible plan, you are almost always billed the full amount for every expense incurred. This will typically cost a lot more than a copayment; it could be anywhere from $75 to $200 for a typical visit. The benefit is that those payments count toward your deductible, reducing your total liability. Of course, this is only a benefit if you actually exceed your deductible, at which point you will have no more liabilities at all for that benefit year.

Nevertheless, experts tend to agree that if you are young and healthy, you are better off with a high-deductible plan. Since you should not count on spending a great deal on medical expenses, you should lower your monthly premium liability. If you are older, have health issues, or are covering several family members, you might be better off with a lower-deductible plan. To see which plan is best for you, compare plan options that are available under a variety of spending scenarios and try to determine which scenarios are most likely for you or your family.

You might still be wondering, though, what the "benefit" of a high-deductible plan is, if you regularly utilize only a small amount of healthcare. Why pay a monthly premium when your expenses fall well short of your deductible, meaning you are paying all of your expenses out of pocket?

There are three answers to this question. First, there is a benefit to having insurance, whether or not you are paying out of pocket. Having insurance means *you are paying lower rates for services than you would pay as a walk-in patient.* When you receive a bill for services, you will see a charge listed, as well as another column with a lower number called the "allowable amount." This is the amount that the insurance company has agreed to pay the provider, and it is often substantially lower than the amount that was billed. Insurance companies can negotiate lower prices through sheer size and market power. Without insurance, you would likely be billed higher amounts for services.

Second, even young and healthy individuals get sick and have accidents. An emergency room visit will cost thousands of dollars; a long-term hospital stay will run into the tens of thousands. Your $5,000 deductible will feel like a drop in the bucket if and when catastrophe strikes, and you are facing tens of thousands in medical bills. Even if you don't think something will happen to you, keep in mind that you put the financial stability of those that love you at risk if you don't keep insurance. What would your parents do if you were in an accident, but you did not have health insurance?

Finally, high-deductible plans make it possible for you to do your healthcare spending pretax, much like your retirement contributions. There are savings accounts dedicated to medical spending that families can use to budget for medical expenses. The choices available for this will be discussed in chapter 3, "The Decision to Save."

If all of this sounds confusing, it is. Healthcare is complicated, particularly in the United States. The fact that your own healthcare utilization will play a role in what kind of health plan is best can make it a little more difficult to compare offers from different employers. And most employers will offer you at least two options, which makes things even trickier. Know this, though: healthcare packages from two employers can be as different from each other as night and day. Some packages are very good, and others provide only basic coverage. If you have a job offer from an employer that provides a "Cadillac style" healthcare plan, it may well be worth a slightly lower salary.

I Got My First Paycheck! Where Did All My Money Go?

You have just landed your first job offer. The job pays $48,000 per year, which is a reasonable starting salary in a lower-cost-of-living area. You have set aside 3 percent of your own salary, pretax, toward the company retirement plan, which will match that 3 percent. You have signed up for the high-deductible healthcare plan, since you are young and healthy and only need coverage for yourself. The premium is $50 per month. You have also decided to save another $50 pretax toward healthcare spending. How much money will you actually bring home?

Let's assume you get paid monthly, although biweekly (twice-per-month) payment schedules are also quite common. Using monthly payments will make the math easier to understand, though, since your healthcare and retirement contributions are usually specified on a monthly basis.

$48,000 comes out to $4,000 per month. This is your *gross income*—income before taxes and everything else that comes out of your paycheck. If you are single, this salary puts you in a 12 percent federal tax bracket. You will likely also pay state income tax, as only a few states don't have one (Alaska, Florida, Nevada, New Hampshire, South Dakota, Texas, Tennessee, Washington, and Wyoming). In Ohio, for instance, you will pay around 3 percent in state income taxes.

Finally, Social Security and Medicare will account for another 7.65 percent of federal taxes taken out of your check, with your employer also paying 7.65 percent to these programs on your behalf. Often, your paycheck will simply note these expenses as FICA, which stands for Federal Insurance Contributions Act. These are taxes that will entitle you to income benefits and healthcare when you retire. Your taxes today go to pay retirees today. When you retire, the workers then will be paying for your benefits. More on this in chapter 7, "The Decision to Retire!"

Your retirement contributions and healthcare spending come out *pretax*, which means they are taken out of your gross income. You will see something similar to table 2.1 in your pay stubs. In the first column, you will see an itemized list of the various deductions from your paycheck. In the second column, you will see the amounts that these correspond to. Finally, in the third column, you will see how much your paycheck is reduced by each deduction. After all deductions have been accounted for, you are left with *net income*. Net income is what you will receive in your paycheck, or what will actually be deposited into your bank account via direct deposit. Notice that at around $3,000, your net pay ends up being approximately three-quarters of your gross income. I have found that, as a general rule, net income ends up somewhere between two-thirds and three-quarters of gross income—depending on how much you have coming out of your check in deductions and withholding. These will be discussed in more detail in the next chapter, chapter 3, "The Decision to Save."

TABLE 2.1 Reading Your Paycheck: Gross versus Net Income

Gross Income		$4,000.00
401(k) (Retirement Contribution): 3 percent of $4,000 applicable gross	($120.00)	$3,880.00
Healthcare premium	($ 50.00)	$3,830.00
Health savings account	($ 50.00)	$3,780.00
Federal income tax: 12 percent of $3,780 applicable gross	($453.60)	$3,326.40
State income tax: 3 percent	($113.40)	$3,213.00
FICA (Social Security and Medicare): 7.65 percent of $3,900 applicable gross	($298.35)	$2,914.65
Net Income		**$2,914.65**

The net pay represents how much you have available for spending—on housing, food, transportation, and everything else. This topic, budgeting, will be discussed in chapter 4, "The Decision to Spend." For now, it is important to keep in mind what your net income will likely be for budgeting purposes, as you consider various job offers and the cost of living in different cities. Take your salary, multiply it by .7 (70 percent is a good approximation of net income), and then divide by 12. This will tell you about how much money you will have to spend each month.

Now you should have a good idea of what you can expect to make when you hit the job market. The US Bureau of Labor Statistics website provides excellent data on median salaries and the growth rate of various occupations.[15] But you have also learned that salary is not the only thing you need to consider. Total compensation includes retirement and healthcare benefits as well, and the wealth that any salary will provide depends to a great extent on the cost of goods and services in the location where you are working.

Finally, monetary compensation is only one kind of utility that employment will provide to you. This book will continue to argue strongly that financial security is an important component of well-being and that it will likely become increasingly important to you as you move through the various stages of life. But there are other forms of utility that employment can provide—flexibility, the potential for advancement, and a sense of meaning and purpose. Only you can determine how to maximize these utilities.

Key Takeaways

Directions: Review the following list of key takeaways to help you remember what you learned in this chapter:

- The decision to work is a decision about how to balance life and work, how to live your values, and how to maximize your well-being.

15. Go to the "Occupational Outlook Handbook," a website hosted by the US Bureau of Labor Statistics, where you can look up profiles for different occupations to learn about the job and the entry-level requirements, the work environment, and pay levels (https://www.bls.gov/ooh/management/home.htm).

- Your college major is not the only determining factor in what kind of work you do or what kind of salary you can expect.
- Salary is only one component of total compensation. Healthcare and retirement benefits are critically important to consider. A high cost of living can make a higher salary less attractive.
- Your net income will be significantly lowered by various deductions and taxes; you can expect to receive around 70–75 percent of your gross income in net income.

Application Opportunity: Do This Now!

Directions: Complete the activities below to apply what you have learned in this chapter.

Activity 1

Go to the "Occupational Outlook Handbook" on the US Bureau of Labor Statistics website: https://www.bls.gov/ooh/management/home.htm.

Find your desired career as well as an alternative career (start in the Occupational Groups category and drill down to the actual careers there).

Report the median salary and growth rate for each occupation you have chosen.

Occupation #1________________________________

Median Salary: $_________ Growth rate:__________ percent

Occupation #2________________________________

Median Salary: $_________ Growth rate:__________ percent

Now, for the #1 career of your choice, investigate a bit deeper. Describe the work environment, the job setting, the hours:

- What is the job market like for this occupation?
- What are the employment trends for this career field?
- What are the advantages and disadvantages to this career?

Activity 2

Go to the CNN Money cost-of-living calculator: https://money.cnn.com/calculator/pf/cost-of-living/index.html.

Where do you want to live?________________________

A typical starting salary for a college graduate is around $50,000. If you were to move to Lexington, Kentucky, after graduation and earn this average salary, what would you need to earn in the desired city to be as well off as you are in Lexington?

$__________

If that salary is higher, it means the place you want to live will tend to be a little more expensive; thus, you will need a slightly higher salary to enjoy the same living standard as you would in Lexington.

If the salary is lower, it means that the city you want to live in is less expensive than Lexington. You don't need the $50,000 to maintain your Lexington living standards. You need less! Thus, if you get the $50,000 in the desired city, you will enjoy a higher standard of living.

Now let's look at city choice from the opposite direction. Choose a new city that you might really like. Assume that you live in that city and earn $50,000 there. What would you need to earn in Lexington in order to have the same standard of living as in the new city you have chosen? Report the place and the salary below.

New Desirable City:____________________

Lexington Comparable Salary:____________________

If the choice of city were based only on the cost of living, which of the three cities considered here would be the best? Explain your reasoning.

Activity 3

Consider the typical starting salary for the place you are interested in living in. Go to First Destinations for the College Class of 2018: https://www.naceweb.org/job-market/graduate-outcomes/first-destination/class-of-2018/interactive-dashboard/.

The report for the college class of 2018 provides information about where graduates at the undergraduate and graduate levels land within six months of graduation. New graduate outcomes include various types of employment (full or part time, contract, temporary, etc.), additional education, entrance into the military or other service, still seeking (not employed, not continuing education), and not seeking. The report also provides starting salary data for those employed full time.[16]

16. NACE Staff, "Average Salary for Class of 2019 Up Almost 6% over Class of 2018's," National Association of Colleges and Employers, September 4, 2020, https://www.naceweb.org/job-market/compensation/average-salary-for-class-of-2019-up-almost-6-percent-over-class-of-2018s/.

You will see seven tabs at the top of the report.

Steps for skimming the report:

1. Under the Class of 2018 tab, read the summary of the report. What are three takeaways for you? Briefly explain why each takeaway stands out to you.
2. Under the Region tab, compare the outcomes for the southeast region with another region of your choice (perhaps a region you would like to live in) for the bachelor's degree. What three comparisons are notable to you? Explain your choices.
3. Under the Academic Program tab, compare the bachelor's degree outcomes for three different disciplines/majors. You should choose your intended major and two other combinations of your choice. How do the mean starting salaries compare? What surprises you in this activity? Explain why.

Now that you understand total compensation, which job would you take?

Job A

- Salary: $40,000 per year
- Retirement: 6 percent employer contribution plus 1 percent match up to 10 percent total
- Healthcare: $100 premium with $1,500 deductible

Job B

- Salary: $45,000 per year
- Retirement: 4 percent employer contribution; no additional match
- Healthcare: $300 premium with $2,000 deductible

Activity 4

Answer the following questions regarding the pay stub below:

1. What is the employer's contribution to the employee's retirement plan, as a percentage?_____ percent
2. What is the employee's contribution? _____ percent
3. What was the employee's federal tax rate, as a percentage?_____ percent
4. What are the employee's total deductions and net pay? Fill in the boxes in the pay stub. Make sure you are only calculating the totals for the **employee**. Deductions include both personal deductions and taxes.

5. Now, a tricky one. What would the employee's net pay be if they had not participated in the employer's retirement or health savings plan? To determine this, add those amounts back into the employee's "applicable gross" and recalculate **federal taxes** at the rate you determined above (don't worry about the other taxes). Then recalculate net pay.
6. What is net pay now? $_____ How much *more* did the employee make? $______
7. How much *less* did the employee save for healthcare spending and retirement? $______
8. How much net income is the employee left with if they save this same amount of money *now*? $_____

Payment Summary

Type	Current Period
Gross Amount:	$5,000
Total Personal Deductions:	$
Net Amount:	$

Earnings

Job	Earnings	Shift	Hours or Units	Rate	Amount
Xxx	Regular Pay	1			$5,000.00
Total:					$5,000.00

Benefits, Deductions, and Taxes

Benefits and Deductions	Employee	Employer	Applicable Gross
Deductions before Federal Tax			
401(k)	$300.00	$400.00	$5,000.00
Health Savings Account	$300.00	$ 0.00	
High Deductible Health Plan	$200.00	$800.00	
Taxes			
Local Tax	$47.00	$ 0.00	$4,656.00
Federal Withholding Tax	$420.00	$ 0.00	$4,200.00
FICA Medicare	$ 65.00	$ 65.00	$4,500.00
FICA Old Age	$279.00	$279.00	$4,500.00
State Tax	$135.00	$0.00	$4,200.00

Bibliography

Abel, Jaison R., and Richard Deitz. "Do Big Cities Help College Graduates Find Better Jobs?" Liberty Street Economics, Federal Reserve Bank of New York. May 20, 2013. https://libertystreeteconomics.newyorkfed.org/2013/05/do-big-cities-help-college-graduates-find-better-jobs.html.

Abel, Jaison R., and Richard Deitz. "Agglomeration and Job Matching among College Graduates." *Regional Science and Urban Economics* 51 (March 2015): 14–24.

Broadbent, John, Michael Palumbo, and Elizabeth Woodman. "The Shift from Defined Benefit to Defined Contribution Pension Plans–Implications for Asset Allocation and Risk Management." Reserve Bank of Australia, Board of Governors of the Federal Reserve System and Bank of Canada, December 2006, 1–54. https://www.bis.org/publ/wgpapers/cgfs27broadbent3.pdf.

Burning Glass Technologies. "What Can You Do with a Liberal Arts Degree? Plenty, with the Right Skills." February 20, 2018. https://www.burning-glass.com/category/liberal-arts/.

Card, David, Alexandre Mas, Enrico Moretti, and Emmanuel Saez. "Inequality at Work: The Effect of Peer Salaries on Job Satisfaction." *American Economic Review* 102, no. 6 (2012): 2981–3003.

CNN Money. "Cost of Living: How Far Will My Salary Go in Another City?" Accessed January 15, 2020. https://money.cnn.com/calculator/pf/cost-of-living/index.html.

NACE Staff. "Average Salary for Class of 2019 Up Almost 6% over Class of 2018's." National Association of Colleges and Employers. September 4, 2020. https://www.naceweb.org/job-market/compensation/average-salary-for-class-of-2019-up-almost-6-percent-over-class-of-2018s/.

NACE Staff. "First Destinations for the College Class of 2018," National Association of Colleges and Employers, accessed March 15, 2019, https://www.naceweb.org/job-market/graduate-outcomes/first-destination/class-of-2018/interactive-dashboard/.

Pasquerella, Lynn. "Yes, Employers Do Value Liberal Arts Degrees." *Harvard Business Review*, September 19, 2019. https://hbr.org/2019/09/yes-employers-do-value-liberal-arts-degrees.

Ryan, Camille L. and Kurt Bauman, "Educational Attainment in the United States: 2015," US Census Bureau, March 2016, https://www.census.gov/content/dam/Census/library/publications/2016/demo/p20-578.pdf.

Smith, Aaron, and Janna Anderson. "AI, Robotics, and the Future of Jobs." Pew Research Center. August 6, 2014. https://www.pewresearch.org/internet/2014/08/06/future-of-jobs/.

US Bureau of Labor Statistics. "Number of Jobs, Labor Market Experience, and Earnings Growth: Results from a National Longitudinal Survey." Economic news release. August 22, 2019. https://www.bls.gov/news.release/pdf/nlsoy.pdf.

———. "Occupational Outlook Handbook." Accessed February 19, 2021. https://www.bls.gov/ooh/management/home.htm.

Verma, Sanjeev, "Career Guide: A Third of Fortune 500 CEOs Have this Degree," *Friday Magazine*, December 7, 2020, https://fridaymagazine.ae/life-culture/ask-the-experts/career-guide-a-third-of-fortune-500-ceos-have-this-degree-1.2310482.

CHAPTER 3

The Decision to Save

Invest by Paying Yourself First

Imagine...

Congratulations! You have achieved the job of your dreams. Or perhaps you are simply on your way. Okay, maybe you just don't hate getting up in the morning. But you have accepted a job offer, and, calculating net pay, you know that you will have about $3,000 to budget. You plan to rent, and luckily, you have a used car to drive, so you won't need to make a car payment. But you don't want to rent forever, and the car is getting old.

- What if you know the transmission is likely to fail in six months? Will you be able to pay for this? What if this is your only way to get to work? Will you have $1,000 to cover the expense?
- What if you know you will be married and thinking about having kids in three years? Will you be ready to buy a house? Will you have $30,000 for the down payment?
- What if you own a house five years from now and the A/C unit fails—right in the middle of summer? Will you have $5,000 to get it replaced?

These scenarios are all too common. You will encounter them, or similar ones, many times in your financial life. They are also the kinds of scenarios that can send financially stable and responsible people deep into debt and set them back years on their financial goals.

Introduction

Automate your saving, pay yourself first, and recognize that building wealth is a journey, not a destination. The big lesson of this chapter is that, before you spend money on anything else, you should pay yourself first. How do you pay yourself? By saving. Saving is a personal investment. It's an investment in your financial security, and, when you consider the devastating consequences of debt, an investment in your psychological well-being. It is the single most important thing you can do to secure your financial future. Pay yourself first—invest in yourself. Save.

In this chapter, you will learn that saving is not a singular activity. There are many kinds of saving for many different purposes—saving for short-term, unexpected needs (e.g., car repairs); longer-term expected needs (a down payment on a house); and, of course, retirement. There is also saving for healthcare spending, childcare, education, and college. There are many ways to save, and many different kinds of vehicles and investments that can be used for saving, all of which you will learn about in this chapter.

You don't have to save big in order for saving to build your wealth. Indeed, when you approach the decision to save as if it were an all-or-nothing proposition, the process becomes too overwhelming to manage. It can be much better to keep the process small at first, as small as 3–10 percent of your income, so you don't even really notice that you're missing out on that money. Make saving automatic and make it the first transaction you do when your paycheck comes into your bank account. Then step back and let time do the work. Add to your contribution slowly, over time, and allow the saving process to become a good habit, something you automatically do.

Chapter Objectives

After reading this chapter, you will be able to:

- Understand that saving is, in essence, an *investment in yourself* that protects you from financial instability, and that savings should therefore be the first place you spend your paycheck.
- Distinguish between emergency savings, both *soft* and *hard*, other savings goals, like a house, and retirement savings.
- Create a savings plan for emergencies, and attend to your other savings goals, using *online savings accounts*.
- Distinguish between different savings/investment vehicles for your retirement fund, such as stocks, certificates of deposit, government Treasuries, bonds, and various types of retirement accounts.
- Identify your *tolerance for risk* and generate an *asset allocation* for retirement savings/investment that reflects and respects that level of risk.

Save? I Am Finally Making Money ... I Want to Spend!

Before you do any spending at all, you need a sustainable, long-term savings plan. A plan sounds big and complicated, but it can really be as simple as automatically committing a small percentage of your paycheck to a separate account every time you are paid. As you grow into the habit of saving, you can add layers to the savings plan.

Think of saving as an investment and a way to ***pay yourself first***. Most of your paycheck will disappear to rent, bills, groceries, gas, the occasional Starbucks latte, that brand new iPhone release, a weekend shopping spree at the mall, the impulse purchase on Amazon ... you get the idea. Your money is going to the landlord. To Netflix. Kroger. Apple. *Where is the share that goes to you?*

Make a commitment to regular saving, every time you get paid. Don't just make a commitment; automate it. This is easy to do. Make that money disappear as fast as you get it. You'll never see it. You'll never know you had it. But you are paying yourself, and it is yours. And it will be there for you when you need it. Unlike that latte, which only lasted fifteen minutes. Or that new iPhone, which probably broke a month after the manufacturer's warranty expired.

Okay, Save for What? And How Much?

A good aspirational guideline for savings is 10 percent of your *gross* salary, but if you must start with 1–3 percent, that is enough for the process to become a habit. The amount you save does not all have to come from you. Most of us save through a company-sponsored retirement plan, and often, the company offers to match your savings as part of your job benefits. But collectively, 10 percent is an excellent benchmark, and if you *can* start there, you will set yourself up for excellent savings success down the road.

Being a bit conservative, let's say you land a job with a starting salary of $40,000 per year. You should aim for $4,000 in annual savings. Perhaps you contribute 4 percent to your company-sponsored retirement account which gets you $1,600 in savings. This leaves $2,400 for you to save on your own, which comes out to $200 a month. If you get paid biweekly, this works out to $100 per paycheck—a reasonable target.

Of course, you need to live, so whether you can afford this or not depends on a number of factors—most importantly, cost of living. Rent will eat up the biggest portion of your paycheck, so this will be your number one barrier to achieving the target. Challenge yourself to get as close to the target as possible, while acknowledging that it may or may not be realistic. What is most important is that you save *something*—even if, starting out, you can only afford to put aside $50 or $100 a month.

You have four critical savings goals; one of them is immediate, and the remainder can be pursued simultaneously. Each is highlighted in the text box and discussed in more detail below.

WHAT DO I SAVE FOR ... AND WHY?

- **A "soft" emergency fund**. Everyone needs a minimum of $2,000 set aside for the bad luck that comes our way. This is the first savings goal, because getting caught here—needing an auto repair, or facing some other unexpected expense—can set your finances back in a way that can be quite difficult to recover from.
- **A "hard" emergency fund**. Working adults need six to nine months of expenses set aside for emergencies like medical costs or losing a job. If you get pushed out of work for some reason, you need financial stability to get back on track. This type of savings is important given how volatile the economy can be, so it should be the second-highest priority.
- **A house**. Not everyone wants a house, but if that is part of your American dream, you will want to start saving for it well before you go house-hunting. You will want to put 20 percent down on a house, so $30,000–$40,000 is not a ridiculous amount. Having a good down payment makes buying the house much easier.

- **Retirement**. This savings goal seems far away, but most people will have the opportunity to start a retirement savings plan as part of their employer's benefits. Make the employee match to your 401(k)! If you don't, you are leaving part of your hard-earned salary on the table.

Your first savings goal is what I call a *soft emergency fund*. This should be about $2,000, or more if you drive an older vehicle that is unreliable. This is essentially a rainy-day fund that you have at the ready for spending circumstances that are beyond your control. And if you use any of these funds, they should be replaced immediately. Divert any future savings—for your hard emergency fund or your mortgage fund—directly back to this soft fund until it is replenished.

In 2017, 60 percent of Americans reported that they would not have enough money to cover an unexpected expense of $500.[1] The percentage increased in 2020, amid the COVID-19 pandemic, to 84 percent![2] That's right. Six out of ten, which was not great, increased to over eight out of ten, albeit in a pretty tough year financially. In a normal year, car repairs average at least $500, usually more. Medical bills for relatively simple procedures can easily top $500. And if you are a homeowner, routine repairs can run into the thousands.

An emergency expense is more than a concern that you might not be able to pay a bill. Large, unexpected expenses can make the difference between financial security and poverty. In the book *Scarcity: Why Having Too Little Means So Much*, the economist Sendhil Mullainathan and the psychologist Elda Shafir document the various conditions that perpetuate poverty.[3] One factor is simply getting behind. Falling behind on expenses can lead to a cycle of debt that is very difficult to break.

Imagine that your car breaks down just a few months after you finally start earning a real paycheck, and the repair is $1,000. What do you do? If you follow the guidelines in this book, you should have that amount ready to cover this cost in your soft emergency fund after a few months of working. If you don't, you are left with using a credit card, or hitting up Mom and Dad—something that, by the way, doesn't work as well once you've graduated!

Low-income individuals, though, often lack the friend- and family-support networks that might make borrowing an option in an emergency like this. Their friends and family members also lack financial security. They also may not have credit in good standing, having already maxed out their credit in similar situations. One recourse of last resort is the payday lender, who can offer you a one-week advance on your paycheck. An

1. Kathryn Vasel, "6 in 10 Americans Don't Have $500 in Savings," CNN Money, January 12, 2017, https://money.cnn.com/2017/01/12/pf/americans-lack-of-savings/index.html.
2. James Royal, "Survey: Nearly 3 Times as Many Americans Say They Have Less Emergency Savings versus More since Pandemic," Bankrate, August 20, 2020, https://www.bankrate.com/banking/savings/emergency-savings-survey-2020/.
3. Sendhil Mullainathan and Eldar Shafir, *Scarcity: Why Having Too Little Means So Much* (New York: Macmillan, 2013).

individual who goes this route, however, is now significantly short on their typical budget, and will run out of funds even earlier over the following months. Inevitably, this leads to more borrowing and more debt.[4]

Payday lenders are actually counting on this happening because they are more than happy to perpetuate this cycle of indebtedness. They make a lot of profit from it. One estimate says that families pay $3.4 billion in fees every year to payday lenders, and that 75 percent of those fees come from a debt trap, a rollover from a previous loan.[5] As long as you always have a soft emergency fund, you will likely never have to worry about falling into the pattern of debt and borrowing that creates so much heartache for too many people.

As a young, single individual who is renting, aim for $2,000 in soft emergency funds—a goal you should be able to reach in your first year of working without too much difficulty. As previously stated, you might need more if you have a particularly unreliable vehicle. If you are already a homeowner, or if you have children (who are more likely to land you with unexpected medical bills), you should have even more than $2,000.

This soft emergency fund is the most essential source of savings you will ever generate.

The Psychology of Saving Makes It Harder Than It Should Be

Saving is an easy idea, no doubt, but a difficult thing to do. As we have seen, because of our tendency to *discount the future*, we tend to prioritize spending now over saving later. This is because of conflicts between "the head and the heart," so to speak. Our emotions are powerful and can sometimes prevail over our cooler-headed notions about longer-term benefits. This is especially true when it comes to spending. Marketers work very hard to make their products push our emotional buttons and to provide us with many tempting reasons to buy. Saving requires *executive functions,* as psychologists say. These functions include resisting temptation, self-regulation, planning, and so on.

Think back to the marshmallow test we discussed earlier, which provides a simple measure of executive functioning. We know that people who can pass the test are much more successful over the long term on a number of different life outcomes. But we also know that a lack of trust can make it harder for kids to "pass" the marshmallow test.

In fact, a great deal of research suggests that many different kinds of insecurity can influence people's tendency to spend now versus save for later. This includes income insecurity, social insecurities, and emotional and ego insecurities. We will discuss some of this research in the next chapter, "The Decision to Spend." But for now, simply consider the fact that income insecurity can make saving more difficult. In some ways, this is quite obvious—if you are experiencing income insecurity, you simply may not have the funds to save in the first place. Indeed, it could be entirely rational to focus on spending, to the extent that it meets your basic needs for survival. But other consequences are more indirect. People spend for lots of reasons besides those related to meeting their basic needs. The emotional stress of income insecurity itself can make resisting temptation difficult, for instance.

4. See Mullainathan and Shafir, Chapter 5, "Borrowing and Myopia," for a critical understanding of the ways that borrowing can sneak up on us.
5. Center for Responsible Lending, "The State of Lending: Payday Loans," September 10, 2013, https://www.responsiblelending.org/state-lending/payday-loans.

For a parallel example, consider the restricted dieter, who spends the entire day trying to overcome temptation and live on a reduced number of calories. Research shows that this kind of dieting is doomed to failure because restricted eating almost always leads to overindulgence.[6] After the dieter spends a great deal of time being worried and stressed about calories, the brain's executive functions are a bit worn down, and it becomes much harder for that person to resist the temptation to indulge.

Something similar can happen when it comes to money. Not having enough money leads to chronic stress and worry, which can, perversely, make splurging a little more likely.[7] What is perhaps more worrisome is that income insecurity early in life can have lasting, longer-term effects, making saving and resisting temptation more difficult even when financial stability is achieved. It's as if the brain learns how to operate in an environment of scarcity—an environment in which prioritizing spending over saving is perfectly rational. These learned patterns of behavior persist and can be difficult to unwind, especially if you are not aware of their influence on you.

Falling on Hard Times Requires Hard Emergency Savings

Once you have ensured you will not fall behind on your expenses by building a soft emergency fund, turn your attention to establishing a more substantial fund for a longer-term setback. This "hard" emergency fund will primarily be a buffer against a loss in employment.

Losing a job can be one of the most difficult things that happens in your life. According to one major stress index (the Social Readjustment Rating Scale), a layoff is listed eighth out of forty-three stressful life events—just behind the death of a family member, experiencing a major illness, or getting married.[8]

Unfortunately, a job loss is more common today than it once was. Long gone are the days of the "company man," who worked thirty years for the same corporation and retired on a pension. According to the most recent data available from the Bureau of Labor Statistics, today's workers spend only about 4.1 years, on average, with a given employer. Even among those with college degrees, average job tenure increases only to about 5.2 years.[9] Now, not all of these people changed jobs because they were laid off—much of this movement is due to fundamental changes in the way employment is structured. Millennials, in particular, change jobs frequently to take advantage of new opportunities and maximize career potential. One recent survey showed that on average, today's younger workers have had four jobs by the time they are thirty-two.[10]

6. See, for example, A. R. Green, M. Larkin, and V. Sullivan, 2009, "Oh Stuff It! The Experience and Explanation of Diet Failure: An Exploration Using Interpretative Phenomenological Analysis," *Journal of Health Psychology* 14, no. 7 (October 2009): 997–1008.
7. Mullainathan and Shafir call this the bandwidth tax (*Scarcity: Why Having Too Little Means So Much*, 43).
8. Saul McLeod, "SRRS—Stress of Life Events," *Simply Psychology*, 2010, accessed February 26, 2021, https://www.simplypsychology.org/SRRS.html.
9. US Bureau of Labor Statistics, "Employee Tenure Summary," economic news release, September 22, 2020, https://www.bls.gov/news.release/tenure.nr0.htm.
10. Guy Berger, "Will This Year's College Grads Job-Hop More Than Previous Grads?" LinkedIn Official Blog, April 12, 2016, https://blog.linkedin.com/2016/04/12/will-this-year_s-college-grads-job-hop-more-than-previous-grads.

But layoffs can and do happen with regularity, particularly when the economy is in recession. For instance, 20 percent of American workers lost their job at some point during the period from 2009–2014.[11]

As bad as losing a job can be, number sixteen on the list of stressors is a major change in one's financial state. Number 21? Foreclosure on a mortgage. Having a hard emergency fund can prevent a stressful situation from becoming much more stressful than it has to be. It is one thing to lose your job; losing your ability to meet your basic financial needs and losing your home could make a bad situation untenable.

There is little good data on how long a typical job search takes. One general rule suggests one month per $10,000 of income, or six months for a $60,000-a-year job. Some research shows that the average length of a job search is three months. So, expecting a three- to six-month search is reasonable, and planning to save for six months of living expenses is a secure strategy. More recently, with the experience of more extreme economic downturns, personal finance experts have been promoting nine months of monthly expenses as a reasonable hard emergency fund guideline. To a large extent, the savings goal you choose will be a function of your job. If you have a very stable job—for example, if you are a teacher with a yearly contract—you may be fine with the six-month fund. If you are a contractor or a gig worker, having a bigger emergency fund can serve you well.

To estimate the size of your hard emergency fund, first consider only your necessities. With no income, what will you absolutely have to have available to meet your basic expenses? This should include your rent or mortgage payment, utilities, and groceries, of course. Beyond that, think of what you really need and what you can live without. You can certainly eat out less or eliminate restaurants altogether. You can make coffee at home. You can go without cable or Netflix. But you might need your internet connection or smartphone for job searching. You may also need some funds for job search expenses such as interview clothing and travel.

Do not forget to consider healthcare expenses. You may keep your health insurance for a period of time after losing your job, or you may not. If you lose coverage, you have the ability under the federal COBRA act to keep it—if you pay the entire premium yourself. Or you could look at buying a high-deductible plan on the open market, which may be cheaper, depending on how good of an insurance plan you had with your employer. Either way, though, this could add hundreds of dollars to your monthly expenses. Your health is not something to take a risk on after a job loss.

For a young, single renter with $800 rent, $2,000 per month should be more than sufficient—maybe a little less. So, expect to save at least $10,000 toward your hard emergency fund. If you are married and/or have children, and if you own a house, it will inevitably be more—say, $20,000 for a family of four.

This is a sizeable sum of money, so obviously, this savings goal could take a lot longer to achieve. Do not necessarily divert retirement savings to establish your hard emergency fund, especially if your employer matches some portion of your income, given the critical time value of money to the growth of your savings. One possibility would be to split your savings evenly between retirement and your living expense fund, after you cover the income match.

As with your soft emergency fund, once you have a hard emergency fund, don't touch it. And if you do lose your job and have to draw it down, begin to replace it immediately upon becoming reemployed.

11. Jim Puzzanghera, "One-Fifth of U.S. Workers Were Laid Off in Past Five Years, Study Says," *Los Angeles Times*, September 24, 2014, https://www.latimes.com/business/la-fi-layoffs-unemployment-jobs-economy-20140924-story.html.

Saving for a House or Something Else...

Once you have established both a soft and a hard emergency fund, your final near-term goal might be a down payment on a home—assuming you wish to be a homeowner. In chapter 5, "The Decision to Owe," you will learn a great deal more about how much money you can expect to spend on a house, and when you should consider buying one. The amount you will need for a down payment could vary greatly, depending on the cost of housing where you live and the structure of the mortgage. Given a median sale price of around $215,000 in 2019 for first-time home buyers, a good target would be about $40,000—or 20 percent of a $200,000 home.[12] However, it is possible, if not always desirable, to put much less than 20 percent toward a down payment. Furthermore, housing makes the single greatest difference in cost of living for different locations. The range of what you need for a down payment could quite realistically be anything between $5,000 and $100,000.

Saving toward a down payment, or toward something else that's important to you, occurs ***after*** the soft and hard emergency funds are in place and in tandem with saving toward retirement. How quickly you choose to reach your target should depend on several factors, such as the amount you are trying to save, the cost of renting versus buying a home, and other factors that will be discussed at length in the chapter on borrowing. But your down payment on a home will quite likely be the single greatest expense you ever incur, and it will take a while to save for it. Your retirement savings cannot wait that long, so you will have to do the third and fourth savings goals, house and retirement, in tandem.

How Do I Create a Savings Plan?

You don't want to put your emergency money in a cookie jar, stuff your mattress with it, or bury it in the backyard. It is not a bad idea to have it in a place that takes some effort to get to, a place where the money is walled off from immediate access. If you simply swipe a card in your wallet in a moment of weakness, you might spend it for something you really want in the moment. To avoid feeling guilty later, put the funds in a place that takes a couple of days to access. When you add a few steps to accessing the money, you force yourself to evaluate whether you really want to use it for any given purpose.

You want your savings accessible but not too accessible. You want your emergency savings to be safe, but it would be nice if the funds earned a little bit of interest. ***Online savings accounts*** can make these goals easy to achieve while providing access when needed.

Online Savings Accounts

Any traditional bank will allow you to set up a savings account that you monitor and manage online. If you are saving, however, you should be getting some kind of a return, as previously discussed. Many banks that only offer online services, such as Synchrony and Ally, offer particularly good interest rates—at least by comparison. The post–Great Recession and postpandemic years have been particularly hard on savings interest rates, due in part to federal monetary policies that encourage spending over saving. A 1.25 percent

12. NAR Staff. "2019 Profile of Home Buyers and Sellers," National Association of Realtors (2019) accessed June 28, 2021, https://www.nysar.com/wp-content/uploads/2020/01/2019-NAR-HBS.pdf.

interest rate may not sound like much, and indeed, it may not be enough to completely mitigate the effects of inflation. But it is much better than the .10 percent interest rates that are typical of traditional savings accounts these days. And the rates fluctuate. Prior to the recession, 4 percent interest on online savings was not uncommon, though that would be impossible to find in 2021.

Online banks can offer higher interest rates for a simple reason. They lack the overhead costs associated with the brick-and-mortar retail spaces of traditional banks. They also tend to offer a much more limited set of options and streamlined services, further reducing costs. Finally, compared to local or regional banks, they have access to higher amounts of capital because anyone, anywhere can save their money with an online bank. There are many virtues of having a local bank or credit union, but for emergency savings, online bank accounts are ideal.

Once you have an account with an online bank, it is easy to set up additional ones, and the bank will be happy to have you do so. You could easily have a separate account for each emergency fund, and even a third for a mortgage fund, all in one place. You could even contribute $25 a month to a Corvette Stingray or Gibson Les Paul account, if it helps you keep the money straight. And online banks make the saving part easy. You can link your checking account (or whatever account your paycheck is deposited into) directly to your online bank account and set up automatic deposits. Set those deposits up to go through a day or two after your paycheck arrives, and you will never even see or miss the money.

The Mental Accounting of Saving and Spending

In many ways, setting up separate accounts for separate savings purposes is a good strategy because it mirrors the way we think about saving and spending, psychologically. In a now-classic study, the behavioral economist Richard Thaler presented people with a scenario in which they had to make a decision about whether to spend $20 on a theater performance. There was a catch (of course): In one case, people were asked to imagine that they had brought $40 with them but discovered they had lost $20 on the way to the performance. In the other case, people were asked to imagine they had already purchased a $20 ticket but discovered they had lost the ticket on the way to the performance.

Notice that in both cases, people had "lost" $20 worth of value—the only difference was whether or not that lost $20 had already been spent on a ticket. Both were faced with essentially the same choice: whether to spend an additional $20 on a new ticket. Who do you think was more likely to buy a new ticket?

It was the individuals who had lost $20 but had not already purchased a ticket.

According to Thaler's work as well as subsequent research by others, this is due to a phenomenon known as *mental accounting*.[13] Psychologically, we set up different accounts for different purposes—once an account has been "filled" or "tapped," it can be difficult to close or reopen. People who imagined losing a ticket they had already purchased "closed" the mental account for this purchase. For those who lost $20, the account was still open. From the perspective of an economist, this is completely irrational behavior. Psychologically, though, it's how we think about money—and we can make saving easier by going with the grain of human nature instead of against it. Our savings account will be well served if we can find ways to keep it open.

13. Richard Thaler, "Mental Accounting and Consumer Choice," *Marketing Science* 4, no. 3 (Summer 1985): 199–214.

The lesson from mental accounting for savers is that as income increases, savings should also increase, even if only by a small percentage. When you get a raise, consider saving it instead of spending it. Or, if that feels like too much, save an additional percentage each year. If you are saving 10 percent, make it a practice to increase that by 1 percent each year for five years, no matter what raise you get.

Keep Emergency Savings Safe

Savings in a bank carries lower risk because the money is covered by the Federal Deposit Insurance Corporation (FDIC). The Banking Act of 1933 created the FDIC to protect consumers in the wake of the Great Depression, when so many people rushed to withdraw their savings at once that many banks collapsed. FDIC protects savings at any insured bank up to $250,000. That is, if the bank goes under, the government will replace your losses. FDIC also applies to some other low-risk investments, such as money market accounts and Certificates of Deposit. FDIC insurance does *not* cover higher-risk investments, such as stocks and bonds. If a company in which you are a stockholder goes bankrupt, chances are you could lose the entire value of your stock holdings.

You need to have your emergency funds available at a moment's notice. The lingo in finance is that you should keep your emergency funds *liquid*, which is why you do not want to buy stocks with them. There is no guarantee that you will be able to sell your stock investments at the exact moment you need the cash, as those stocks may have lost value since you purchased them. Furthermore, most brokerages will hold your funds for some period after you sell stock before you can access the cash. But your retirement savings will not have the same liquidity consideration as your emergency funds. Add to this that you would like to earn a larger return on these savings so that you do not have to save quite so much, and a little more risk becomes justifiable, if not palatable.

Beyond your online savings account, you may also want a brokerage account for a different type of savings—*the savings you invest in order to build your retirement.* Navigating the retirement process will require you to understand some more complicated savings vehicles! You will find more detail on preparing for retirement in chapter 7, "The Decision to Retire," but understanding how to *start saving for retirement* is the first step, and what you need to know to get started is next.

Where Can I Invest My Retirement Savings?

A big financial decision you will face is how to allocate your retirement savings among asset classes such that ***you earn a high enough return over time to retire, while still being able to sleep at night.*** Retirement savings are longer-term and should be placed in higher-return savings vehicles, more commonly referred to as investments. In general, the longer term the investment, the higher the return you can expect to earn. However, higher returns usually mean greater risk. Some investments, such as stocks, can both gain and lose value over time, and others, such as bonds, do not come with any guarantee of return or repayment on the initial investment. Because retirement is far in your future, you will have the time to overcome shorter-term losses, and the higher returns will significantly cut down the amount you have to put back out of each paycheck. Higher returns allow you to save a lot less, as demonstrated in chapter 1, "The Decision to Be Financially Literate." But because the return is not guaranteed, you are assuming some risk when you invest.

We will discuss investing in the stock market at greater length in chapter 6, "The Decision to Own Shares." Below, we simply define the various asset classes of savings and investment options that are available in the typical retirement account. It is essential to point out that savings and investment can often be used interchangeably in the media and among friends, but there is a notable difference between the two activities: ***Investment involves more risk than savings.***

It is nice to earn a little return on savings, but it is usually more important to keep savings liquid and safe. Investment for retirement has the time to grow, and most people will need to take advantage of the higher returns that a little risk adds to the expected return. The next section considers the places where savings for retirement can be invested, starting with the least risky and the lowest returns and moving up from there.

Money Market Accounts

Money market accounts differ little from traditional savings accounts. Historically, interest rates on money market accounts were better than those on savings accounts; today, however, the rates can be the same on both types of accounts. At the time of this writing in 2021, a typical savings account might pay around 0.145 percent, whereas a money market account pays .4 percent and a good online savings account is paying .5 percent.[14] Most financial institutions offer access to money market accounts. These accounts have higher savings rates but are basically like checking accounts for banks. They make a pool of funds available for banks to borrow on a short-term basis. Just like with a checking account, the saver can deposit or withdraw the funds at any time and write checks on the money five or six times a month. Your brokerage account will be linked to a money market account, and this is the vehicle through which you deposit and withdraw cash in and out of investments.

Certificates of Deposit

Typically known as CDs, these investments make funds available to financial institutions for longer-term borrowing needs. Because of their longer-term nature, CDs are a little less liquid than money market funds. That is, when you invest in a CD, you are agreeing to have your money held for a given period—typically, three months, six months, or somewhere between one and five years. The longer the time frame, the higher the interest rate. In early 2021, for instance, a three-month CD averages around .4 percent, while a five-year CD rate is around 1 percent.[15] If you need the cash from a CD, you can withdraw your funds, but you will pay a penalty. In many cases, you may forfeit some of the interest that you have earned. Like money market accounts, CDs are insured by the FDIC. Though CDs were popular forty years ago, they have become less used because the rates they pay have fallen so much. You give up a lot when you park your money and get such a low return.

14. Lending Tree, "High Interest Online Savings Accounts," accessed February 27, 2021, https://www.lendingtree.com/banking/savings/.
15. Matthew Goldberg, "Best CD Rates for May 2021," Bankrate, accessed May 19, 2021, https://www.bankrate.com/banking/cds/cd-rates/.

Treasury Securities

Treasury securities come in three varieties: T-bills, T-notes, and T-bonds. These securities provide funds for the government to borrow. While not FDIC insured, Treasury securities are "backed by the 'full faith and credit' of the US Government."[16] Therefore, they are considered to be among the lowest risk of all investments. Treasury securities act as *fixed-income* investments, which means they pay a fixed rate of interest, known as the *yield*, on a given amount purchased. T-bills are the shortest-term securities, held for periods of one year or less. The time is so short that T-bills do not pay interest but are sold at a discount to their par value, which is what they pay when they mature. The investor makes money by lending less than is received when the bill matures. T-notes have maturities between one and ten years, and T-bonds are issued for periods of thirty years. Generally, T-bills pay the lowest and T-bonds pay the highest interest rates, and when the maturities are shown along a horizontal axis and the expected interest rates of return are on the vertical axis, you get what is known as the yield curve.

In figure 3.1, four different patterns for the yield curve have been captured for four different days across the last twenty years. The shape of the yield curve is often an early indicator of the economic cycle and reflects market expectations for the larger economy. The three bottom graphs of the yield curve for different days from 2007 to 2018 are generally upward sloping, where short-term rates of return are lower than long-term rates. This curve shape implies that people require a higher return for parking their cash in a Treasury for longer. It makes sense that a rational investor would want more return for lending their money over a longer time. When the curve is flatter, as it was on October 22, 2007, all Treasury maturities are offering approximately the same yield. We call this a flattening, and it suggests that the economy could be slowing. The economy did slow quite a bit in 2008 with the housing crisis. When the yield curve is very steep, like on February 15, 2011, an economic boom may be close at hand.

But when the yield curve inverts—when short-term maturities pay more than long-term maturities—it can be a leading signal that the economy is headed for a recession in the next six months or so. This was the case for Treasury yields represented by the top line in the graph below, marked July 10, 2000. Indeed, the economy did move into a recession seven months later, between March and November of 2001. This pattern of the yield curve may be important to watch once you become a stock investor in chapter 6, "The Decision to Own Shares."

16. FINRA, "U.S. Treasury Securities," accessed June 15, 2021, https://www.finra.org/investors/learn-to-invest/types-investments/bonds/types-of-bonds/us-treasury-securities.

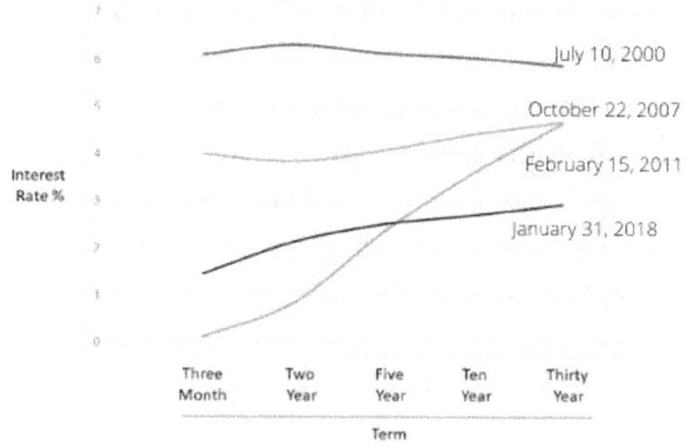

FIGURE 3.1 Yield Curve Shapes

Because Treasuries are considered very safe investments, their yields are typically much lower than what one could obtain with a similar kind of investment in corporate bonds. In fact, it is common to refer to the ten-year Treasury note as the best approximation of the *risk-free rate*. This is the return that must be earned for "parking your money" without worrying about default, or the possibility of not getting your principal back. This feature of safety makes Treasuries very useful for preserving the principal and creating very predictable cash flows for an investor. Further, when the future of the market seems uncertain and there are fears of market losses, there can be a flight to safety into Treasury investments. Investors will watch the ten-year Treasury rate carefully as a measure of market confidence. When the ten-year Treasury note rises to a level beyond current economic expectations, this signals to market participants that the economy could be on track to overheating because investors are taking their money out of Treasuries to earn the big returns promised by the stock market. When the ten-year yield falls, that is an indication that the demand for Treasuries is increasing as more demand pushes up the price and the yield drops. Thus, expect market watchers to talk about the position of the ten-year note in daily recaps of the stock market activity for the day.

Bonds

Bonds work similarly to Treasury securities. They are fixed-income investments that pay a regular interest rate, usually twice a year or semiannually. Whereas Treasury securities are provided by the federal government, bonds can be issued by any entity to raise funds for financing the organization. Local governments issue bonds, called *municipals* or *munis*, to build infrastructure and sports arenas. Corporations issue bonds to fund new ventures. Foreign governments, financial institutions, and even school districts issue bonds. Bonds are considered a lower-risk investment than stocks; however, their risk can vary widely. They are also not FDIC insured.

Bonds are typically issued at a given principal rate known as the *par value*. For instance, a $1,000 bond would have a par value of $1,000, meaning that this is the amount that will be paid at *maturity*. The maturity date is the time for which the bond can be traded—typically thirty years or less. The *coupon* amount is the bond yield, or the amount of annual interest paid to the investor. Bonds can be purchased at par value but may often be selling at a discount or a premium—that is, at a lower or higher value than par. This occurs because of trading in bond markets that raises and lowers the value of the investment. Finally, bonds may have a *call provision*, which allows the borrowing institution to pay the bond back early. The borrower will do this if market interest rates fall, and they can borrow money cheaply at the going market rate.

The riskiness of a bond investment is captured by its yield. Bonds that are considered riskier are those that have a greater chance of default and must offer a higher rate of return in order to be held. All bonds are given a credit rating by one of three credit rating agencies: Moody's, Standard & Poor's, and Fitch. Institutional investors are often required to invest only in investment-grade bonds, which means they are not allowed to invest in bonds with ratings below B+. Bonds with lower grades are viewed as too risky and are often called ***junk bonds***. A person who is averse to risk will want to avoid these as well.

Aside from their differences, all of these savings vehicles have two things in common: they provide funds for institutions to borrow so that they might grow, and they offer a return to offset the cost of savings to the saver. The holder of the bond becomes a creditor for the institution and is called a debtholder, a bondholder, or a lender. If the organization goes bankrupt, the bondholders are paid first if any funds are left. Notably, the bondholder does not get a bigger return if the organization does well; the return is specified up front. Equities, on the other hand, offer a different kind of investment: a share of *ownership* in a company.

Equities

The most common form of equity investment is *stock*, represented by a share of ownership in a company or corporation. The word equity indicates a level of ownership stake in the firm, while stock is what you physically trade to increase or decrease your equity stake in a firm. Know that investors will interchangeably refer to equity investments or stock investments, and when they do, they are almost always referring to the same concept. Chapter 6, "The Decision to Own Shares," will explain how stock investments work in much greater detail. For now, simply understand that companies issue stock in the form of stock ownership shares to raise capital for their operations. Unlike bonds, however, stocks provide more than money for borrowing. Investors are literally buying a piece of the company; when you invest in stock, you become a shareholder, a stockholder, and an owner in the firm.

Your investment return will rise and fall with the success and failure of the underlying firm. This happens because stocks are bought and sold in a market, like any other product or service. Stock prices rise and fall for the same reason that the prices of goods rise and fall: supply and demand. When investors expect that a company will perform well, they may expect that the value of the company will increase, through greater sales and revenue or some other mechanism. They may also expect that other investors will reach the same conclusion and decide to buy the stock to capture the increase in value. As more investors decide to buy the stock, the increased demand for the limited supply of ownership puts upward pressure on the price, and the price of the stock increases.

The opposite happens when investors expect the company to do poorly. In this case, fewer investors are interested in buying the stock, which puts downward pressure on the stock price due to decreased demand. Current stockholders may see the declining price and decide to sell too, either to realize whatever gain they may have made from purchasing the stock at a lower price or to avoid further losses. This increased supply puts further downward pressure on the price of the stock.

Because the value can fluctuate so easily, equities carry more risk than bonds, Treasuries, CDs, or money market investments. In fact, it is possible to lose everything you invested if a company goes out of business. And like bonds, stock investments are not FDIC insured. Despite this, there is simply no surer path to long-term financial security than investments in stock markets. In fact, it is almost certain that your retirement funds will be invested in the stock market, and this is true whether you are in a defined contribution *or* a defined benefit plan. Most of us cannot save enough to retire without the stock market.

How Do I Allocate My Savings for Retirement among These Choices?

What you will have to decide is how you wish to allocate your retirement savings among the categories described above. Most of us do this, at least initially, through a retirement plan offered by our employer. On the first day on a new job, human resources personnel may ask you how much of your paycheck you want to put into the company's retirement savings plan for each pay period. Including the employer's offer to match some of this savings, you want to aim to budget 10–15 percent of your gross paycheck to retirement savings. This may be more than you can budget for at first, but that is OK; simply work to increase the percentage over time until you reach the target range.

Given the percentage you contribute to retirement savings, you will also get to think about how you want your portfolio allocated among asset classes. There is no one-size-meets-all answer to this choice, but your uninformed, first response might be to look at the investment options offered by the employer and simply split your allocation among the choices provided in equal amounts—say, 25 percent to money market, 25 percent to Treasuries, 25 percent to bonds, and 25 percent to equities. You might think, "I am not sure what is best, and this way, I will have a little invested in each thing." The investment industry calls this strategy ***naïve diversification***. The problem with this strategy is that you can put too much of your savings into vehicles that will not earn you the return you need to retire well. Plus, you are treating all the investment options as if they were equal, and this is a mistake because of the differences in risk and return that were discussed above.

Choosing the asset allocation for your retirement portfolio is a much more nuanced and important choice than it may seem on that first day of work, when your focus and excitement is really all about the new opportunity to work. Ultimately, your asset allocation choices will be guided by your attitude towards risk. Your ***tolerance for risk*** is measured by your ***ability*** and ***willingness*** to handle the variability of the returns in your retirement account over time. If your investments drop 10 percent or more very quickly, will you feel huge amounts of anxiety and want to sell before the investment drops even more? It is exceedingly important to have a notion of your tolerance for risk before you begin your retirement savings plan, so that you can make asset allocation choices consistent with your level of risk. Consider how to determine your risk tolerance in the text box below.

RISK TOLERANCE—ABILITY VERSUS WILLINGNESS

The wealth management industry distinguishes between the *ability* to take risk and the *willingness* to do so.

Ability: The ability to take risk will be a function of your age, your time horizon, your career flexibility, and the amount of wealth you have.

Age: The younger you are, or the farther you are from retirement, the more able you are to handle and recover from a downturn in your portfolio.

Investment time horizon: The longer the time period before you need your money, the more able you are to take the risk for achieving higher returns. If you need the money within five years, you do not want to place it in equities because the value might be down when you need the funds.

Career flexibility: If you are in a job that you love and there are no constraints on when you retire (e.g., a professor with tenure), you have a better ability to take risk. However, if your job is physically demanding and your skills will not easily translate to a different career option (e.g., a construction worker), you will have a lower ability to handle risk.

Wealth: If you have other resources beyond these investments, you have a greater ability to take risk. The more wealth you have access to, the easier it is to accept risk. A very regular income can help here. If you are living paycheck to paycheck and are doing contract work that could be seasonal, you will not have as much ability to accept risk.

Willingness: Your willingness to accept risk is more about the anxiety you would experience if there were losses in your investment. If you are focused on stability and income from the portfolio—if you can't sleep at night if the investment decreases—your willingness to take risk is lower.

How would you feel if ... ?: Questions about how you would feel if an investment fell by 10 percent, 20 percent, or 30 percent establish your willingness to take risk. They are all questions to try to understand how you feel about the trade-off between risk and return. Most people do not like risk, but some can be paid to take risk. The rule is this: the higher the risk, the higher the expected return must be in order to take it. But some people really don't like risk, and taking risks impacts the quality of their life.

What would you do if ... ?: The other way to understand your willingness to take risk is to answer questions about what you would do if the returns on your investments fell by a lot. The more likely you would be to sell the investment immediately after a fall, the lower your willingness to accept risk. The more likely you are to trust your plan of investment, the asset allocations, and stick with it, the higher your willingness to take risk.

By far, the greatest thing in your favor is your age and the time you have before retirement. These two factors give you a lot of tolerance. Most of us need to accept some risk, especially early in our careers, to grow our retirement savings to a level sufficient to support us in our old age. Even so, it is worth paying attention to how you feel and to how you would react to a down swing, because the wrong response could compromise your goals. If you sell at the bottom of the market because you have anxiety about losing even more, you can really hurt your goals for retirement—and lose a lot of money!

If you are interested in exploring what your risk tolerance is, there are a number of free "investor profile quizzes" online, which will ask you ten to fifteen questions that assess your risk tolerance and help you decide on your asset allocations between cash, bonds, and stocks. Simply search for "risk tolerance and asset allocation."[17] This opportunity provides only a general guideline, however, because hypothetical questions about how you *might* react do not always capture how you *do* react.

Ultimately, your risk tolerance will range between conservative, moderate, and aggressive. Table 3.1 provides suggested percentages for investments in asset classes, given your risk tolerance. This can serve as a guideline for the investment strategy you take with your retirement savings.

TABLE 3.1 Asset Allocations for Risk Tolerance

	Conservative	**Moderate**	**Aggressive**
Cash	15–30 percent	5 percent	5 percent
Bonds	45–50 percent	30–35 percent	0–10 percent
Stocks	20–45 percent	60–65 percent	85–90 percent

There are ranges under each risk tolerance category, and your only constraint is that the percentage allocation you choose must add up to 100 percent.

If you have a risk tolerance that is ***conservative***, you hold a lower percentage of stock so that the return on your portfolio does not move around as much. You may tend to hold a greater proportion of your resources in cash, or you may be a newer investor! Remember: you are saving the cash for an emergency first, so it is OK if your cash percentage is a little higher when you start out. Your position in bonds offers some return but adds a lot of stability to your annual returns. You still hold stocks, though, because you will need the returns

17. A particularly nice risk tolerance quiz, where you don't have to sign up for anything, can be found at Charles Schwab, "Investor Profile Questionnaire," 2018, https://www.schwabmoneywise.com/public/file/P-4038840/InvestorProfileQuestionnaire.pdf.

that come with stocks to get that compounding of savings discussed earlier. Almost every young person will put the largest percentage in stocks in order to capture the expected returns.

At the other end of the spectrum, you might be categorized as ***aggressive*** if you are among those with a lot of risk tolerance. You have a little bit of cash (including your soft and hard emergency funds) but are focused on growth and the appreciation of your investments. You are in the market for at least ten years and don't plan to need the resources before then. You may have to watch the value of your investments move around quite a bit. Sometimes, you may have to live with the fear that the returns will not rebound. Think about how you would have felt in March 2020, when the stock market fell 26 percent with the realization of the COVID-19 pandemic. If you can handle a 30 percent drop in value without panicking and selling, you might be considered aggressive.

Your ability to handle movements in your retirement savings must be balanced against your desire to reach your savings goal. Many will caution you to choose a little less risk until you really understand how you would react to a downturn. The better you understand the ways the market moves, the less risk averse you may become.

You may be thinking, "This is so not my wheelhouse!" If so, that is OK, really. You can allocate your retirement savings to what is known as a ***target-date fund***. A target-date fund sets your allocation according to how far away you are from retirement. As you near the end of a thirty- or forty-year working career, the target-date allocation automatically adjusts the asset mix toward less risky investment vehicles. At the most basic level, you start with more stocks at the beginning of your career, and as you get closer to retirement, the allocation becomes more focused on bonds and/or retirement annuities. This allows you to get both the growth you need early on and the stability that helps you sleep at night as you reach retirement. If you plan to retire in 2070, your target-date fund might invest 95 percent in various equity classes and 5 percent in fixed income. The high weight to stocks reflects the low trade-off between risk and return when you are early in your career. Twenty years later, the bonds portion of the portfolio will be as high as 10 percent, with no cash allocation. But after thirty years of working, the target-date fund will automatically be rebalanced so that as you near retirement, you might have 25 percent in cash, 10 percent in bonds, and 65 percent in equities. The key is time. The fund recovers after a market pullback with time, and as the worker nears retirement, the asset mix becomes less volatile.

This is a great solution for those who do not wish to pick individual classes of investment but wish to start saving for retirement. Different investment styles are considered more carefully in "The Decision to Own Shares," but target-date funds are a very good example of ***passive investing***. A passive investment strategy is designed to earn the return on the market and recognizes that beating the market is hard and is often not worth the costs. The goal is to earn the market's return; the plan will have a loss in some years, but over time, retirement savings will grow, on average, at the average market rate, between 6 percent and 10 percent.

Target-date funds are selected by workers who want to "set it and forget it," and they became exceedingly popular between 2010 and 2020. One report estimates that at the time of this writing in 2021, nearly $1.5 *trillion* dollars is invested in target-date funds, mostly through employer-sponsored defined contribution plans.[18] Vanguard reports that 77 percent of retirement plan participants use these funds as part

18. Mike Palmer, "Why Target Date Funds Miss the Mark," Kiplinger, March 25, 2021, https://www.kiplinger.com/investing/602499/why-target-date-funds-miss-the-mark.

of their retirement savings plan, with two-thirds of that group holding *only* target-date funds.[19] If you don't pick a mix for your asset allocation, your firm will often place you in one of these funds, because the firm has a fiduciary duty to protect your choices if you don't choose for yourself.

Many individuals do all of their saving toward retirement in an employer-sponsored retirement plan, especially when they are just starting their career. There is good reason for this, which will be explored next.

How Do I Start My Retirement Plan?

Your employer's retirement plan is a great place to begin your retirement savings not only because of matching benefits and ease of entry for signing up and making contributions, but also because of the ***tax advantages*** in these plans. As you have already learned, it is possible to realize very large gains—$1 million or more—with relatively small monthly savings contributions to an investment account. Additional income will mean new taxes.

"Nothing is certain except death and taxes."[20] A good retirement plan will push the first circumstance well into the future and the second as low as legally possible. Understanding the tax implications of your investment choices is critical for protecting your returns.

Tax-Advantaged Accounts

Because the stock market is so critical to retirement savings, and because we are not naturally inclined to save on our own, the federal government offers important tax incentives to savers. As you learned in the last chapter, like healthcare premiums, retirement contributions can be deducted from *gross* income, before taxes are applied, and the money grows tax-free. This essentially makes it possible to save money that would have been absorbed by the tax man, allowing you to keep a bigger share of your income, though you will have to wait to spend it after you retire! Be aware, however, that because this is such an attractive offer, the government limits the contribution amount that can be made tax-free in any given year. These contribution limits are high enough, though, that they shouldn't have any impact on your savings until well into your career. And the IRS does want its tax slice at some point, so it will require you to spend some of your savings once you reach a certain age (in 2020, that age is seventy-two years); the amount is called the *required minimum distribution* or RMD. Because the time value of money also applies to taxes, legally deferring them until later gives you a valuable opportunity! The text box below provides an example of how tax benefits can be captured through the employer's retirement plan.

19. Vanguard, How America Saves 2019: Vanguard 2018 Defined Contribution Plan Data, June 2019, https://pressroom.vanguard.com/nonindexed/Research-How-America-Saves-2019-Report.pdf.
20. Benjamin Franklin gave us this idiom in 1789 when referring to the expected durability of the newly written Constitution of the United States, but it seems worth noting as we consider aspects of retirement savings and investment.

THE TAX BENEFITS OF THE EMPLOYER'S RETIREMENT PLAN

Imagine that you make \$5,000 per month gross (a \$60,000 salary)—once again, before taxes and other deductions are taken from your check. Now imagine that you contribute 6 percent of your pay to your 401(k) plan, or \$300 per month. Your taxable income is \$4,700—or \$5,000 minus the \$300 contribution. If you have no other pretax deductions and your federal tax rate is 15 percent, your tax liability is \$705 (\$4,700 × .15). This leaves you with a net income of \$3,995.

Had you not made a 6 percent contribution to your 401(k), you would owe 15 percent federal taxes on the full \$5,000 amount, or \$750, leaving you with a net income of \$4,250. If you were to then save the same \$300 amount, you would have only \$3,950, or \$45 *less* than you would have if the contribution had been made pretax. Another way to think of this is that you were able to save \$300 for a cost of only \$255! Notice that this \$45 difference is the 15 percent taxes applied to the \$300 amount that was not set aside pretax. So, you can always calculate the size of the pretax benefit by simply calculating federal taxes on your savings amount.

Of course, this example considers only the effect on the federal income tax liability. Most states also levy state income taxes, and many of these states do not tax your retirement contributions. And as you have already learned, healthcare premiums and healthcare savings are not subject to federal and state taxes. Considering the combined impact of pretax savings, the benefits can easily reach hundreds and perhaps even thousands of dollars per year. If state taxes were an additional 5 percent and combined healthcare premiums and savings totaled \$300, a total of 20 percent in taxes would be levied on \$4,400 of income. This amount of \$880 is a full \$120 less than the taxes on a gross income of \$5,000 would be if no pretax deductions were made (20 percent of \$5,000 = \$1,000).

Most salaried positions offer a 401(k). Even jobs that provide a defined benefit plan will offer a supplemental 401(k)—they just might not make any employer contributions to it. But taking advantage of it will still allow you the pretax benefits of automatic paycheck deductions. You should also be aware that if you are in education, government, or nonprofit work, you may be offered a different kind of account—a 403(b) or a 501(c). These accounts work essentially the same way as a 401(k)—all the principles we have discussed here apply.

In addition to these options, you can also set up your own retirement account outside of work. This is known as an Individual Retirement Account, or an IRA. People who are self-employed will usually go this route, using a Simplified Employee Pension Plan (SEP). If it is not a company-sponsored plan, the contributions cannot be made via payroll deduction, before taxes, which means you make the contribution "after tax." For instance, if you contributed 5 percent of your salary to your own IRA on a \$4,000 monthly income, you would have contributed \$200 per month, or \$2,400 for the year, of your total \$48,000 salary. You can effectively "get back" the taxes you paid on that \$2,400 when you complete your federal income taxes for the year. Your 20 percent combined federal and state income tax liability would garner a $480 tax return. To summarize, when contributions are made to an IRA, they are typically subtracted from income taxes at tax time.

Saving for retirement means you get to keep more of your own paycheck and allow it to grow ...

you just must wait to spend that money until after you retire.

Roth IRAs

Another option would be to make your after-tax contributions to a Roth IRA, in which case your contributions cannot be deducted from your tax liability. Why would you want to forgo this tax savings? Whereas traditional IRAs and 401(k)-style contributions are made pretax, withdrawals made at the time of retirement are taxed as regular income. That is, these accounts will allow your contributions to grow tax-free, but when you retire, you will be taxed whenever you withdraw cash from the account.

Withdrawals from a Roth, on the other hand, are made tax-free.

In other words, both plans come with significant tax benefits. It's simply a matter of when taxes are applied—on the withdrawals or on the contributions. Finance experts disagree on which types of accounts are better. Some argue that traditional plans are better, because as you have seen, pretax contributions allow for a greater amount of saving up front, which increases the principal amount that will realize investment returns over time. Others argue that because that greater amount is taxed as regular income at withdrawal time, that benefit does not outweigh the benefit of tax-free withdrawals from a Roth. Still others argue, however, that the tax benefits end up being similar enough over the long term that the difference doesn't much matter. The truth is that the actual benefits will depend heavily on the amounts contributed and the amount of realized gain—the latter of which is difficult to predict—and whether your tax rate is higher or lower during your working life compared to your retirement life.

Here is one recommendation: make sure you qualify for your employer's maximum contribution to your 401(k) plan. This means that you want to take full advantage of any employee match. If the employer will match up to 5 percent of your salary, make sure you are contributing that 5 percent to get a total of 10 percent going toward retirement. For any additional retirement savings, open a Roth. This way, you can capitalize on both types of tax benefits. The amount that you can contribute to a Roth is more limited than your employee 401(k) plan, anyway, so it may not be that difficult to max out your Roth contribution. Then you can increase your personal contribution to your company-sponsored plan if you like.

Federal guidelines change yearly, but for 2020 the maximum Roth IRA contribution is $6,000, which works out to $500 per month. The employee-sponsored plan limit is much higher, at $19,500 per year (historically, it has increased by $500 each year). This, by the way, includes Roth contributions, so if you max out a Roth IRA, the effective cap on your personal contributions to a 401(k) is $13,500. This cap does not include your employer's contributions, though. However, when employer contributions are considered, the combined limit is $57,000. Most people will never come close to that amount—at least, not until well into their careers.

Because these tax benefits are provided to encourage retirement savings, there are some restrictions on how early you can access the money without penalty. In 2020, that age is 59½. Any withdrawals made before that time will be subject to taxes as well as an additional 10 percent tax penalty. This could be enough to eliminate any realized investment gains under some conditions. Needless to say, these accounts are for long-term savings, and any contributions you make should be funds that you will not need for emergency spending, a mortgage down payment, or any other shorter-term financial goals.

Of course, you do not want to put off saving for retirement, given that the greatest benefits accrue for those who begin the process in their twenties. This is why it is strongly recommended that you build your soft emergency fund before you do anything else at all. Then, max out your employer match while building your hard emergency fund. Finally, you may consider simultaneously splitting your mortgage down payment and any additional retirement contributions you want to make, such as to a Roth, until you own a house with at least 20 percent equity. At that time, you may want to maximize your savings to retirement, but realistically, you may have other needs at any point along the way of this plan.

Key Takeaways

Directions: Review the following list of key takeaways to help you remember what you learned in this chapter:

- Save for the rainy day. You need a "soft" emergency fund and a "hard" emergency fund.
- Make saving as automatic as possible.
- You don't have to be wealthy or achieve a certain level of income before you start saving. Saving is for everyone, but the amount saved will be different. Recognize that saving is a process and that making it a habit is the key to success.
- There are many different kinds of savings vehicles for your retirement savings. The major asset allocation classes are cash, bonds, and equities. Picking the asset allocation for your savings is chiefly a function of risk tolerance and the saver's preferences.
- Employer-sponsored retirement savings plans, generally known as 401(k)s, are an important mechanism for workers' retirement savings and offer important tax advantages.
- Take advantage of the tax benefits of saving, to whatever degree possible.

Application Opportunity: Do This Now!

Directions: Complete the activities below to apply what you have learned in this chapter.

Activity 1

Look back at your answers for the exercises from chapter 2, "The Decision to Earn." Then apply that info to thinking about emergency savings by answering the following questions:

1. How much money will you need for your hard emergency fund? To solve this, you need to know the salary you expect to earn once out of college. It might be that average of $50,000, or it might be more specific if you really know what job you want to pursue. Now apply the guidelines from this chapter for how much hard emergency money you need to set as a savings goal.

2. How long do you think it will take you to save this amount? Think about how much of your salary you will be able to save each month. How many months will it take for you to get to that emergency savings goal?
3. In which type of account do you think it is best to save your emergency fund? Why?
4. After you accumulate the money you need for your soft and hard emergency funds, what do you think you will save for?
5. Would you want to save these additional funds in the same type of account as the emergency savings? Why or why not?

Activity 2

Now take a look at your current spending habits. Identify three ways in which you could change those habits so that you might be able to save some of your income today.

Activity 3

What does your risk tolerance tell you about *how* you should save for retirement?

Most people do not like risk. They hate to lose on anything, especially money. But most people will not be able to save enough principal to provide the savings they need for retirement. Some risk can help get you to the savings you need, and most people will take risk if they are paid enough.

GOAL: Understand what factors the industry uses to assess your risk and what the industry might do with that knowledge to suggest how you should save. Fill out investor profile questionnaires online. A nice one from Charles Schwab can be found here: https://www.schwabmoneywise.com/public/file/P-4038840/InvestorProfileQuestionnaire.pdf

Take the quiz a couple of times, trying to score in different risk tolerance ranges, so that you can see what factors are driving the results. Be honest with yourself and see what the questionnaire tells you about your own risk tolerance level.

Activity 4

Make an investment strategy for retirement savings! Slide down the Charles Schwab page to see options for an investment strategy, given your risk tolerance. An alternative site to consider can be found here: https://smartasset.com/investing/asset-allocation-calculator

What is your suggested investment strategy asset allocation? Do the parameters track with your comfort level? Why or why not?

Bibliography

Berger, Guy. "Will This Year's College Grads Job-Hop More Than Previous Grads?" LinkedIn Official Blog. April 12, 2016. https://blog.linkedin.com/2016/04/12/will-this-year_s-college-grads-job-hop-more-than-previous-grads.

Center for Responsible Lending. "The State of Lending: Payday Loans." September 10, 2013. https://www.responsiblelending.org/state-lending/payday-loans.

Charles Schwab. "Investor Profile Questionnaire." 2018. https://www.schwabmoneywise.com/public/file/P-4038840/InvestorProfileQuestionnaire.pdf.

Federal Reserve Economic Data (FRED). https://fred.stlouisfed.org/

FINRA. "U.S. Treasury Securities." Accessed June 15, 2021. https://www.finra.org/investors/learn-to-invest/types-investments/bonds/types-of-bonds/us-treasury-securities.

Goldberg, Matthew. "Best CD rates for May 2021." Bankrate. Accessed May 19, 2021. https://www.bankrate.com/banking/cds/cd-rates/.

Green, A. R., M. Larkin, and V. Sullivan. 2009. "Oh Stuff It! The Experience and Explanation of Diet Failure: An Exploration Using Interpretative Phenomenological Analysis." *Journal of Health Psychology* 14, no. 7 (October 2009): 997–1008.

Lending Tree. "High Interest Online Savings Accounts." Accessed February 27, 2021. https://www.lendingtree.com/banking/savings/.

McLeod, Saul. "SRRS—Stress of Life Events." Simply Psychology. 2010. https://www.simplypsychology.org/SRRS.html.

Mullainathan, Sendhil, and Eldar Shafir. *Scarcity: Why Having Too Little Means So Much*. New York: Macmillan, 2013.

NAR Staff. "2019 Profile of Home Buyers and Sellers," National Association of Realtors (2019) accessed June 28, 2021, https://www.nysar.com/wp-content/uploads/2020/01/2019-NAR-HBS.pdf.

Palmer, Mike. "Why Target Date Funds Miss the Mark." *Kiplinger*, March 25, 2021. https://www.kiplinger.com/investing/602499/why-target-date-funds-miss-the-mark.

Puzzanghera, Jim. "One-Fifth of U.S. Workers Were Laid Off in Past Five Years, Study Says." *Los Angeles Times*, September 24, 2014. https://www.latimes.com/business/la-fi-layoffs-unemployment-jobs-economy-20140924-story.html.

Royal, James. "Survey: Nearly 3 Times as Many Americans Say They Have Less Emergency Savings versus More Since Pandemic." Bankrate. August 20, 2020. https://www.bankrate.com/banking/savings/emergency-savings-survey-2020/.

Smart Asset. "Asset Allocation Calculator." Accessed June 14, 2021. https://smartasset.com/investing/asset-allocation-calculator.

Thaler, Richard. "Mental Accounting and Consumer Choice." *Marketing Science* 4, no. 3 (Summer 1985): 199–214.

US Bureau of Labor Statistics. "Employee Tenure Summary." Economic news release. September 22, 2020. https://www.bls.gov/news.release/tenure.nr0.htm.

Vanguard. *How America Saves 2019: Vanguard 2018 Defined Contribution Plan Data*. June 2019. https://pressroom.vanguard.com/nonindexed/Research-How-America-Saves-2019-Report.pdf.

Vasel, Kathryn. "6 in 10 Americans Don't Have $500 in Savings." CNN Money. January 12, 2017. https://money.cnn.com/2017/01/12/pf/americans-lack-of-savings/index.html.

Figure Credit

Fig. 3.1: Copyright © by Farcaster (CC BY-SA 4.0) at https://commons.wikimedia.org/wiki/File:U.S._Treasury_Yield_Curves_-_v1.png.

CHAPTER 4

The Decision to Spend

Invest in Your Well-Being Today

Imagine...

Have you ever heard that money can't buy happiness? Do you believe it?

Imagine yourself in a ten-million-dollar mansion on the California coast. You've built a successful finance company from scratch, and you are enjoying its rewards. You have several cars in the driveway, including a rare Italian sports model. Your kids have everything they want. In fact, you must force them to do chores so they will develop some sense of responsibility, because otherwise their every desire is granted. When you can actually take time off (which isn't often an option), you can go anywhere you want—Paris, London, Rome, or a private Mediterranean island accessible only by boat.

Would you be happy?

In 2008, at the outset of the Great Recession, CNBC produced a documentary entitled *Rise of the Super Rich.*[1] In it, billionaire hedge fund managers, real estate tycoons, and Wall Street financiers describe their spending habits and their relationship with money. One by one, they list their exorbitant purchases: rare Italian sports cars bought only at auction, million-dollar weddings, and yachts that cost more than entire city blocks. In one evocative scene, the founder of a multi-million-dollar mortgage lending firm even admits to owning homes he has never visited. Rhetorically, the CNBC reporter asks, "You have a great life, don't you?" Almost as if trying to convince himself, the lender notably pauses. Only half-looking at the camera, he quietly agrees, "Yeah, I have a great life."

Now, it's impossible for the viewer to know whether or not this man truly has a great life and whether he additionally believes this to be the case. What does seem clear is that the answer is not obvious to him, and he is not sure how to respond. Even in the exact moment at

1. , David Faber. "Untold Wealth: The Rise of the Super Rich." CNBC Original Production, October 13, 2009. https://www.youtube.com/watch?v=TNRwERkZhjs.

which he is thinking specifically about how much money he has, this information alone is not enough for him to agree enthusiastically and without hesitation.

In addition to profiling the who's who of the nouveau riche, the documentary features a very different kind of figure—a psychiatrist, who specializes in working with high-income individuals. He describes a specific set of problems that seems to be characteristic of the very wealthy: narcissism, fragile egos, and damaged relationships. Some of these problems are likely related to the characteristics that explain why certain people are driven to succeed financially at a high level. Research shows, for instance, that psychopathy is higher among CEOs.[2] But the larger point is that wealthy people are still humans, with very human problems—the kinds of problems that Italian sports cars and yachts—while nice to have—are not well-suited to solving. So, it is true, right? Money doesn't buy happiness, as we have always been told? Wrong.

Introduction

For the wealthy, privileged few, money doesn't buy happiness, because wealthy people have a lot more of what they need and what they want. For most of the rest of us, though, a little more money wouldn't hurt at all, and might actually help quite a bit.

To say that money doesn't buy happiness is, in some ways, an important point about the true nature of human well-being. Wealthy individuals clearly have the means to buy the things they want. They may or may not have deep, meaningful relationships and time to enjoy the things their money can buy them. On the other hand, that statement about money and happiness can be a condescending and naïve perspective on the plight of hardworking middle-class and lower-income individuals. What matters is not how much money one has, but what one does with it. As previously discussed, having more money to save for the future may not enable you to buy a yacht, but it will help buy you some piece of mind in a more comfortable and secure retirement. And that is worth a little bit of human happiness, by any definition of well-being. The yacht? It may or may not be.

The goal of this chapter is to help you think about how to spend money in a way that will maximize well-being. This may involve buying the things you want—things that will likely bring you some degree of pleasure. But in order to have those things, it is first necessary to meet your more basic financial necessities. Having the latest model of iPhone may bring you some fleeting joy, but not having it is unlikely to cause you any major distress. Having your cell service cut off because you couldn't pay the bill will cause you some stress. Being unable to pay your rent or defaulting on your student loans will cause you more. And spending at the expense of your long-term savings goals for retirement could result in negative consequences that are impossible to undo, given the importance of a long-term time horizon for investing. Don't forget: this is why saving comes before spending.

2. Paul Babiak, Craig S. Neumann, and Robert D. Hare, "Corporate Psychopathy: Talking the Walk," *Behavioral Sciences & the Law* 28, no. 2 (2010): 174–93.

Chapter Objectives

After reading this chapter, you will be able to:

- Discern between wants and needs.
- Create a household budget that syncs with your level of expected earnings, desired living location, and anticipated expenses.
- Understand the role of insurance in hedging risks and allow your spending budget and your savings to work for you.
- Identify the types of insurance that a young adult should consider and evaluate the pros and cons of these types with respect to individual needs.

If Money Doesn't Buy Happiness, What *Does* It Do?

As you have seen in previous chapters, money is worth only the "subjective utility" that it can purchase for you. This might mean the satisfaction of a good meal and the alleviation of hunger. It might mean feeling comfortable and safe in your home. It could come in the form of good feelings, fun experiences, positive memories, and stronger relationships. It could simply be the relief of anxiety, or the psychological security, of knowing that you can pay your bills, that you have reliable transportation to get you to work, and that your savings are in secure financial instruments. At the end of the day, this is all money can do for us—it can provide us with the good feelings that come from psychological security and, perhaps more importantly, help us avoid the stress and anxiety of psychological insecurity.

Many people are familiar with Maslow's hierarchy of needs, which is represented in figure 4.1.[3] Abraham Maslow was a humanistic psychologist in the 1960s who believed that all humans were motivated to achieve their highest potential—what he called *self-actualization*. But in order for them to do so, it was first necessary that they attend to more basic needs. First among these are physiological needs, such as hunger and thirst. Humans, like all animals, need to consume in order to survive, and this need takes precedence over all others. Indeed, humans will resort to extreme circumstances when food is not available for long periods of time. Next are safety and security needs, such as the need to be safe from physical harm and to seek shelter from the elements. Third, humans have social needs; they need to be loved and cared for by family and friends. Fourth, humans have ego needs; they need to feel good about themselves. And only when people have all of these needs met, according to Maslow, can they achieve their highest potential. Indeed, Maslow saw all of human existence as a struggle to transcend these more basic physical and social needs.

3. Abraham Harold Maslow, "A Theory of Human Motivation," *Psychological Review* 50, no. 4 (1943): 370.

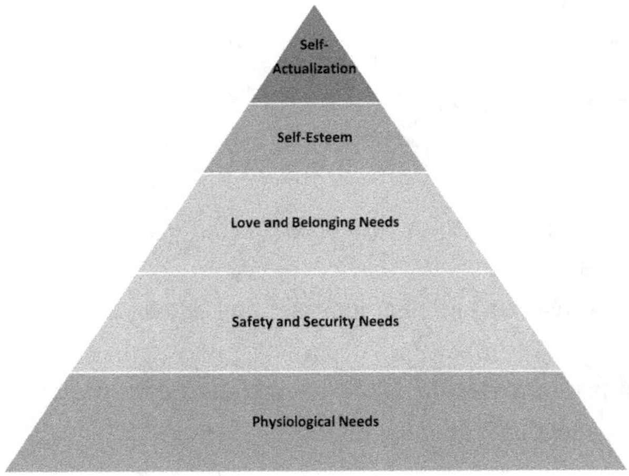

FIGURE 4.1 Maslow's Hierarchy

So, what does a hierarchy of our most basic requirements have to do with money? Well, in a consumer-driven capitalist society, we are taught that spending money is the way to meet these needs. Indeed, the very health of our economy depends on this being true to some degree or another; consumer spending accounts for the largest proportion of our nation's gross domestic product (GDP), the primary measure of the economy's health. In fact, when spending dips enough that GDP growth begins to fall, businesses lose money and lay off workers. This can result in a recession, which causes an enormous amount of financial and psychological distress. It's a bit of a vicious cycle that capitalist societies find themselves caught up in.

Strictly speaking, it is necessary to consume to meet our needs, particularly our more basic physical needs. We consume calories that we obtain by spending money at the grocery store and at restaurants. We spend money on rent and on homes to provide physical shelter, and we spend money on food and shelter for our children because we love them. In modern society, spending to meet our basic needs is unavoidable. For this reason, marketers and advertisers are more than happy to tell us exactly how their products can help us.

While nobody would doubt that we do in fact *need* food, we don't necessarily need Big Macs and Snickers bars. We might *want* those things, and because these wants fulfill more basic needs, it is easy to sell them. We may need reliable transportation—because the ability to get to work provides the financial security to meet more basic physical needs—but we don't need to drive a Mercedes. More likely, we buy a Mercedes to feel good about ourselves, which is something we need, but once again, we don't need luxury products to feed our egos. Marketers count on this. Any student in a consumer behavior class learns exactly how to pair specific products with specific basic needs, with the goal of selling the product, to create desire.

Take the smartphone, for instance—perhaps the single most successful new product to be developed in the last two decades. As far back as 2012, a Pew Research poll showed that 90 percent of people considered a cell phone a necessity.[4] Of course, cell phones are now smartphones, and even globally speaking, most people consider a smartphone a necessity. But when people say they need their smartphone, what are they

4. Aaron Smith, "Cell Internet Use 2012: Main Findings," Pew Research Center, June 26, 2012, https://www.pewresearch.org/internet/2012/06/26/main-findings-9/.

really saying? Do they really need an iPhone 12 as opposed to an iPhone 11? Or a Samsung S10? Or, for that matter, a laptop computer and a landline?

It's not so much the product that we need, of course. It's all the things we can do with a smartphone. In one single, compact, portable device, the smartphone provides for all the needs in Maslow's hierarchy. It allows us to quickly search for restaurants when we travel somewhere new, or find grocery stores, to meet our basic physiological needs. It allows us to call for help if we are stranded in a remote area or our car breaks down, providing for our security needs. Perhaps most important of all, it provides us with social connection—through its calling function, of course, but increasingly also through email, text, and social media. Social media, in turn, feeds our ego needs; it allows us to not only share with one another but also receive social validation when we do. We can use our smartphone to aid in just about any goal we might choose to pursue, including self-actualization, as there are apps that help us achieve goals for self-improvement and apps like Headspace that teach people to meditate. No wonder the smartphone is likely the most successful product ever marketed in the history of capitalism!

So, you could live on Big Macs and Snickers, but there are far healthier ways to eat. Similarly, while you could drive a Mercedes to work, there are less expensive ways to get there! The trick is to learn how to differentiate between your wants and your needs.

One very simple way to do this is to imagine the effects of buying something on your happiness. Getting a want might make you happier than you already are. Getting a need simply keeps you from being unhappy. How do you determine this?

Consumer behavior researchers distinguish between two different mechanisms that motivate purchasing behavior: noticing that you could be better off than you already are, or noticing that you have become less well-off than you were. Consider these different sources of motivation for buying a car. In one case, you drive a high-mileage older car that is unreliable, and it breaks down. You have to make a decision about whether to spend additional money fixing the car or put the money toward a new one. In another case, you have a car that runs fine; maybe it is not brand new, but it is also not very old. It is a good car—say, a Toyota Camry. But it is not a Lexus, which is what you really want.

In the first case, a new car purchase is better thought of as a necessity. You need reliable transportation; having a broken-down car will make you worse off than you were before. In the second case, a new car purchase would really be better thought of as a want. It would be nice to have a Lexus—it might even make you happier than you were before—but you don't need a car, because you have a perfectly reliable one.

That's not to say you should never buy out of want—not at all. But you should understand your psychological motives for buying, to better determine that you are making good decisions. If you buy out of want, make sure you understand that what you are buying is a want and not a need. This will help you make better purchase decisions because if you are not buying out of a sense of necessity, you may think more deeply about whether or not you should buy it, plan your purchase more carefully, and budget appropriately.

With the understanding that what you are buying is a want, you will also be more certain that you are not mistaking wants for needs, because many times needs can be better met in more fulfilling ways than by buying things. If you want to buy a Lexus, are you fulfilling ego needs that could be met in other ways—by taking on a new project at work that makes you feel competent and capable with respect to your work colleagues, for instance?

This is a point worth elaborating. A huge body of research shows that many people who seek happiness in buying things—often known as materialists—are less happy.[5] A reason for this might be that materialistic individuals are often driven by various types of psychological insecurities, and that they may be buying to compensate for or fill the gaps of loneliness, or of a lack of meaningful social or parental relationships.[6] Table 4.1 in the text box below shows some sample items commonly used to measure materialism.

MATERIALISM

Answer each question on a scale of 1 to 5, from *strongly disagree* (1) to *strongly agree* (5).[7]

TABLE 4.1 How Materialistic Are You?

	Item	Response
1	I admire people who own expensive homes, cars, and clothes.	
2	The things I own say a lot about how well I am doing in life.	
3	Buying things gives me a lot of pleasure.	
4	I like to have a lot of luxury in my life.	
5	I would be happier if I could afford to buy more things.	

At the most basic level, materialism is driven by experiences with material insecurity and even poverty in childhood.[8] You may think that materialism is associated with luxury consumption and thus more likely among those with a great deal of wealth. While it is obviously true that wealthy individuals have greater means and are more likely to spend their wealth on luxury goods, it is also true that many people who relentlessly pursue wealth are themselves individuals driven by various sorts of insecurities, as documented by *Rise of the Super Rich.*

In sum, buying a lot of wants, or mistaking wants for needs, is not just bad for your bank account. It also may not contribute greatly to your overall happiness. It is true that wants, by definition, are things that

5. Emily G. Solberg, Edward Diener, and Michael D. Robinson, "Why Are Materialists Less Satisfied?" in *Psychology and Consumer Culture: The Struggle for a Good Life in a Materialistic World*, eds. Tim Kasser and Allen D. Kanner (Washington, DC: American Psychological Association, 2004), 29–48, https://doi.org/10.1037/10658-003.
6. J. Ian Norris, Nathaniel M. Lambert, C. Nathan DeWall, and Frank D. Fincham, "Can't Buy Me Love?: Anxious Attachment and Materialistic Values," *Personality and Individual Differences* 53, no. 5 (2012): 666–69.
7. Marsha L. Richins, "The Material Values Scale: Measurement Properties and Development of a Short Form," *Journal of Consumer Research* 31, no. 1 (June 2004): 209–19.
8. Lan Nguyen Chaplin, Ronald Paul Hill, and Deborah Roedder John, "Poverty and Materialism: A Look at Impoverished Versus Affluent Children," *Journal of Public Policy & Marketing* 33, no. 1 (2014): 78–92.

make us "better off" than we are. In many cases, they may actually bring us joy and delight. The pleasure one derives from driving a brand-new Lexus is sure to exceed that of driving a five-year-old Camry. The problem is that the pleasure won't last. So, while it will be nice for a while, we can't count on material things to bring us any kind of lasting, sustainable happiness. New things get old, innovative products become outdated, and today's fashions and trends become yesterday's embarrassments.

On this note, the next section presents a broader discussion of the relationship between money and happiness, followed by some lessons on how we can buy to best maximize our well-being.

Money and Happiness—Coda

We've all heard that money can't buy happiness. But hey, a little more would sure be nice. So, what's the problem here?

First of all, we know from the research literature that our income satisfaction is a relative phenomenon. As discussed above, we have a tendency to adapt—a nice new car contributes greatly to happiness now, but eventually that will wear off, and we will have our eye on a newer, better, more expensive model.

This is also true of income. We can never have enough, because our tendency is always to compare ourselves with those who have more—making us feel like we don't have enough, no matter how much we have! The good news is that we have some control over the comparisons we make. We can compare ourselves to those who have less and feel grateful for what we have. We can compare our current and future selves to our past selves and feel proud at how far we have come.

That said, there are clearly absolute effects of income on happiness. People in wealthier countries are, on average, happier than people in less wealthy countries.[9] There is even more variance within countries: wealthier people, on average, are happier than less wealthy people. But there are also diminishing marginal returns to the effects of money on happiness. This means that money matters more at lower levels of income than at higher levels. Once you reach a certain level of material comfort, additional increases in income continue to add to happiness, but less and less so.[10] Imagine that you make $50,000 a year. Increasing your salary by 20 percent would have a pretty big impact on your income—it would increase to $60,000. If you made $200,000, the same $10,000 increase wouldn't be that noticeable. At this salary, a 20 percent increase would correspond to $40,000, but that bump in income would not make you as happy as the 20 percent bump at the lower income.

In addition to financial contexts, happiness is also important in philosophical, social-psychological, and even religious contexts. And at the end of the day, much of what we know about money and happiness dovetails nicely with what we know about happiness more generally from our philosophical and religious traditions.

One of the big three "practices" of happiness is altruism—doing things to make other people happy. And as it turns out, a great deal of research demonstrates that spending money on others contributes more

9. John F. Helliwell, Richard Layard, Jeffrey Sachs, and Jan-Emmanuel De Neve, eds., "World Happiness Report 2020." New York: Sustainable Development Solutions Network. (2020)
10. Michael R. Hagerty, "Social Comparisons of Income in One's Community: Evidence from National Surveys of Income and Happiness." *Journal of Personality and Social Psychology* 78, no. 4 (2000): 764–71. doi:10.1037/0022-3514.78.4.764.

greatly to happiness than spending money on ourselves does.[11] You will have the opportunity to explore how to incorporate happiness from altruism more in a section of chapter 7, "The Decision to Retire," but for now, know that one way to avoid overindulging in our own materialistic pleasures is to think about the needs of others, which might make us a little less indulgent. And our happiness might come from the happiness we are contributing to others.

Second, we know that experiences make people happier than material things. So, when you do have extra money to spend beyond the necessities, you might be happier spending it on vacations than on luxury goods. There are many reasons for this. A simple one is that the happiness we get from experiences doesn't "wear off" the same way it does with material things, which get old and outdated. Experiences live on in our memories and become more central to our identities than material things do.

Another reason why you might choose vacations over goods is that we are a lot less likely to engage in harmful comparisons when it comes to experiences. Remember the research studies discussed back in chapter 2, "The Decision to Earn," in which people were asked whether they would prefer to make more money in real dollars, but less than everyone else, or less money in real dollars, but more than everyone else? Most people preferred to make less money, knowing that their happiness with income would depend on comparisons with others. But this was not so when it came to vacations! More vacation is better, regardless of how much vacation everyone else has.

The point of this section is not to tell you that it is never OK to indulge in a bit of luxury or to buy nice things. Rather, the point is to help you understand your own motives for buying and your own psychological relationship to money. This can only help you have a healthier and happier relationship to the things you choose to buy. By all means, when you can afford it, buy the car of your dreams! Just don't buy it out of some false belief that it will lead to enduring happiness, which will lead you into an endless cycle of buying, dissatisfaction, and buying again. Knowing what you want and why you want it will help you find the means to achieve it.

Follow the guidelines in this chapter, and you can budget for anything that you might want.

How Do We Spend Money?

If you are reading this book, you were not profiled on *Rise of the Super Rich*—although I hope you will be one day! Understanding how everyday Americans spend their money can provide you with a snapshot of where you can expect your money to go. It can also point to some pretty hard financial lessons.

Average Household Spending in the United States

According to a 2019 study produced by the US Bureau of Labor Statistics, the average US household spent a total of $63,036 on an average pretax income of $82,852. Of this amount, nearly $20,679—or roughly a

11. Oliver Scott Curry, Lee A. Rowland, Caspar J. Van Lissa, Sally Zlotowitz, John McAlaney, and Harvey Whitehouse, "Happy to Help? A Systematic Review and Meta-Analysis of the Effects of Performing Acts of Kindness on the Well-Being of the Actor," *Journal of Experimental Social Psychology* 76 (May 2018): 320–29.

third—went to housing, indicating an average mortgage or monthly rent payment of a little over $1,700. Other major spending categories included transportation (17 percent), food (13 percent), healthcare (8 percent), and entertainment (5 percent).[12] Altogether, these five categories amount to over 75 percent of budgeted spending, leaving little for *discretionary spending*—that is, spending not already committed to something that is to some extent considered a necessity. In some ways, this makes budgeting fairly easy, because you have a sense of where the big chunks of your spending will go, and individually, you just have to figure out what is important to you.

When considering the impact of taxes, it is also clear that the average household had little left over for saving, after all discretionary spending is considered. The average American worker contributed 29.8 percent of their earnings to income taxes, Medicare, and Social Security in 2019.[13] This helps to explain the difference between pretax income and spending. Given how much of your money will be destined for taxes, housing, food, and other necessities, it is all the more critical to exercise careful oversight of your finances in order to meet your saving and spending goals. Of course, this is a reference to everyone's favorite personal finance topic: budgeting!

Guidelines for a recent college graduate, based on a pretax income of $50,000, might look something like the budget in the text box below.

Notice this "budget" is not really a budget, but more of a way of trying to establish a framework for what kind of spending might be reasonable at a given income level. This also does not include every possible category of spending that is tracked by the Bureau of Labor Statistics. For one thing, it does not include any spending that goes to debt service beyond mortgages and car loans, which are included in housing and transportation costs, respectively. Payments made to student loans or credit cards are not reflected here.

Finally, keep in mind that these amounts are based on pretax income, given that this is the way the government collects and reports the data. This means that the remaining $1,417 is not all discretionary—some of this, though not all of it, will go to federal, state, and local taxes. Nevertheless, staying under the average percentage of spending in each category should leave enough slack for saving. In fact, when constructing an actual budget, you will want to make your savings a line item; ideally, it will be the *first line item* in the budget.

12. US Bureau of Labor Statistics, "Consumer Expenditures 2019," economic news release, September 9, 2020, https://www.bls.gov/news.release/cesan.nr0.htm.
13. Beverly Bird, "How Much Does the Average American Pay in Taxes?" The Balance, updated May 26, 2021, https://www.thebalance.com/what-the-average-american-pays-in-taxes-4768594.

NEW COLLEGE GRADUATE BUDGET

TABLE 4.2 Budget

	Actual
Income (pretax)	$50,000
Monthly (pretax)	4,167
Housing	1,200
Transportation	400
Food	400
Healthcare	300
Other	200
Entertainment	150
Apparel and services	100
Remaining:	$1,417

Consider the Major Line Items in the Budget

Before constructing an actual budget, though, let's look at each of the biggest spending categories in more detail.

Housing

Housing will be your single largest expenditure. In fact, your house might be the single most expensive thing you ever purchase in your life, although your college education may be a close competitor! While actual average spending on housing is around 33 percent, most experts recommend that it not exceed 30 percent, or, even better, 25 percent. The reality is that housing costs have increased dramatically in recent years, and that you can reasonably expect to pay a lot for a decent place to live. In the next chapter, we will look more closely at housing costs, but the example salary and budget above should suffice in a city with a moderate cost of living. The median rent nationwide for a one-bedroom apartment in 2021 is $960.[14] This is just under the 25 percent benchmark for a pretax salary of $50,000. Of course, there are drastic differences in housing costs—it is simply unavoidable that in places like New York, San Francisco, and Seattle, you will pay more, much more, than 25 percent of your pretax income. You will likely make a higher salary in these cities, yes,

14. Igor Popov, Chris Salviati, and Rob Warnock, "Data & Rent Estimates–National-Level Historic Estimates (2017–Present)," Apartment List, February 24, 2021, https://www.apartmentlist.com/research/category/data-rent-estimates.

but that does not usually make a big enough difference to fully compensate for the difference in housing costs. Having a roommate can instantly enhance your standard of living. Two- or three-bedroom apartments may cost 20–50 percent more, but a roommate will cut your costs in half.

If you have a mortgage, the median amount spent on housing—over $1,500 per month nationwide—includes all components of your mortgage payment, plus other monthly housing expenses.[15] That is, it includes interest on the mortgage loan, property taxes, homeowner's insurance, and mortgage insurance. It also includes the costs of repairs and updates. It does not include any part of the mortgage payment that goes to principal, or the amount you actually owe on the house. The basic idea is that principal payments increase your ownership of the home, which is considered an asset, or an investment, as opposed to a cost. Your mortgage payment could be a little higher than the benchmark you set for yourself, so long as you consider the portion going to principal to be part of your savings and investment strategy.

This means that smart spending should dictate home ownership, right? This is usually the case, but not always. There are many costs of ownership that have to be considered carefully—some that are simply part of the buying process itself. The costs of buying and selling a home is documented in more detail in chapter 5, "The Decision to Owe."

Transportation

In 2019, the average American spent about $10,742 on transportation.[16] Of this amount, about $2,000 was spent on gas, and about $4,400 on vehicle purchases. The remaining amount went to repairs, maintenance, and related costs. The $4,400 works out to a $366 per month car expense in your budget. This corresponds to a vehicle worth around $20,000, depending on the terms of the loan. If you were to have a $300 car payment or less, you would have $100 per month for gas, repairs, and maintenance at a $400 transportation allotment, putting you well under the 17 percent national average for transportation costs. You can achieve this goal by purchasing a new low-cost vehicle, such as a Honda Civic, or a moderately priced but gently used one, such as a three-year-old Toyota Camry.

Whether such an allotment is viable depends on the length of your commute, of course, as well as the cost of gasoline. In fact, leaving some slack here is particularly important in this era of volatile energy prices. In 2012, gas prices nationally were around $3.60 per gallon. By 2016, they had fallen close to $2 per gallon. By 2021, they had slowly crept back up above $3 per gallon again. Indeed, over the last few years, it has not been unusual to see swings of 50 percent or more in prices over a one-year timeframe.

Your allocation to transportation will depend on what you can reasonably afford. It will also depend on your needs. If you live in San Francisco or New York, for instance, owning a car may be more expensive than it is worth. Parking charges alone could rival your car payment. If you live in a place where car ownership is not necessary, though, you will still need to factor in transportation costs for mass transit, regional trains if you commute from outside the city, and ride-hailing services like Uber.

15. US Census Bureau, "American Community Survey (ACS)," 2018, accessed March 5, 2021, https://www.census.gov/programs-surveys/acs.
16. US Bureau of Labor Statistics, "Consumer Expenditures 2019."

Food

American households spent around $8,169 on food in 2019.[17] Of this, about $4,643 was food consumed at home and another $3,526 was food eaten away from home. This corresponds to about 43 percent of food expenditures, and in terms of the example budget, about $175 a month. At an average price of $15 per meal, which would account for take-out and fast-food meals in the $10 range as well as some more expensive sit-down meals that include an entrée and a tip, you could eat out for about eleven or twelve meals per month, or three meals per week. Assuming a typical person eats twenty-one meals per week, or three meals per day (which might not be an accurate assumption), American households are eating only a fraction of their total number of meals outside their own kitchens yet spending almost as much money on them. The implication is clear: it is much, much more expensive to eat away from home.

Given that this is the second or third biggest category of expenditures for most people, it represents an excellent opportunity for savings. It is also one of the most difficult categories to trim. For one thing, people eat out more than ever because they are busier. It takes time to prepare meals, particularly when prior planning has not taken place.

Nevertheless, eating more meals at home is the single greatest thing that one can do to trim the food budget. And the payoff is not just financial: meals eaten out are almost always less healthy than those made at home. All it takes is a little planning. Once a week, perhaps the night before you typically go shopping, list each meal you plan to make each night of the week, and then build a shopping list. Knowing what you are going to make ahead of time makes a big difference: no rummaging around trying to figure out what you have ingredients to make, no last-minute decisions to stop for fast food because you are not sure what you have at home. In fact, just having a shopping list at all can be an effective way to manage a food budget. People spend more when they shop without having clear objectives in mind. Make a list and stick to it. And don't go to the store hungry because that is when you buy items on impulse!

Healthcare

Healthcare is one of the fastest-growing areas of expenditure for American consumers. In 2016, total healthcare spending was over $10,000 per individual in the United States.[18] This was more than a fivefold increase over 1970, when it was $1,762 (adjusted for inflation). In that same time span, the cost of many other goods and services decreased (once again, in inflation-adjusted dollars). Healthcare and college educations were exceptions.

As previously discussed, there are some key principles for managing healthcare expenses that are essential to a sound saving and spending strategy—for instance, taking advantage of a company-sponsored health savings or flexible spending account. Conducting a thorough assessment of your healthcare and family situation is necessary to determine what kind of coverage is best suited to your needs. Many of you reading this book are probably young, single, and healthy and will be best served by a higher-deductible, lower-premium plan with a regular monthly health savings contribution.

17. US Bureau of Labor Statistics.

18. Robert Pear, "National Health Spending to Surpass $10,000 a Person in 2016," *The New York Times*, July 13, 2016, https://www.nytimes.com/2016/07/14/us/national-health-spending-to-surpass-10000-per-person-in-2016.html.

While housing, transportation, and food will consume the majority of your budget, the bright side is that these are relatively predictable expenses. Your rent or mortgage will cost the same each month. You will use a similar amount of gas and eat a similar amount of food each month. Not so with healthcare spending. It is impossible to know when you will get sick, or worse, have an accident or develop a more severe illness. That is why regular health savings contributions are absolutely critical and should occupy a line item in your budget. You may save $1,000 before you have any out-of-pocket health expenses at all, but one MRI could cost half that amount in one thirty-minute visit to the clinic. Be prepared. Medical bills cannot be sent to collections as long as you are paying something toward your balance, and it is possible to pay high medical bills on low-payment, zero-interest payment plans. But you cannot simply ignore medical bills. You want to minimize monthly liabilities to better meet your monthly savings goals. So, allocating a regular, consistent amount of your monthly check to pay for future medical bills will go a long way toward being ready when and if they do come.

While much of your healthcare spending is unpredictable, some of it should not be. The Affordable Care Act of 2010 mandates that insurance providers pay the full cost of a yearly preventive care health check-up. Take advantage of this. If you have something that requires attention, it may show up here, in this free appointment, before it becomes a bigger (and more expensive) problem. And any spending you do that contributes to your physical health and wellness should likewise be considered preventive care. A gym membership, good running shoes, a yoga class—these are positive expenditures that could mitigate against the liability of greater medical costs down the road.

The beginning budget you establish is the framework you can use to adjust later as you learn about your spending needs and personal preferences. This may take some time to see, but you will never understand your spending habits until you start paying attention to them. Try not to ignore the savings requirements. This is a bill you send yourself, and it needs to be paid, preferably first. There may be some room to maneuver in other parts of the budget, chiefly transportation, food, and apparel. Early in your career, these are the places with the greatest amount of give.

Who Has the Time to Make an Actual Budget? Anyway, Broke Is Broke!

So, let's be honest: budgeting is about as boring as financial literacy gets. But it is absolutely essential. Many people might think that budgeting doesn't apply to them because they have so little income or money to budget. That thinking is exactly backward. When you have very little to work with, being smart with it can make a big difference. People who have a lot of money have a lot of slack in their budget, so they can fritter away money foolishly and suffer very minor consequences. People without that slack can, if they eliminate poorly chosen spending, create a little "loose" or "extra" money that can allow an additional meal out or enough gas for an extra trip home one month. After all, squeezing out a little extra so you can buy a little more or something you really want, or need, is far more important when you are getting by on very little. If you budget when times are tough, you will create a habit and attitude for when times are better. Budgeting is the most fundamental step toward healthy saving and spending habits because it is the first place where you can rationally discern between the things you need and those that you might simply want.

Our brains do a pretty poor job of tracking what is in our bank accounts, even if we think we know. For one thing, we tend to be unrealistically optimistic about how much money we have. Though optimism is usually a good thing, here it leads to spending more than we immediately have at the moment. Consider that only 45.44 percent of American households reported that they spend less than they make each month.[19] That means that more than half of the households out there are saving nothing, or spending more than they earn, on a regular basis. This is not only a poor spending strategy, but also a sure path to serious ***financial distress***. Accidental overspending can lead to debt and to living beyond one's means. A budget puts you in control of your money and can help to relieve a cycle of debt.

There are many excellent tools available online to help you. Mint.com is one of the original tools and still one of the best, according to NerdWallet.[20] Many are available as smartphone apps that actually track your spending habits in real time. A couple of the apps do this for free, but they may require you to link your banking and credit card accounts to the app. The Federal Trade Commission, a government organization whose mission is to protect American consumers, provides a good budgeting tool as part of their website on financial literacy education.[21] No doubt, budgeting has come a long way from the days of Excel spreadsheets and purchases scribbled on the backs of checkbooks.

Smart Budgeting in Three Steps

Online apps can go a long way toward getting you started in your budgeting. Over time you can develop a sense of where your money goes and think about where you would rather have it go. This approach to budgeting can be nice because you can get started right away. The apps take you through the budgeting process automatically, and in some ways, they are doing the heavy lifting for you. Some may not like to connect their financial accounts to an app, and this is understandable in this age of hacking and identity theft. The good news is that you can think through the steps of budgeting yourself, and that awareness may help you stick with the activity. The budgeting apps are taking you through the following three steps, in some ways simultaneously.

Step 1: Start the budget process by ***tracking your spending***. You might keep a notebook with you for a period of time and write down every purchase you make or use a notes app on your phone. By linking to your bank accounts, budgeting apps track your spending for you, and as long as you are using a debit or a credit card, they keep you pretty honest. You see, our brains tend to gloss over things they don't perceive as important, like the second latte of the day. Even worse, your mind may selectively "forget" purchases you were conflicted over, just to make you feel a little bit better about having spent money you were not sure you should spend (this is what psychologists call *cognitive dissonance*). So, take the reins and force yourself to pay attention. You might be surprised by what you learn. One thing you will certainly notice is that small

19. The Pew Charitable Trusts, "Survey of American Family Finances: Top-Lines Accompanying 'Americans' Financial Security: Perception and Reality,'" March 2015, https://www.pewtrusts.org/~/media/assets/2015/03/fsm-poll-results-toplines_artfinal_v3.pdf.
20. NerdWallet, "The 7 Best Budget Apps for 2021," NerdWallet, December 21, 2020, https://www.nerdwallet.com/article/finance/best-budget-apps.
21. Go to consumer.gov to see the resources provided by the Federal Trade Commission. Consumer.gov, "Consumer Protection Basics ... Plain and Simple," accessed June 14, 2021, https://www.consumer.gov/.

purchases can really add up. A wise high school teacher once pointed out that given the price of a pack of cigarettes at the time, the same amount of money over ten years could buy a decent used sports car. Of course, that was in the early 1990s. Today, quitting smoking will buy you a small house! You could run a similar scenario for your daily run to Starbucks or your weekly take-out lunch.

One simple way to track your ***small*** purchases without writing everything down is to give yourself a ***cash budget***. Take $100 (for instance) out of the ATM at the beginning of every month and use this cash strictly for frivolities. If you want a pack of gum, use the cash. If you want an ice cream cone, use the cash. For anything small, use the cash budget. When that is gone, your free cash frivolity is done too. Over three months, you can start to see the influence that little things have on your budget. You will get a sense of what to prioritize, even in this area, and you can adjust the cash balance allocation over time as you start to recognize your priorities and see the trade-off of not saving. You simply have to stick to the rule: when the cash is gone, easy spending stops. This way you won't have to write down every item or input every item into an app, but you will still have a sense of your small spending.

Step 2: Having documented your daily purchasing habits, ideally over three months, ***construct your monthly budget***. If you add together the three months' worth of expenses and divide that by three, you get your monthly expenses. Perhaps it is obvious, but the first thing to check is that your monthly expenses are lower than your monthly income. Typically, average expenses are 75–80 percent of the average income. Remember that your net income will be about 85 percent of the gross income; in other words, 15 percent of your income will be deducted from your gross paycheck before you ever see it. At least part of that will include retirement savings and health insurance premiums. Most of the rest will be taxes.

Some of your spending will be the same every month: rent or mortgage, insurance premiums, and car payments. These amounts are static, or fixed, and you need to be sure that you do not spend the part of your paycheck that is allocated to these items. Some people automatically deposit this part of the paycheck in one account, their savings allocation in a separate account they will not easily touch (as discussed in chapter 2, "The Decision to Save"), and the rest in a third account. This third part of your income will include budget areas where there is more flexibility. Maybe one month you won't buy soda, or you will color your hair. The budget can be manipulated in this area to reflect your priorities because there may be some places where you can cut back on expenses or add to them as needed.

Back in the day, households used envelopes to allocate their cash money, to separate budget items. One envelope said rent; another said groceries. When the bills were paid, the envelopes emptied, and people simply did not spend anymore. Now you can easily have different accounts, which act like envelopes, and you can track your spending by looking at your balance online. Or you can go to the envelope method and try it. This works for some people.

Step 3: Once you allocate your spending to the different budget categories, spend some time ***living your budget***. Often, there can be a big difference between what you believe your budget should be and what your budget actually is. When we first lay out our budget categories, we censor ourselves a bit because we may not know what we actually spend money on. Or we may start our budget in one place and need a bit of time to get our spending allocated, according to individual priorities. Try not to feel like the only outcome is perfection, and it must be immediate. Immediate perfection is a difficult bar to live up to. And if failure to achieve the ideal spending habits right away makes you quit, because "what is the point?" then you will miss the opportunities to learn about your spending and your priorities and to adjust them over time. Just like saving, the act of budgeting is really more of a practice or a process. It is rarely a one-and-done arrangement. Once you set things up, though, it really does not take a lot of time to manage your choices.

To manage your budget, one thing you can do is compare your spending to the averages for other American households. Remember the Bureau of Labor Statistics report? The next text box shows you the major percentage spent in each area by the average American household.[22]

TABLE 4.3 Budget Category Shares for Average Annual Expenditures, 2019

Budget Item	Percentage Spent
Housing	32.8
Transportation	17.0
Food	12.9
Personal Insurance and Pensions	11.4
Healthcare	8.2
Entertainment	4.83

Work to stay well under the average percentages listed in the table. Once you add up your expenditures, take what you spend in each category and divide that amount by the total expenditure number. If your total expenses for the year add to $50,000 and you spend $1,500 on monthly rent, your housing expense share is: ($1,500 × 12) / $50,000 = .36 or 36 percent.

If your spending is a bit higher than the average of 32.8 percent for housing in the previous table, you can then think about why that might be. Are you living in an expensive area? Are you living above your means? Should you get a roommate? Keeping your spending at or below the national average is a good way to be sure that you are spending within your means. The better you are able to do this, the more you will have available for both saving and discretionary spending.

Of course, it may be the case that your spending in any single category reflects a higher priority to you. Perhaps your apartment is close to work and the location is important to your lifestyle. Only you can know if this is a need or a want. Look honestly at where you land, relative to the overall picture. If where you live is a lot more important to you than what you wear, then maybe there is room to maneuver a bit. Spend a little less in one place and a little more in another. The key is to be aware of these choices and to periodically reassess your priorities.

22. US Bureau of Labor Statistics, "Consumer Expenditures 2019."

As you already know, people are not good at thinking over long-term time horizons. Another strategy for living in your budget is to set yourself up with a shorter-term goal. Perhaps making coffee at home for a month will net you $100. So up your savings by $50 per month, and then reward yourself with a thirty-minute massage or a couple of tickets to a game. Such rewards will reinforce good spending and saving habits. The small budget changes will add up and move you toward a better longer-term allocation.

Inevitably, you may reach a point where you want to track your ***cash budget*** more closely. If any of this spending can be reasonably cut—such as your daily latte or weekly take-out meal—limit yourself and devote more to savings.

What Kinds of Insurance Do I Need?

How could there be another expense in the budget? It is already feeling pretty stretched. Still, there is no denying that a health setback or a catastrophic accident can create a financial crisis that ruins everything you are working towards. In order to protect the life and standard of living that you are in the process of creating, think through the types of insurance that may mitigate the impact of bad luck.

Insurance is protection. You spend a little today and have protection if you encounter something outside your control that your budget and your savings can't handle. Prudent financial planning suggests that you manage the risks we all face in life. The insurance company absorbs the risk for a small premium, knowing that not all of its customers will experience a problem at the same time.

Below is a list of the types of insurance every working person should examine and think about having as part of their financial protection plan.

Medical: Even if you are a very healthy person, you really need to have medical insurance. This one can seem like an easy thing to skip, but a car accident or an unexpected illness could become a catalyst to financial ruin very quickly. A Harvard Study cowritten by Senator Elizabeth Warren argued that over 62 percent of consumer bankruptcies are related to medical catalysts.[23] When you are young and healthy, you can feel invincible. It may be easy to skip over insurance products so that you can budget more toward discretionary spending like entertainment and travel!

At a minimum, enroll in a high-deductible plan that will cover your expenses in the event of a catastrophic health event. These plans tend to be less expensive at the level of the premium, though you will pay more out of pocket when you use medical care services, especially before the plan deductible is met. If you already know that you have an ongoing medical situation that requires care, you will want a more expensive medical plan. Many times, your employer-supplied medical plans will be the most cost effective for you because often the employer will pick up some portion of the cost of your plan as part of your benefits (see chapter 2, "The *Decision to Earn*").

If you have a chronic health condition or must take expensive medications on a regular basis, you will want a *richer* health plan with higher premiums. Your history will tell you what is best here. If you have small children, you are likely to get the benefits out of a more expensive plan as well. A colleague with lots of

23. David U. Himmelstein, Deborah Thorne, Elizabeth Warren, and Steffie Woolhandler, "Medical Bankruptcy in the United States, 2007: Results of a National Study," *The American Journal of Medicine* 122, no. 8 (2009): 741–46.

children once quipped, "we reach the family deductible by February," meaning that children will often have unexpected medical events and that a comprehensive health plan is very valuable for families with many, busy children.

A good thing about medical insurance is that you can reappraise your health situation once a year, and change plans if you need to, during a period known as *open enrollment*. This means that if a health procedure is not an emergency, you may be able to plan for it by switching to a richer plan in years when you will need it. Perhaps this might be the case if you plan to become pregnant and start a family. There are also *qualifying life events* that can open a window to changing plans—marriage or divorce, a dependent losing medical coverage, or the death of a spouse—but you will have to check your plan to see what the parameters are.

Work to save the deductible in your emergency savings in case you need it. A Health Savings Account (HSA) is a very nice way to do this. With an HSA, unlike with a Flexible Savings Account (FSA), you do not have to spend the money you put in during that year or lose it. Your HSA funds stay available for any medical-based spending. Some of these savings plans have become quite innovative, allowing you to invest the savings in different mutual funds when you are not using them. This means that your savings fund for medical expenses is growing in a tax-advantaged way. Because medical costs continue to rise, it is inevitable that having a stash of funds ready to help you cover unexpected health expenses is a plus. If you have a high-deductible medical plan, saving toward the maximum out-of-pocket costs for any given year can provide a nice margin of safety, in case anything unforeseen were to happen to your health.

This can be the type of insurance that young people try to skip. Really think it through, though. Would you want to cripple your parents' finances if you had a car accident? Do you think they could leave you to manage alone if something happened to you? Under current law in 2021, young people can stay on their parents' medical plans until the age of twenty-six, and that may be worth doing. You neither have to live with your parents nor have to be financially dependent on them in order to share their health coverage. This may be a reasonable choice for you, and less expensive, even if you pay your part of the premium to your parents! Look at all the options, before bad luck finds you and you leave the people who love you in a financial bind because you were willing to risk not having medical insurance.

Home or Renter's: You want to protect your stuff. If you own a home and have a mortgage, it is likely your mortgage will require homeowner's insurance. Given the average age of the reader here, however, it is more likely that you are renting, or will be when you start your career. Even though you may not think that your stuff is valuable enough to warrant insurance, you should get it because renter's insurance also includes personal liability coverage if someone is hurt in your apartment or sues you because your dog nipped them. And if your apartment is damaged from a fire or made uninhabitable by a covered event, renter's insurance can pay for the additional living expenses incurred while you wait to return to your rental.

By all accounts, renter's insurance is fairly cheap, considering the protection it provides. The typical renter's policy will cost between \$20–\$40 per month and will protect \$20,000–\$60,000 of your personal property, with liability coverage from \$100,000–\$300,000.[24] So if a guest wipes out on your wet kitchen floor and breaks a leg, your renter's insurance will cover their medical bills, using the liability coverage. If the pipes

24. Michelle Megna, "How Much Is Renter's Insurance?" Insurance.com, January 28, 2021, https://www.insurance.com/average-renters-insurance-rates.

in the apartment burst and your TV is destroyed, your policy will provide funds to replace the television. If a fire rips through your apartment complex, you may need funds to relocate while the landlord repairs the damage to your apartment. Your renter's insurance will help to cover additional costs.

Look for policies that cover replacement value, adjust your coverage as your income grows, and stay aware of policy limitations. A policy that pays cash value will pay for the item only after depreciation, and you want to be able to replace your items. The additional cost in the premium to insure replacement value is pretty minor. You can reduce the premiums by choosing a higher deductible amount; anticipate between $500 and $1,000 that you will have to cover yourself before the insurance kicks in. But overall, you can get decent coverage for as little as $250–$300 per year. As your wealth increases, consider upping your coverage. State Farm reports that the average value of personal possessions is $35,000, which is more than most people realize.[25] If you have really expensive possessions, like jewelry or art, you may want a special "rider" policy. You will have to talk to the insurance agent to make sure you follow the procedure for covering such items.

Life: When you are young and responsible for taking care of only yourself, you may want to look at getting enough life insurance to cover your funeral expenses.[26] In deciding on this one, think about the loved ones you would leave behind if something happened to you. Could they afford to pay for the funeral?

Once you have a family and children, life insurance becomes a bigger consideration. Life insurance helps your dependents move through life without you. If you are the primary bread winner, your family may count on your income to pay off the mortgage, send your kids to college, and pay monthly expenses. Even if your partner stays home, you may need life insurance to replace the activities that your partner covers at home, such as cleaning, home maintenance, and taking care of the kids. The need for coverage will be specific to your family and will reflect annual expenses, debt, education requirements, funeral expenses, and so on. From these needs, subtract liquid assets to find the right amount of coverage for you. Consider the following text box to see one method of estimation you can use to determine the appropriate coverage.

THE DIME METHOD FOR DETERMINING LIFE INSURANCE COVERAGE

You know you should add up your big expenses, the ones that your family would have a hard time covering if you were not here, but what are they? DIME[27] is an acronym used in the

25. State Farm, "How Do I Know How Much Renters Insurance to Buy?" Simple Insights, accessed March 8, 2021, https://www.statefarm.com/simple-insights/residence/how-much-renters-insurance-do-i-need.
26. The National Funeral Directors Association reported that the median cost of a funeral was $7,640 in 2019, but it could run upward of $9,000 with a cemetery burial. National Funeral Directors Association, "Statistics," updated July 18, 2019, https://nfda.org/news/statistics.
27. Amy Danise, "How Much Life Insurance Do You Need?" Forbes Advisor, February 5, 2021, https://www.forbes.com/advisor/life-insurance/how-much-life-insurance-do-you-really-need/.

insurance industry as a checklist for potential expenses you might want to cover with the life insurance plan.

D is debt. Do you have credit card debt, student loans, car payments? Any debts you have will pass to your partner when you are gone (one exception is federal student loans)? You want to total these debts and add the cost of the funeral here, to make things easier to pay off after you pass.

I is income. Your beneficiaries may miss your income without you. You want to provide enough income coverage so that your partner can raise the kids, at least through high school. The younger the kids are, the bigger this number will be. Take your income minus the mortgage payment and multiply by the number of years before the youngest child turns eighteen.

M is mortgage. Do you own a house and a have a mortgage? Many would want to remove this burden from the family's shoulders and will include the debt from the mortgage here. The amount will be a function of what you still owe for the house. You can get the payoff amount by looking at your escrow statement.

E is education. Again, you may want to be sure that the kids will have what they need for daycare, school activities, and maybe even college. You know how expensive college is! Consider how much you want to contribute to that, and add it to the total.

Beyond the amount of coverage, you must choose between ***term life*** and ***whole life***. Term life insurance is for a period of years, usually twenty to forty years, corresponding to the amount of time you want your family to be covered. You want to set the term long enough to see the kids through college, pay off your mortgage, and build your savings to a level sufficient for the needs of your partner. Generally, the premium does not change over time, and each year, you may have the opportunity to increase the amount of the insurance coverage in line with your increased needs. But when the term of the policy is up, so is the coverage. The idea is that you won't need the coverage anymore.

Whole life insurance lasts throughout your life. There is a built-in investment process to this type of insurance that the policyholder can borrow against and sometimes draw dividends from. This policy type builds cash value over time, and once you are older, it can be cashed out for its value if you need the money. The premium money you must pay for this policy would likely earn a bigger average annual return if it were saved in other investment vehicles, but the benefits from this type of insurance are guaranteed when you die, as long as you don't let the premium payments lapse.

Whole life insurance is much costlier than term life insurance, as much as twelve to twenty times more,[28] because of the built-in benefits and policy length. You might want to pay more if you have a dependent with disabilities and want to ensure care after your passing, but most of us get the coverage

28. Andrew Marder, "Term vs. Whole Life Insurance: How to Choose," NerdWallet, February 23, 2021, https://www.nerdwallet.com/article/insurance/term-vs-whole-life-insurance#what-is-term-life-insurance.

needed for an average cost of $40–$55 per month.[29] The premium you pay will go up with the size of the death benefit and the length of the policy term; it will be higher if you are male and will also depend on how old you are when you purchase coverage. The younger you are, the less it costs starting out. Your health history can impact your premium rates, but often you can pick a term life plan without answering health questions.

Long-Term Disability: This is the type of insurance that can easily slip by a healthy and young person's notice! If you were to have an accident, become very ill, or have an injury away from work and become unable to work, what would you do? The Council for Disability Awareness reports that 25 percent of twenty-somethings—that is, one in four—will experience disability before they retire due to serious illness or back injury. Further, the typical duration of the disability is almost three years![30] These statistics suggest that looking into coverage for such an eventuality is financially prudent.

The long-term nature of this insurance means that you would not be able to claim it for the first three to six months of a disability event. This insurance is designed to kick in after you have used the hard emergency fund money but find yourself in a situation where, medically, you cannot work.

You want a policy that will replace 50–75 percent of your monthly income, with five years of coverage. The insurance is not terribly expensive, on average costing between 1–3 percent of your annual salary.[31] Sometimes your employer may offer this type of insurance and help pay for the premiums. Be aware that any benefits realized from tax-advantaged policies will face taxation.

In such a situation, though it might take a while to work through the governmental system, you might also be able to apply for Social Security disability benefits (SSDI), but the amount paid to you would almost certainly be much less than the paycheck you lost. Thus, the need for long-term disability insurance is twofold: the money comes more quickly, and it can be used to buttress the government benefits. Be aware that some policies might expect you to file for SSDI benefits and would lower your payments once those payments started. So, if you expected $1,500 per month in disability insurance payments, and SSDI paid you $500, the insurance payment would be reduced to $1,000. That form of the insurance is much less useful, so avoid that when you are signing; make sure that your disability payments couldn't be *reduced* with other insurance claims.

Long-term disability insurance fills in the gap so that you can maintain a reasonable standard of living while you are unable to work and helps pay the costs not covered by your medical insurance. This is insurance that you do not want to have to use, but it is important to be ready for catastrophe should it arrive at your door.

This list of insurance types looks pretty long, and there are many other forms that insurance can take, notably car or boat, pet, cancer, and umbrella policies for liability. Some of these may be important and necessary for you, but not for everyone. Your case is unique, and what works for you may be different from

29. Liz Knueven, "The Average Life Insurance Rate by Age, Sex, and Coverage Type," Business Insider, Personal Finance, February 4, 2021, https://www.businessinsider.com/personal-finance/average-life-insurance-rates.

30. Council for Disability Awareness, "You, Disabled? What Are Your Chances?" accessed March 8, 2021, https://disabilitycanhappen.org/overview/.

31. Colin Lalley, "How Much Does Long-Term Disability Insurance Cost?" Policygenius, March 16, 2018, https://www.policygenius.com/disability-insurance/learn/how-much-does-long-term-disability-insurance-cost/.

what is important for someone else. The types discussed here are specifically about averting financial ruin. Even with insurance, you face ***wants*** and ***needs***. It is important to think through the risks you are willing and able to take and to protect yourself where necessary.

Key Takeaways

Directions: Review the following list of key takeaways to help you remember what you learned in this chapter:

- Money and happiness are clearly linked, but more money will not always add to happiness. Focus on the income necessary to cover your needs and a few wants.
- As much as 75 percent of your budget will not be discretionary spending, so learning how to budget within the range of the average for housing, food, transportation, and entertainment will provide more room for allocating toward wants.
- Smart budgeting is a process rather than an activity. To be successful, it must be done with your preferences in mind.
- No one really wants to spend money on insurance, but several types are worth considering so that you can secure all that you are working toward.

Application Opportunity: Do This Now!

Directions: Complete the activities below to apply what you have learned in this chapter.

Activity 1

Go to consumer.gov to download the budget worksheet from the Federal Trade Commission. A blue tab on the site will say "Toolbox." Click that. Then choose "Worksheets and Presentations." Finally, click "Make a Budget—Worksheet." Use the techniques we have developed in this chapter to create a budget for you as a **student**. Insert your expenses for the most recent month, and use those to create a budget for next month.

Activity 2

Now create a second budget, using the data you gathered in your Career Worksheet (chapter 2) and your Savings Plan (chapter 3). This is an aspirational budget for your first year of working. What are the challenges you notice?

Bibliography

Babiak, Paul, Craig S. Neumann, and Robert D. Hare. "Corporate Psychopathy: Talking the Walk." *Behavioral Sciences & The Law* 28, no. 2 (2010): 174–93.

Bird, Beverly, "How Much Does the Average American Pay in Taxes?" The Balance, updated May 26, 2021, https://www.thebalance.com/what-the-average-american-pays-in-taxes-4768594.

Chaplin, Lan Nguyen, Ronald Paul Hill, and Deborah Roedder John. "Poverty and Materialism: A Look at Impoverished Versus Affluent Children." *Journal of Public Policy & Marketing* 33, no. 1 (2014): 78–92.

Consumer.gov. "Consumer Protection Basics ... Plain and Simple." Accessed June 14, 2021. https://www.consumer.gov/.

Council for Disability Awareness. "You, Disabled? What Are Your Chances?" Accessed March 8, 2021. https://disabilitycanhappen.org/overview/.

Compound Interest Calculator. *Investor.Gov: U.S. Securities and Exchange Commission.* Accessed July 17, 2022. https://www.investor.gov/financial-tools-calculators/calculators/compound-interest-calculator

Curry, Oliver Scott, Lee A. Rowland, Caspar J. van Lissa, Sally Zlotowitz, John McAlaney, and Harvey Whitehouse. "Happy to Help? A Systematic Review and Meta-Analysis of the Effects of Performing Acts of Kindness on the Well-Being of the Actor." *Journal of Experimental Social Psychology* 76 (May 2018): 320–29.

Danise, Amy. "How Much Life Insurance Do You Need?" Forbes Advisor. February 5, 2021. https://www.forbes.com/advisor/life-insurance/how-much-life-insurance-do-you-really-need/.

Faber, David. "Untold Wealth: The Rise of the Super Rich." CNBC Original Production, October 13, 2009. https://www.youtube.com/watch?v=TNRwERkZhjs.

Hagerty, Michael R., "Social Comparisons of Income in One's Community: Evidence from National Surveys of Income and Happiness." *Journal of Personality and Social Psychology* 78, no. 4 (2000): 764–71. doi:10.1037/0022-3514.78.4.764.

Helliwell, John F., Richard Layard, Jeffrey Sachs, and Jan-Emmanuel De Neve, eds., "World Happiness Report 2020." New York: Sustainable Development Solutions Network. (2020).

Himmelstein, David U., Deborah Thorne, Elizabeth Warren, and Steffie Woolhandler. "Medical Bankruptcy in the United States, 2007: Results of a National Study." *The American Journal of Medicine* 122, no. 8 (2009): 741–46.

Knueven, Liz. "The Average Life Insurance Rate by Age, Sex, and Coverage Type." *Business Insider*, February 4, 2021. https://www.businessinsider.com/personal-finance/average-life-insurance-rates.

Lalley, Colin. "How Much Does Long-Term Disability Insurance Cost?" Policygenius. March 16, 2018. https://www.policygenius.com/disability-insurance/learn/how-much-does-long-term-disability-insurance-cost/.

Marder, Andrew. "Term vs. Whole Life Insurance: How to Choose." NerdWallet. February 23, 2021. https://www.nerdwallet.com/article/insurance/term-vs-whole-life-insurance#what-is-term-life-insurance.

Maslow, Abraham Harold. "A Theory of Human Motivation." *Psychological Review* 50, no. 4 (1943): 370–96.

Megna, Michelle. "How Much Is Renter's Insurance?" Insurance.com. January 28, 2021. https://www.insurance.com/average-renters-insurance-rates.

National Funeral Directors Association. "Statistics." Updated July 18, 2019. https://nfda.org/news/statistics.

NerdWallet. "The 7 Best Budget Apps for 2021." December 21, 2020. https://www.nerdwallet.com/article/finance/best-budget-apps.

Norris, J. Ian, Nathaniel M. Lambert, C. Nathan DeWall, and Frank D. Fincham. "Can't Buy Me Love?: Anxious Attachment and Materialistic Values." *Personality and Individual Differences* 53, no. 5 (2012): 666–69.

Pear, Robert. "National Health Spending to Surpass $10,000 a Person in 2016." *The New York Times*, July 13, 2016. https://www.nytimes.com/2016/07/14/us/national-health-spending-to-surpass-10000-per-person-in-2016.html.

The Pew Charitable Trusts. "Survey of American Family Finances: Top-Lines Accompanying 'Americans' Financial Security: Perception and Reality.'" March 2015. https://www.pewtrusts.org/~/media/assets/2015/03/fsm-poll-results-toplines_artfinal_v3.pdf.

Popov, Igor, Chris Salviati, and Rob Warnock. "Data & Rent Estimates–National-Level Historic Estimates (2017–Present)." Apartment List. February 24, 2021. https://www.apartmentlist.com/research/category/data-rent-estimates.

Richins, Marsha L. "The Material Values Scale: Measurement Properties and Development of a Short Form." *Journal of Consumer Research* 31, no. 1 (June 2004): 209–219.

Smith, Aaron. "Cell Internet Use 2012: Main Findings." Pew Research Center. June 26, 2012. https://www.pewresearch.org/internet/2012/06/26/main-findings-9/.

Solberg, Emily G., Edward Diener, and Michael D. Robinson. "Why Are Materialists Less Satisfied?" In *Psychology and Consumer Culture: The Struggle for a Good Life in a Materialistic World*, edited by Tim Kasser and Allen D. Kanner, 29–48. Washington, DC: American Psychological Association, 2004. https://doi.org/10.1037/10658-003.

State Farm. "How Do I Know How Much Renters Insurance to Buy?" Simple Insights. Accessed March 8, 2021. https://www.statefarm.com/simple-insights/residence/how-much-renters-insurance-do-i-need.

US Bureau of Labor Statistics. "Consumer Expenditures 2019." Economic news release. September 9, 2020. https://www.bls.gov/news.release/cesan.nr0.htm.

US Census Bureau. "American Community Survey (ACS)." 2018. https://www.census.gov/programs-surveys/acs.

Figure Credit

Fig. 4.1: Copyright © by Androidmarsexpress (CC BY-SA 4.0) at https://commons.wikimedia.org/wiki/File:Maslow%27s_Hierarchy_of_Needs2.svg.

CHAPTER 5

The Decision to Owe

Invest in Your Well-Being Tomorrow

Imagine...

You've graduated from college and are about to start your first job (Congratulations!). Because you have followed the advice in this book, you have carefully selected a job with great benefits. You have already built a budget you can follow, based on your estimated net monthly income. You have even built up a small soft emergency fund from your part-time job during college.

You have allotted a conservative 25 percent of your budget for housing needs. You are hoping for a two-bedroom so you have room for a home office and some guest space for friends and family. But browsing the rental properties on the web, you notice that it will be hard to find even a decent one-bedroom apartment in your price range. This is surprising to you, because you have friends that have already purchased houses, and you know they are paying less per month toward their mortgages than you are looking at paying in rent. Should you think about buying a house? You don't have money for a down payment, but you do know there are some special government programs that will allow you to buy a house for very little in up-front costs.

You also have transportation needs. The used car you've been driving since high school is on its last legs and will have to be replaced soon. Right now, you need new tires, and if you don't get them, it won't be safe to drive much longer. It is a good thing that you have the $500 in your soft emergency fund to purchase them, but it will wipe you out. You applied for a credit card in college, but you've never used it. Is now the time? Or should you look at taking on a car payment? You think you can get a decent used Corolla for about $200 a month.

Pretty soon, you will have to start paying on your student loans as well. Now you are getting a little worried—will your income be enough for rent, a car payment, and a student loan payment? Maybe you should get a master's degree to boost your earning potential. But that will require even more borrowing—is that a good idea, when you hope to be able to buy a house before too long?

Introduction

At some point, as it is inevitable for most, you will have to finance your financial future. You have made good financial choices so far; you have a solid savings plan, a manageable budget, and good spending habits. But some of the most important purchases that you make in life—a house, a new car, an undergraduate or advanced degree—are simply not always possible to make from savings and income alone. How do you know when it makes sense to borrow? How do you balance saving, spending, and borrowing? The topic of borrowing comes along with a whole new vocabulary: credit, FICO, amortization ... how to make sense of all this?

This chapter is about *borrowing*, which is, essentially, taking money now that will have to be paid back later. Hopefully, by this point in the book, that generally sounds like a bad idea, and it often is. There is a reason to think about saving and budgeting before thinking about borrowing: the goal of saving and budgeting is to make borrowing unnecessary. And yet, there are times in your life where it will almost certainly be necessary.

Chapter Objectives

After reading this chapter, you will be able to:

- Appreciate the danger and usefulness of debt, evaluate credit statements, and make sound credit card spending decisions.
- Understand what a FICO score is, recognize the components in its calculation, and demonstrate some proficiency about understanding what determines credit.
- Be able to demonstrate financial fluency with interest rates and loan amortization regarding mortgages and car loans.
- Make good decisions about investing in education with student loans.

Is Borrowing Ever a Good Idea?

As with all the other topics in this book, you can think about borrowing as an *investment*—an investment in your financial tomorrow. In order to understand when and why this can be beneficial, consider how businesses think about investment. In business, borrowing is an important part of *financing*, or figuring out how to pay for long-term projects. Businesses care primarily about profitability, so every long-term project is evaluated in terms of how much money it might make for the company over the investment's life. In general, projects that have the potential to return a lot of money are also quite big, risky, and expensive, such as developing a new product or building a new manufacturing facility. Companies might not always have all the money they need up front to finance them. But that doesn't necessarily mean they shouldn't make the investment. As with anything else, if the expected payoff of making the investment is sufficiently greater than the cost, the company will likely take on the project. But if they don't have all the cash up front, the cost won't only include the amount of money to build the factory (for instance). It will also include the cost of borrowing the money to pay for the factory over time.

You learned in earlier chapters that when you save, you will earn a return on your investment, often paid in the form of interest or dividends on savings. The reason you earn this return is to reward you for making your money available to someone else, like a business when it wants to invest in a project. The interest you earn, then, is a cost to whoever borrowed the money.

Like any business that borrows money, you will also pay a cost to do so, in the form of interest. As you will learn, for some kinds of borrowing, those interest rates are so high that it almost never makes sense to take on those costs, such as with credit cards, and worse, payday lenders. But when it comes to things like houses, cars, and education, it can certainly make sense to borrow. Just as a business makes a decision to take on the cost of borrowing for some better, longer-term payoff, you might make the same decision when you are investing in your future. In fact, if you are reading this, you have likely already made that decision. According to recent data from the US Bureau of Labor Statistics, the median salary (overall; not starting salary) for a college graduate is around $65,000, compared to $39,000 for a high school graduate.[1] This is a difference of $26,000—or, said another way, college graduates make about 67 percent more than high school graduates over the course of their career.

The college graduate had to devote time, energy, and money to earn the degree, however, and that may make it a more difficult decision to evaluate. On the downside, the average college student's debt is around $32,000.[2] On a ten-year payment plan at a 4.6 percent interest rate, this amounts to a $334 monthly payment—or a total amount of *roughly* $40,000 ($334 × 120 months). This means that over the course of ten years you will pay an additional $8,000 ($40,000 – $32,000) back in interest. It should be immediately obvious that the total cost of the loan, principal plus interest, is less than two years' worth of the college graduate's salary premium of $26,000. Over a lifetime of working, after the loan is repaid, the payoff on the degree is in the hundreds of thousands of dollars.

Technically speaking, the $8,000 borrowing cost is not the only cost to consider; there are opportunity costs as well, as economists like to say. There is the money you are not earning while you are in college. And there are the budgeting constraints of that loan payment once you start working, which could set you back on your long-term savings goals and delay financing another major purchase, such as a house, for a few years. But even after accounting for these opportunity costs, you will almost surely find that the cost of borrowing to finance a college undergraduate education is one that is worth the investment. In fact, education is not just a *financial* investment—hopefully, the value goes well beyond what it can do for you salary-wise. Hopefully, you will study something that you are passionate about and have a career that you find interesting and meaningful. It will make you a better citizen and help you determine how to live a happier, more fulfilled life.

This is the way to think about borrowing:

It is the cost of an investment in your financial future.

1. US Bureau of Labor Statistics, "Learn More, Earn More: Education Leads to Higher Wages, Lower Unemployment," Career Outlook, May 2020, https://www.bls.gov/careeroutlook/2020/data-on-display/education-pays.htm.
2. Federal Reserve, "Report on the Economic Well-Being of U.S. Households in 2016–May 2017," Board of Governors of the Federal Reserve System, June 2017, https://www.federalreserve.gov/publications/2017-economic-well-being-of-us-households-in-2016-education-debt-loans.htm.

You Don't Always Deserve the Credit

One day, while strolling across campus as an undergraduate, I came across a booth set up on the quad. Giant stacks of free T-shirts naturally caught my attention, so I wandered over. All I had to do, the friendly vendor told me, was fill out a short application, and I could have whichever shirt I wanted. I had my eye on the one with the image of John Belushi from *National Lampoon's Animal House*, emblazoned simply with the word "College," so I set down my backpack and got to work. That day, I walked away with, I think, five free T-shirts, one for each of the credit cards applications I had filled out, with only the dimmest awareness of what I had just signed up for.

These credit cards, with their ridiculously low credit limits and ridiculously high interest rates, sat in my desk drawer for several years. Every once in a while, I would get a new one in the mail and just toss it in the drawer along with the others, without even removing that little sticker with the phone number you have to call to activate it. Honestly, I wasn't even sure what to do with them! Unfortunately, I soon discovered their use when I needed money and didn't have any. At the urging of a graduate school roommate, who also did not want to put up with a broken washing machine any longer, I bought a fancy new one that came in just under my $500 credit limit. The plan was to pay it off in a year, which would cost each of us about $20 per month. That was about the cost of a plate of fajitas and a beer at Ruby Tequila's in Lubbock, Texas. Seemed reasonable!

One thing about graduate students, though, is that they often find themselves without a lot of money. And that desk drawer kept calling. I may not have had much left to spend on one credit card, but there was always another sticker to be ripped off and a fresh $500 to spend! And while I honestly didn't realize just how financially irresponsible this was, the strategy seemed to work for a while. Twenty dollars a month on this one, $30 on this one, another $10 here. In total, the payments were less than my cable and phone bill. That was the justification I told myself as I racked up debt on a few desirable *wants*.

As the monthly payments began to escalate, I realized that I was paying more than I had to. Forty dollars a month was enough to pay off the washer in a year. But I noticed that my credit card statement was telling me I only had to pay twenty—"minimum payment due: $20." It was exhilarating! Like the first moment I scanned a credit card and came home with a new washing machine. This effectively made it possible to squeeze in a whole extra monthly payment on another credit card.

Until, one month, I forgot to pay one of the bills altogether. In those days paying bills was no fun. I mean, it was even less fun than it is today. Back then, you had to actually physically mail in a check, or call in with your bank information, in which case you might spend a great deal of time on hold. We younger GenXers and older Millennials were a little too hip and internet savvy for such antiquated methods. Unfortunately, the internet was also still young, and slow dial-up and poor-quality webpages didn't make online payment much easier. In any event, when you are managing multiple bills, it is certainly easy to miss one when those are your payment options.

I didn't even notice until I got my next bill, and I saw that it hadn't budged from the previous bill. Indeed, it was higher than the month before! This was due in part to a $25 late fee that had been tacked on. But given that I had also gone a month without making a minimum payment, I had not paid down any of the principal either.

It slowly sank in that the minimum payments on some cards were not enough to keep the balance going down, because the interest was higher, in some cases, than the minimum payment. Add in a few late fees, and in one case, the balance went over the credit maximum of $500. Now an additional overlimit fee was tacked on, and the minimum payment wasn't even enough to get the balance under the credit limit. This meant another overlimit fee the next month.

When it comes to credit, it is easy to get in over your head, fast. The interest rates are so high that it can be tough to pay down the principal; throw late fees and overlimit fees into the mix, and it can be overwhelming. I was lucky that, although I was managing payments on multiple cards, the balances were low. I was able to pay them down and get myself out of trouble, and I've never once carried a credit card balance past a month since.

You won't find the credit card hawkers out on the quad anymore. Legislation passed in the wake of the Great Recession severely limited the ability of banks to market to younger individuals, and many banks have decided that young consumers are too risky to offer credit to anyway. Hopefully, this makes it harder for young people to find themselves in credit trouble that comes from not reckoning with *wants* versus *needs*.

My story might lead you to vow never to use credit cards at all, thinking, "if I don't have them, I won't fall into that trap," but know that it is difficult in our society today to avoid credit altogether. In fact, building credit is often an integral part of a healthy personal finance strategy. Having a high credit score will make it possible for you to get a mortgage to buy a house and to get the best interest rates on that mortgage. Likewise for car loans. So long as you are paying bills, such as your cell phone bill, you are building credit. But credit card utilization factors particularly heavily into credit scores. Using credit regularly and using it wisely is one of the best ways to build the best possible credit score that you can. Use it irresponsibly, as I did, and it can wreak havoc on your financial well-being. Not only can you end up way over your head in terms of what you owe, but high balances, late payments, and overlimit fees will also destroy your credit score. In the very-worst-case scenario, *bankruptcy* can be a necessary step toward eliminating your debt. But it will tank your credit for the next seven to ten years, making a mortgage or car loan effectively impossible.

Know the Danger in Using a Credit Card

Now that you are sufficiently scared—as you should be!—it's time to turn the tables and talk about the necessary but wise and responsible use of credit. Consider a concrete example: the credit card statement in figure 5.1.

	CREDIT CARD STATEMENT		SEND PAYMENT TO First Bank International Orlando, Florida
ACCOUNT NUMBER	**NAME**	**STATEMENT DATE**	**PAYMENT DUE DATE**
xxxx-xxxx-xxxx-3254	Sally Jones	2/15/2020	3/11/2020
CREDIT LINE	**CREDIT AVAILABLE**	**NEW BALANCE**	**MINIMUM PAYMENT DUE**
$1,200.00	$1,036.76	$163.24	$20.00

REFERENCE	SOLD	POSTED	ACTIVITY SINCE LAST STATEMENT	AMOUNT
486GRT254		20-Jan	PAYMENT THANK YOU	($235.23)
109POT382	19-Jan	21-Jan	Mike's Hot Dog Stand, Tampa, FL	$9.81
215GRE031	21-Jan	23-Jan	La Casa Mexicana Restaurant, St. Petersburg, FL	$35.99
899FTE657	25-Jan	27-Jan	TicketHub Tickets, Orlando, FL	$40.00
900MST769	30-Jan	31-Jan	EZ Mart Gas and Go, Kissimmee, FL	$27.45
142FFF661	4-Feb	5-Feb	Textbooks Plus, Orlando, FL	$49.99

Previous Balance	(+)	235.23	Current Amount Due	$163.24
Purchases	(+)	163.24	Amount Past Due	
Cash Advances	(+)		Amount Over Credit	
Payments	(-)	235.23	Minimum Payment Due	$20
Credits	(-)			
FINANCE CHARGES	(+)			
Late Charges	(+)			
NEW BALANCE	(+)	163.24		

FINANCE CHARGE SUMMARY	PURCHASES	ADVANCES	For Customer Service Call:
Periodic Rate	1.65%	0.54%	1-800-xxx-xxxx
Annual Percentage Rate	19.80%	6.48%	For Lost or Stolen Card, Call:
			1-800-xxx-xxxx
			24-Hour Telephone Numbers

FIGURE 5.1 Credit Card Statement Example

On this statement, you will see several key pieces of information.

Periodic Rate and Annual Percentage Rate (APR)

You will see the applicable cost of borrowing at the bottom of this particular statement. One of the most common metrics used to evaluate credit cards is the annual percentage rate. This is effectively the amount of interest you will pay on a balance in a month times 12. In 2021, typical APR ranges are around 12.99 percent to as high as 29.99 percent, with an average of between 15.56 percent and 22.87 percent.[3] The periodic rate is found by taking the APR divided by twelve—essentially, the corresponding interest on a monthly basis. This rate is the important one, because it is what determines how much interest you pay each month *if you carry a balance.*

Statement Date and Payment Date

Notice that the payment date is nearly a month later than the statement date. The statement date represents the end of the billing period, which is February 15 in this case. This is the last day on which any purchases you made would end up on this bill. In fact, you will see that you actually made the first payment on this bill January 19, at the beginning of this particular billing period. The payment date is March 11—nearly two months after the first purchase! So be aware that even though this bill covers payments made in January, those payments do not come due until February, and don't have to be paid until March.

3. US News Staff, "Average Credit Card APR," *US News and World Report*, March 15, 2021, https://creditcards.usnews.com/articles/average-apr.

Credit Limit, Remaining Credit, Balance, and Minimum Payment

The credit line is set at a limit of $1,200, indicating that this is the maximum amount that can be billed to the card. If you have a balance of $500 and try to make a $800 purchase, the card will be declined, but a $700 purchase will go through.

The total amount of purchases billed to the card in this case is $163.24, which also explains the amount of credit available. Most importantly, though, notice that the minimum required payment of $20 doesn't come close to paying off the current balance of the card. The minimum payment is simply the amount that the bank has determined you have to pay in order to remain in good standing. Any payment less than this amount, or no payment at all by the March 11 date, and the bill will be considered late.

Previous Balance, Payments, and Current Balance

From this information, you can determine that you paid the credit card balance in full the previous month. The previous month's balance was $235.23; you will see in the activity list that this amount was credited to the account on January 20. You can assume the previous bill was due around February 11, as this bill is due March 11; therefore, the payment was on time, reducing the account balance to $0. However, purchases were made during this billing period as well, and you will see that these purchases in the activity list do in fact add up to the current balance of $163.24. Given that the previous balance was paid in full during this billing period, you might expect that the next bill will also show a $163.24 payment in the next billing period.

Notice that there is nothing listed under "finance charges." ***So long as the balance is paid in full each month, you will never pay finance charges***. That is, even though some of these purchases were made in January, even if the full balance is not paid until the day of March 11, there will be no finance charges on the next statement. The amount of the next statement should correspond perfectly to the sum total of purchases under activity, just as this one does.

If the full balance is not paid, however, you will see finance charges on the next statement, which will appear under "previous balance" and thus factor into the "new balance" on the next bill. For instance, imagine that you only make the minimum payment of $20, a trap that many who use credit cards fall into. What will the new balance be on the next bill?

Even if not a single additional purchase is made in the next billing period, there will remain a $143.24 balance on the card, which can be found by taking "previous balance" minus "payments." However, the "current amount due" will be for slightly more than this because you will pay one month's finance charges as well. Given the periodic rate of 1.65 percent (which you need to turn into a decimal for calculation), you can calculate the month's interest as $2.36 (which is $143.24 × .0165). Therefore, the next month's "new balance" will be for $145.60. You paid $20, but you didn't reduce the balance by $20!

This may not sound like much of a difference but consider a few scenarios that are more drastic.

First, what if you fail to make a payment? Assume a $25 late fee is assessed, which is a little less than typical.[4] Will the balance be $188.24 or your current balance plus the late fee? Not exactly—because you will,

4. US News Staff, "Average Credit Card APR." The late fees can be as low as $25 or as high as $39. Some companies charge less the first time you are late, but the fee goes up with additional transgressions. If you have a good record with the company, you can call and get the fee removed if you accidently miss a payment. This won't work over and over again, though.

of course, be charged interest on the carried balance. In fact, you will pay interest on the balance including the late fee, or $3.11, and the balance on your next bill will be $191.35.

Suppose you want to buy a new guitar amplifier for a total of $1,200. If you have a balance of zero, you can indeed make this purchase within your credit limit. Can you pay it off in a year by making $100 payments each month? By this point in the book, you may immediately recognize that this will not be possible, considering the impact of interest. After one month of payments, you will not have a balance of $1,100, but rather $1,118.15, considering the $18.15 worth of finance charges tacked on to your $1,100 balance at a periodic rate of 1.65 percent. By the third month, your balance will be $950.38—about $250 less than your initial balance, even though you will have already paid $300.

In fact, if you run this out until the balance is paid off, it will take fourteen payments, not twelve, and you will have paid an additional $148 in interest. So, this is not a $1,200 amplifier; it becomes a $1,350 amplifier! And it might not be nearly the bargain you thought it was.

Finally, let's run a really drastic scenario. Suppose you have a balance of $5,000 (this is pretty easy to do if you are buying musical equipment). Because you were late on a payment, not only were you assessed a late fee, but your interest was also increased to the maximum rate allowed—29.99 percent. Your minimum payment is $100. What will your balance be the next month?

If you pay the minimum payment, you will be assessed 29.99 percent interest on $4,900. This corresponds to a periodic rate of 2.5 percent, which amounts to $122.50 (which is .025 × $4,900). Your next bill will be $5,022.50, which is $22.50 more than your previous balance, even though you paid the $100 minimum payment! If you continue to make only the minimum payment in this scenario, your balance will continue to grow, and in theory, you will never be able to pay the balance down to zero.

I hope this scenario illustrates the risk of using credit cards unwisely. High interest rates, late fees, overlimit fees, and the minimum payment can easily add up to an unsustainable situation in which you are paying large amounts of money every month without ever making a dent in the debt. This is detrimental to financial well-being, and to personal well-being; it is an extraordinarily stressful situation to find yourself in.

Use Credit Wisely

Yes, credit can get you into hot water, pretty quickly if you are not paying attention. All of this said, you should still use credit. In fact, you should use it a lot, if you are responsible and use it wisely. It might surprise you to hear this, after the disaster scenario described in the previous section. Maybe an analogy would help. When you were a toddler, your mom told you not to touch the oven because it was hot and it could burn you. She did not mean that you should never touch the oven for the rest of your life. Most of us need the oven to eat decent meals. We all learned how to use the oven. The same is true for credit cards. You can get burned, but when used correctly, the credit card is a tool that can make your life better. It is really all a matter of how you think about and use credit. Here is some advice:

Credit cards are NOT for borrowing. They are for spending.

If you make purchases on credit and pay your balance in full every month, you will never pay an extra dollar in finance charges. In fact, you will be building credit for a future home purchase, which will help you save money on mortgage interest rates, and help you ***build long-term wealth*** by investing in a long-term durable asset like a home.

And you will also likely make money in the form of credit rewards. That's right: because the reward of building a good credit score is hard for people to imagine, and because too many people think of credit cards as a way to borrow money, credit card companies offer rewards to consumers who both make purchases and pay their balances. These rewards often go by the name of "cash back" and offer points that can be used for a variety of different purposes. Typically, these rewards correspond to 1 percent or 2 percent of every purchase made. The Citi Double Cash card, for instance, offers 1 percent on every purchase and an additional 1 percent when balances are paid. Someone who puts $1,000 each month on a card like this will essentially make back $240 per year in cash-back bonuses—1 percent of every purchase will correspond to $10 every month, or $20 if the balance is paid off each month. Many cards offer much higher rewards in specific categories, as high as even 5 percent or 6 percent. Travel, dining, grocery, and gas are popular categories.

Not only will you be building a strong credit score, but you will also be getting money back. The catch, of course, is paying your balance in full every month. Missing a payment or paying finance charges for failing to pay the whole balance can quickly undo the benefits of credit rewards, and then some. The best way to avoid this is to link your credit accounts to your bank account, which online account management makes very easy to do. You can set your bill to be paid automatically from your bank account on any day during the billing period. Of course, if you do this, it becomes critical that you manage your budget and stick to it, to ensure that you have the necessary balance to pay the bill. Remember that lesson?

My recommendation? Choose specific categories of purchases to use with specific credit cards. For instance, if you have a card that offers great grocery rewards, use this one for your grocery purchases, and use another card for dining out if it offers better rewards in that category. Stick to purchases that you make regularly, ones that are part of your budget—if you budget $500 for groceries per month and track your spending, then you can be sure you will always have the $500 in your bank account when the credit card bill drafts.

A final point: remember that your bill comes due nearly a month after the closing date, which is a month after the beginning of the billing period. If you operate this way, you will find yourself paying off purchases that may be six or seven weeks old. When budgeting, you should always consider the total credit balance, which will include your statement balance from the previous billing period *and* all the purchases you have made since. There is no reason to pay anything more than the statement balance. But any more recent purchases still count. That is, when you are budgeting purchases, consider the money that you spend on credit to be spent immediately, even though you might be paying for it much later. One thing that might help is setting your bill to draft as early in the payment period as possible instead of paying it on the due date. This way, your current balance will typically be pretty close to your statement balance.

Can I Get Started with Credit Cards Now?

If you are a college student, you may find it more difficult to get a credit card than it was back when companies were handing them out with free T-shirts. But if you use the card correctly, it is not a bad idea to have one. Many banks offer cards that are made for students specifically, with low credit limits and low periodic rates. Another way to go is with ***secured credit***. A secured credit card works more like a debit card—the money has to be available up front, as if it were being deducted from your bank account. For instance, if you were to obtain a secured card through your bank, the bank might "hold" $500 in reserves if you have a $500 credit limit. But in every other way, the card works exactly like a credit card, and you can use it to get used to using credit responsibly and paying your bill regularly.

Secured credit will help you build credit faster, which could come in handy if you need to buy a new car shortly after graduation. You will almost certainly need a car loan to do so, and car loan rates can be quite high; having a good credit score can save you a great deal of money in interest. If you are a college student with a credit card, you might consider using it just for one or two things that are regular expenses in your budget and that stay pretty much the same amount each month, like your phone bill. That makes budgeting easy.

Start with your bank. Give them a call, and just ask what kinds of options they might have available for you. The solid and competitive deals you can get from your local organization may be surprising. Alternatively, *US News and World Report* maintains a website that helps you compare credit cards, and one page is directed to students.[5] Be aware that you do want to look through the entire page, because the news source discloses that they accept advertiser dollars from some of the credit card companies; that may affect where on the site the card is listed, though they say their editorial comments are without bias. The site may still be worthwhile to look through, though, because it can offer you a way to compare card benefits and costs directly. It will give you an idea of things worth considering as you think about the card that is right for your needs.

You don't want to apply for a bunch of credit cards online that you likely won't get as a college student without any income. This matters, because every time you apply for credit it has a negative impact on your credit score. Better to find out the right solution for your situation first.

It's Exciting to Build Credit. Score!

Using credit wisely is important for several reasons. But perhaps the greatest benefit you will personally get out of it is a good credit score. Your credit score will affect your ability to get car loans, a home mortgage, and other types of financing. But even more importantly, it will affect the kinds of interest rates you will get on those loans. In recent years, mortgage interest rates have become very low by historical standards, falling to average rates under 4 percent in 2020 and under 3 percent in 2021. For comparison purposes, due to rampant inflation, rates were as high as the mid-teens in the early 1980s! I recently refinanced my home at a rate of 2 percent, but an earlier generation might have felt lucky to have a rate of 9 percent if they bought the family home in the mid-1970s, or an even higher interest rate in the teens if the house was being purchased in the early-1980s.

Even though recent and current rates are low by historical standards, there is still good variation in the rates offered to individuals, and the difference is based on their credit scores. Credit scores range from 300 to 850 points. Someone with very good credit—defined by scores in the high 700s into the 800s—may get a rate as low as 3.8 percent.[6] But someone with a lower credit score—in the low-to-mid 600s, for example—might

5. Beverly Harzog, "Best Credit Cards for Students," *US News and World Report*, March 26, 2021, https://creditcards.usnews.com/student.
6. Bankrate, "Mortgage Calculator," accessed April 1, 2021, https://www.bankrate.com/calculators/mortgages/mortgage-calculator.aspx.

expect a rate around 5.2 percent. This variance of 1.4 percent is not inconsequential when a loan will be paid back over a thirty-year time horizon, which is typical for a mortgage. On a $250,000 mortgage with a 20 percent down payment, the total interest paid at 3.8 percent over the life of the loan is around $130,000. But with a 5.2 percent interest rate, the total interest paid is around $190,000. The difference of $60,000 is quite significant!

On a monthly basis, that difference corresponds to a payment of $1,160 vs. $1,330—a difference of $170. So, this $60,000 difference will have an immediate impact on your budget. To really drive this point home, remember that there are both costs and opportunity costs of borrowing to consider. Imagine that you were to invest this $170 difference over the thirty-year life of the loan. At a reasonably conservative 6 percent rate of return, you will have roughly $161,280 at the end of those thirty years if you invest the difference. The true cost of having a lower credit score could be almost as high as the amount you mortgaged in the first place: $200,000 (the purchase price minus the 20 percent down payment of $50,000).

I hope this example has convinced you of the importance of credit scores! You have also already learned a little about mortgages, which we will turn to shortly. But first: where do those credit scores come from, and how are they calculated? For official purposes, credit scores generally come from three credit reporting agencies: Experian, TransUnion, and Equifax. The next text box discusses what you need to know about the consumer credit bureau business.

THE POWER TO DETERMINE YOUR CREDIT SCORE

Who decides your credit score?

Experian, TransUnion, and Equifax are three different firms, which compete for the business of your creditors. These three are the major firms in the industry, but there are other, smaller firms out there. The "big three" form the top of an industry that is really an oligopoly (an industry with a few big firms). What they do is behind the scenes, but it is very central to every individual's life.

What is the formula for calculating your credit score?

Each of the firms uses a proprietary formula, which is akin to a "secret recipe," for deciding on your final score. So you may find that your score is a little different from each firm, because the weight they use is different or because the data each has on your payment behavior is different. But each firm relies on the data they have from five key areas to determine your score: payment history, credit usage, credit age, account mix, and recent inquiries (more on these areas below in the text). They then use a scoring model—examples include FICO and VantageScore—to calculate your score.

How do these credit bureaus get your personal information?

Creditors will report to these firms any failures on your part to meet your financial obligations. Banks and credit card companies are obvious examples, but utilities (particularly cell phone providers) and stores where you have a credit account are other examples. The credit bureau will also scan through public records to find information for your credit report, and they may buy or share information, working with each other or with smaller, more specialized credit bureaus. Anything that happens in court, like a bankruptcy or a tax lien, will wind up in your report, too.

You will see many other companies offering free credit reports—surely, you can already hear the jingle for freecreditreport.com in your head! Increasingly, credit card companies and banks also tabulate their own credit score metrics for you each month. These scores are based on similar data to those used by the three credit reporting agencies. But ultimately, only the scores provided by the "big three" are used for official purposes, such as when you apply for a credit card or a home mortgage. Credit scores can also affect insurance rates and your ability to rent an apartment, and sometimes they are even controversially used in employment decisions.

Table 5.1 shows the ranges of credit associated with specific credit scores.[7]

TABLE 5.1 Credit Score Ranges

800–850	Exceptional
740–799	Very Good
670–739	Good
580–669	Fair
300–579	Very Poor

The average credit score is around 710.[8] But the best rates are granted to those with credit scores of 740 and above. Those with scores of 800 or higher are considered to have exceptional credit.

The actual specific formulas used to calculate these scores are calculated with company formulas not readily revealed to the public, which is one reason why the scores provided by sources such as your bank and freecreditreport.com are not considered official. But it is known how various factors will *generally* affect credit. Figure 5.2 demonstrates the approximate composition of factors important to your credit score.

7. myFico, "What Is a FICO® Score?" accessed April 2, 2021, https://www.myfico.com/credit-education/what-is-a-fico-score.
8. Louis DeNicola, "What Is a Good Credit Score?" Experian, February 11, 2021, https://www.experian.com/blogs/ask-experian/credit-education/score-basics/what-is-a-good-credit-score/.

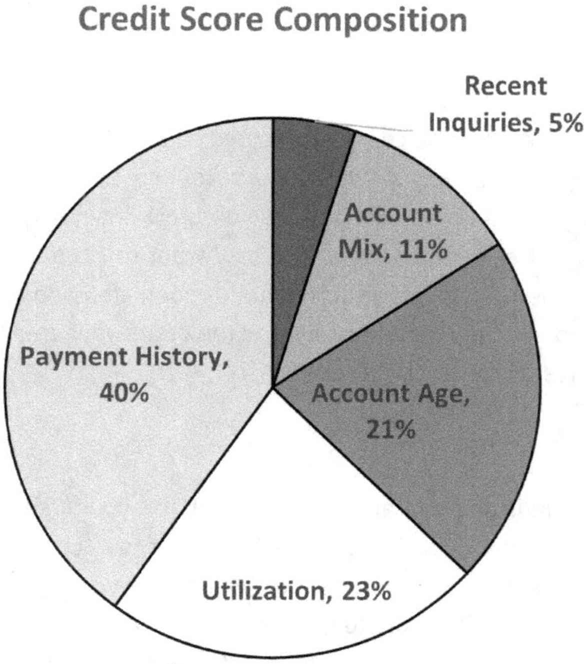

FIGURE 5.2 Credit Score Composition

But what does each factor really indicate about you? The following list explores the details of each credit score factor a bit further, with a few recommendations for improving your score over time.

Payment History

Payment history is determined by whether you pay your bills on time. It helps to have a credit card that you utilize regularly, though paying any bill on time can factor into your credit. This is why it is important to have some bills in your name even while you are in college—such as a streaming subscription bill and a cell phone bill—and to make sure you pay them on time. You will be building solid credit history even before you apply for your first credit card. Indeed, this will help you get your first credit card. Payment history accounts for about 35–40 percent of your overall credit score.

Credit Utilization

This has to do with your credit balance relative to your credit limits. In general, you don't want maxed-out credit cards. For reporting purposes, carrying a balance won't necessarily hurt your credit. In fact, banks actually like it when you carry credit across monthly statements—that's how they make money! Of course, you have learned lots of reasons why you shouldn't carry a balance. A general rule is that balances should not exceed 30 percent of your total credit limit within any billing cycle. This means that if you have a card with a $5,000 credit limit, you should not have more than a $1,500 balance on the card. This issue can impact your credit score even if you pay the card off each month. A red flag is raised when your credit balances move above 30 percent, even in the middle of a credit cycle, so be aware. Of course, as you've learned, you are best off not carrying a balance at all! Credit usage will account for 20–25 percent of your credit score.

Credit Age

One reason to get a card early—even if you can get a secured card while you are in school—is to build history. Having a long-established credit line factors favorably into your credit score. This means that you may want to think carefully before you get rid of a credit card. As you grow financially, you may gain access to better cards, ones with rewards or better periodic rates. You may want to keep the older, less user-friendly card account open, however, and use it just enough to remain in good standing. The greater the length of time with the same creditors, the longer your credit history, and the better your credit score. Credit age can account for approximately 20–25 percent of your credit score.

Account Mix

Having a variety of different kinds of credit also favorably impacts your credit score. That is, you don't want a bunch of credit cards but no other debt financing. Having a car loan or a mortgage represents a different type of loan, known as installment credit, in which you pay a fixed amount each month. This also helps build credit. Of course, you need some credit history to get a mortgage, which might depend primarily on revolving credit, like credit card usage. But once you establish a mortgage and a payment history, you can expect your score to continue to increase.

The credit scoring models give you more points when you handle both revolving accounts and installment accounts. Being able to juggle regular payments every month, while maintaining a revolving credit line such as a credit card, tells the credit bureau that you can handle your credit obligations and that you pose a good credit risk.[9] A mix of credit comprises 10–15 percent of your credit score.

Credit Inquiries

Applying for credit counts against your credit score. If you are applying for a store credit card at a retail outlet, you should ask whether the credit check is a "soft hit" or a "hard hit." A soft hit just returns a score without any detailed information. A hard hit returns a full credit report and will ding your score a few points for a temporary period of time (say, three points off for three months). The actual size of the credit hit is specific to the individual.

Why is this? Reporting agencies view credit applications as a potentially worrisome sign. If you have excellent credit, the hit you take won't affect you much at all. But if you have weak credit and apply for a bunch of credit cards all at once, your score can take a pretty big hit, which sends a signal to banks that perhaps you are not in the strongest financial position.

When you apply for a mortgage, a car loan, or a regular credit card, there will be a hard inquiry on your credit report. If you are looking for a good auto loan, it is possible that several inquiries will be made within a very short time span as potential lenders look at your credit to determine the interest rate to offer you, and those together will likely be considered one inquiry. Take note, however, that several different credit inquiries at once will be a red flag for credit bureaus as to your credit worthiness. They might question the motivation

9. Gerri Detweiler, "Tips for Improving Your Credit: The Types of Accounts in Your Credit Report," Credit.com, October 27, 2020, https://www.credit.com/credit-reports/tips-for-improving-your-credit-types-of-accounts/.

behind trying to access so much credit at once. Inquiries can impact your credit score for twelve months, but they stay on your credit report for two years. Recent applications for credit account for around 5 percent of your final score.

By far the best action you can take to bolster your credit score is to make your payments on time. If you are in a bind, be proactive, and call the lender to discuss options for payment. Do not put your head in the sand and hope it all gets better. It will not get better on its own. If you show that you are intent on meeting your obligations, the lender is more likely to work with you.

The other thing to "do" is to exercise some patience. Credit scores improve over time when you act in financially prudent ways. Try not to fall victim to suggestions to help your score by taking out personal loans, or by applying for a bunch of cards to increase your total credit limit all at once. Taking an unneeded installment loan simply to improve your credit will be costly. Remember that if your credit score is not where you want it, you will pay more in loan costs. And having multiple cards to keep up with erodes your ability to stay on top of your bills; you increase the chances of missing a payment when you have more than three cards to keep up with.

What's Credit Got *in Store* for Me?

Building on the last point about the optimal number of cards in your wallet, be wary of those unbelievable retail store offers for discounts if you "sign up" for the store's card. It seems every retail outlet offers their own credit card these days. This includes diverse companies offering everything from *Lowe's Home Improvement* to *Gap clothing* to *Pottery Barn* furniture. These offers can be quite tempting, with 0 percent introductory APR rates or 10–30 percent off your first purchase when you use the card. Approach these cards with a great deal of caution.

Realize that an offer like 0 percent APR can tempt you into buying things you can't really afford, because you rationalize that you will pay it off monthly. If this is an item you budgeted for and your monthly budget can absorb the cost without affecting your savings, then this might make financial sense. But only if you can structure the payments to pay off the purchase in the introductory period, which is rarely longer than a year. Remember the guitar amplifier example above? Your plan to purchase this amplifier for $1,200 and pay it off in a year would in fact have worked, if you had taken out a credit card at a music store that offered a 0 percent rate for twelve months. The store makes these offers to reduce your purchase inhibitions, and it works. The store does not make this offer out of kindness to you. They know this will hook you, and they are waiting to reel you in.

Not getting the balance paid in full can really backfire. For one thing, store credit often comes with interest rates much higher than those offered by traditional credit card companies. Even worse, if you carry a balance past the introductory rate promotional period, you may be subject to interest on the ***initial*** purchase price. Say you bought that guitar amplifier with the intention of paying $100 per month at 0 percent. One month, due to some unexpected expenses, you only paid the minimum of $20. This means that in the first month after the rate expires, you will still have an $80 balance on the card. Suppose the rate jumps to 19.99 percent after the introductory period. You might find yourself with a $320 bill: the remaining balance of $80, plus a full $240 of interest on the initial $1,200 purchase! This is not necessarily the case. But you need to read the terms of these agreements very carefully, because there is no shortage of nasty surprises out there once you start playing the credit game.

Similar concerns exist for other kinds of promotional offers. For instance, will the savings on a 10 percent introductory rate encourage you to buy things you otherwise wouldn't? From a marketing perspective, that is certainly one advantage for the retailer. Once you have all these store cards lying around, are you likely to continue to use them when you ***want*** things, but don't ***need*** them, and can't afford them? As with any credit card game, it is a dangerous way to play.

If you are smart and selective, it can make financial sense to have a few store cards. Just understand your objectives and have a strategy. For instance, Lowe's offers 5 percent off any purchase made on the Lowe's card, or six months of 0 percent APR. If you only buy things at Lowe's that you would buy anyway and pay the card balance off immediately, then it does make good financial sense to use the card and save 5 percent on every purchase. But if you have a balance that you don't pay off in six months, you might find yourself in trouble.

Another problem is that if you apply for every card that makes you an offer, your credit will take a big hit because of too many inquiries too fast, and you will be left with a bunch of cards that you either use too frequently or don't use enough to build any solid credit history. So once again, be smart, and be selective. Treat credit as you would any other expenditure. ***Credit is for buying things you can pay for immediately, not for borrowing for things you really want but can't afford in the budget.***

Bankruptcy Is a Way Out—but It's a Long Hard Road

This section on credit ends with another note of caution. All the positive benefits of building good credit history can also work in reverse. Using credit poorly can destroy your credit history, making it impossible to buy a house or take out a car loan. In the worst-case scenario, you may even have difficulty getting a rental car contract. If you find yourself in a situation of insurmountable credit card debt, you can work with a credit consolidation agency. But it will have a long-lasting, highly negative impact on your credit score. A consolidation firm essentially pays off all your credit card debt and then rolls it into one lower-interest payment that you make to one lender. For some people, this can be a lifeline. Because debt is consolidated at a lower interest rate, the payment will be lower than all the other payments combined. Furthermore, these agencies can structure the terms of the agreement to make the payments manageable for specific borrowers' situations. If you are in a particularly bad situation and you need help, this can be the best of several very bad options. Be prepared, though, that you will pay exorbitant interest if you need to take out an auto loan and will have to slowly rebuild your credit before obtaining a mortgage.

Under dire circumstances, bankruptcy is an option. Bankruptcy can discharge debt completely, depending on the terms of the arrangement. This legal avenue is most common when excessive debt comes from multiple sources, such as a mortgage that one can no longer afford to pay, crippling medical expenses, or even excessive student loans.[10] Bankruptcy can have the effect of freezing credit altogether; that is, for seven to ten years (depending on the type of bankruptcy), you will be unable to borrow for any purpose at

10. Kat Tretina, "Is It Worth Using Bankruptcy to Free Yourself from Student Loans?" Credit Karma, November 18, 2020, https://www.creditkarma.com/advice/i/student-loans-in-bankruptcy.

all. This, obviously, is an option to be avoided under most circumstances. Bankruptcy can result in foreclosure on a mortgage, in which the bank takes ownership of your home. It can result in cars and other kinds of possessions being taken and sold to pay off debts, in a process known as repossession. And be aware that while most kinds of debt will be discharged, student loan debt is very difficult to discharge, even under bankruptcy.

So far, this discussion of debt has focused on revolving credit. The next section considers installment credit, in which you take out a loan and make fixed payments to pay it off. Installment debt is structured a little differently than credit. To explain, we focus on the biggest purchase most people make in life: a ***house***.

Is Home Ownership Worth the Cost?

When I was in my twenties, nothing symbolized the American dream more than home ownership. There was a time when no middle-class life was complete without a Ford in the driveway and a little house with a white picket fence. Owning a home was not only a safe and comfortable way to raise a family, but also the best and most-used pathway to building wealth. Although most people borrow money to buy a house, a house is an asset—when you own the home, you own the value of the home. And home values have a tendency to increase over time, much like stocks.

While it is still true that home ownership is an important marker of middle-class success, it no longer has the pristine reputation it once did, due to the 2008 housing crisis that served as a catalyst to the Great Recession. By some estimates, around ten million families lost their homes during that financial crisis.[11] There is a lot of blame to go around, but the basic story is that a lot of people bought homes they couldn't afford, because mortgage lenders found increasingly creative and attractive ways to market loans that made houses seem more affordable than they actually were. You see, the initial lender in a mortgage tended to sell the loan to someone else, and one implication of this was that less care was taken to assure creditworthiness. This set off a wave of foreclosures, which caused the investors in something called a mortgage-backed security to lose a lot of money unexpectedly, which caused layoffs in the financial sector, which caused people to pull back on spending, which caused more layoffs in other industries, which caused more homes to be lost, and so on. Like dominoes arranged in a death spiral, down they all went.

The changes to the housing loan market as a response to the financial crisis, and the rise in housing prices due to a shortage of supply, have made it very costly to enter the housing market. Young adults may actually return home after college to live in their parents' basement. A quick look at housing prices makes this understandable. Even after adjusting for inflation, the average home price was $264,676 in 1990. This value rose to $318,922 in 2010 and to $375,850 in 2020.[12] Although it represents a compound annual growth rate of only 1.77 percent, that rise is a nice accumulation of wealth for parents over time but a big hurdle of debt for their kids who are ready to purchase a first house.

11. Colleen Shalby, "The Financial Crisis Hit 10 Years Ago. For Some, It Feels Like Yesterday." *Los Angeles Times*, September 18, 2018, https://www.latimes.com/business/la-fi-financial-crisis-experiences-20180915-htmlstory.html.
12. Joni Sweet, "Timeline: History of the Housing Market over the Last 50 Years," The Simple Dollar, October 6, 2020, https://www.thesimpledollar.com/mortgage/history-of-the-housing-market-over-the-last-50-years/.

In the current landscape, it is financially prudent to carefully consider the decision to buy a house. The upfront costs are higher, the debt load is bigger, and the chances of relocation are greater than what your parents and grandparents faced. It is no longer clear that the American dream is a spouse, two kids, and a house with a white picket fence.

There's No Place like Home ... but Don't Mortgage Your Future

Prior to the financial specifics, this topic requires a little bit of a backstory. Until the 1950s, fewer than half of Americans owned homes. In fact, many of these people would have inherited their homes, or bought them outright—the idea of borrowing to buy a home was not yet standardized or widespread. Many homeowners were farmers who owned property. In the city, most people rented apartments. That began to change in the post–WWII era as people moved out of cities and into brand-new suburbs, which were connected by brand-new highways and interstates made possible by widespread automobile ownership. There is an interesting political anecdote to this: home ownership was framed as a patriotic and capitalist response to the public housing projects of Cold War–era Russia.[13] By the 1960s, a wide variety of legislation and federal policies were in place that standardized the typical mortgage arrangement: a 20 percent down payment, fixed monthly payments spread out over a predetermined period of time (originally ten or fifteen years), and interest amortization, in which all the interest on the life of the loan is calculated and paid up front. The result was that in 1940, just about 44 percent of Americans owned homes; by 1980, nearly 64 percent did.[14]

As rates of ownership began to level off and remain constant, mortgage lenders dreamt up new ways to entice the public into home ownership. First, the fifteen-year mortgage became a thirty-year mortgage, which had the effect of drastically reducing monthly payments (though not by exactly half, as the astute student of financial literacy will note, given the additional interest paid on the loan!). Then the standard down payment began to shrink—in some cases, to as little as 3 percent of the purchase price of the home. Finally, the death blow: the introduction of the adjustable-rate mortgage.

When you take out a mortgage, you will pay a predetermined amount of interest over the lifetime of the loan. These rates are set by market forces and fluctuate over time. As you can see in figure 5.3, interest rates were in the mid-teens as a percentage in the early 1980s, but below 4 percent in 2020. Obviously, you will pay a lot more on your mortgage with a higher rate, so buying is much more attractive when rates are low and a low rate can be locked in for a long period of time, such as thirty years.

The idea behind an adjustable-rate mortgage (ARM) is that the rate is allowed to fluctuate, to some degree, with the market. Typically, an ARM loan will come with a highly attractive introductory rate that is below market averages for a prespecified period of time, such as five years. But after that period expires, the rate is allowed to rise to wherever the market rate is. This will be further unpacked a bit later on, but just imagine the potential consequences.

13. Marisa Chappell, "The False Promise of Homeownership," *The Washington Post*, July 20, 2017, https://www.washingtonpost.com/news/made-by-history/wp/2017/07/20/the-false-promise-of-homeownership.
14. Bureau of the Census, "Tracking the American Dream—Fifty Years of Housing Changes," *Statistical Brief*, April 1994, https://www.census.gov/prod/1/statbrief/sb94_8.pdf.

When you take out a mortgage, your payment will consist mostly of interest on the loan, as well as some principal amount that pays down the amount borrowed. The amount of your payment is obviously affected by the purchase price of the home, considering that you will have more or less principal to pay down depending on how much you borrow. But it will also be quite significantly affected by the interest rate, as you learned in the previous credit section .

Remember that in the earlier example, someone who purchased a $250,000 house at a 3.8 percent interest rate would pay $167 less per month than someone who purchased the same house at a 5.2 percent rate, when the only difference was the interest rate on the loan.[15] But let's say that the person who got the 3.8 percent rate could actually afford to pay $170 more per month. Could they get a more valuable house?

It turns out that a $300,000 house would cost about $1,382 per month at a 3.8 percent interest rate—about the same amount as a $250,000 house at 5.2 percent. So, a lower interest rate will give you a lower payment, or—everything else held constant—it will make it possible for you to buy *more* house.

Now suppose that the person with poor credit is offered the 3.8 percent rate as an introductory rate on an ARM loan for five years. All of a sudden, this person can afford a $300,000 house that they would not have been able to afford with a traditional loan. But remember, after the introductory period expires, the loan payment adjusts to market rates. What if market rates increase significantly over that time period? What if, say, rates rise to 7 percent in year six? A quick calculation will show that the monthly payment on a $300,000 house at 7 percent will be $1,860, or nearly $500 higher than the monthly payment during the introductory period.

This is why people lost their homes between 2008 and 2011. Rates climbed steadily during the early to mid-2000s, so that those who had taken out ARM loans and bought at the top of their budget saw increases of hundreds of dollars per month on their mortgages virtually overnight. And they couldn't afford the payments.

Notice something here: people with ARM loans who lost their homes would have been fine if they had taken out a traditional thirty-year fixed mortgage. They may have paid a higher interest rate from the beginning—5.2 percent—but this rate would have been locked in. The catch is that they would have had to stick to the $250,000 house, rather than the $300,000 house, to stay within budget.

The lesson from this example is to stress how important it is to make sound financial decisions when buying a home. Further, do not assume you can afford the loan just because the banker is willing to give you the money. Your local banker will sell your loan to a bigger mortgage company. Adjustable-rate mortgages are great if rates are falling, but no one knows where rates will be in five years. You add risk to your purchase if you are living on the edge of your budget when you are just starting out. Further, many young people do not include the costs of maintenance and property taxes as they are planning the purchase. A home is a big investment that requires resources in time and money to maintain. It could be the most important, and the most expensive, purchase that you ever make. To bring the significance of this into focus, let's review the basic financials of the home purchase transaction.

15. I used the mortgage rate calculator at https://www.bankrate.com/calculators/mortgages/mortgage-calculator.aspx to get the figures. Assume a 20 percent down payment, a thirty-year mortgage, and average estimates for homeowner's insurance and property taxes included as part of the monthly payment.

Buying a Home Is Complicated and Costly

There are three primary things that will affect the amount that you will spend each month toward your mortgage. There are also a few additional expenses that you might pay either as part of your monthly mortgage payment out of an escrow account (explained below) or separately. Finally, you will pay some up-front costs in the process of buying a house, known as closing costs, as well as some pretty significant costs when you sell. Buying or selling a home is a major decision with financial ramifications that go well beyond the sale price of the house.

This section breaks down the expenses you will face living in the home, beginning with the components of the payment you will make each month toward the mortgage itself. A fourth factor, the length of the mortgage term, will also have a significant effect on the monthly payment. That will be addressed shortly. For now, this discussion assumes a standard thirty-year mortgage.

The Down Payment

Nearly all home loans require a down payment, but certain national programs can help the potential homeowner bypass this requirement. As explained earlier, 20 percent is considered the standard expectation for a down payment. However, it is possible to pay 10 percent, or even 5 percent in some cases, though you may pay a higher interest rate, and you may need better credit. Some government-backed loans make it possible to pay even less. The Federal Housing Administration (FHA) allows you to get a mortgage, known as an FHA loan, with a down payment as low as 3.5 percent.[16] The United States Department of Agriculture (USDA) even makes a zero-down payment loan possible as part of its Rural Development Guaranteed Housing Loan program.[17] Be aware that if you are taking out an FHA, USDA, or other government-backed loan, it is quite likely that you will pay higher *closing costs* when the transaction takes place—significantly so, in some cases.

Keep in mind that the down payment affects the size of the mortgage payment simply because it reduces the amount of money that you borrow. Buying a $200,000 house with a 20 percent down payment would finance $160,000, which corresponds to a monthly principal and interest payment of around $960 at a 4 percent rate. If you only paid 3 percent down, however, you would finance $194,000, which would correspond to a monthly payment of $1,124—a difference of $164 every month!

The Mortgage Interest Rate

As demonstrated earlier, the mortgage rate plays a significant role in the size of your monthly payment. Rates fluctuate according to market forces and depend on government monetary policies. The Federal Reserve is tasked with making monetary policy and has a dual mandate to promote maximum employment and maintain price stability in the wider economy. This is a tough job, because when everyone is employed and the economy is strong, prices may start to rise so much such that families can't afford to buy gas or food.

16. You can view all the details of an FHA loan on their website: https://www.fha.com/fha-down-payment.
17. See the details for the "Single Family Housing Guaranteed Loan Program" at USDA Rural Development website: https://www.rd.usda.gov/programs-services/single-family-housing-guaranteed-loan-program.

Under this circumstance, the Federal Reserve raises the target range for the *federal funds rate*, which is the interest rate that banks charge each other for using excess reserve balances overnight. The Federal Reserve's goal is to slow down the economy enough such that prices stabilize again.

The target range of the federal funds rate becomes the basis on which the interest rates the rest of us pay are calculated, and mortgage rates react very quickly when the Federal Reserve alters this target range. Beyond the foundation of the macroeconomy, many factors affect the rate individuals and firms pay, but in general, rates tend to move higher when the Federal Reserve raises its target due to inflationary pressures in the economy.

When the economy is weaker or in a recession, businesses are less likely to invest in their products and may reduce employment levels. To counteract unemployment, the Federal Reserve will lower the target range for the federal funds rate to encourage business investment and the need for workers. When borrowing is more attractive, the economy can be jumpstarted to become stronger again. Higher levels of employment will encourage consumers to spend money, and the economy recovers.

Figure 5.3 below shows the pattern for interest rates over time.

FIGURE 5.3 Thirty-Year Fixed Mortgage Rates over Time

You can see that rates were much higher in the early 1980s after a tremendous bout with inflation in the 1970s, but have fallen until a new period of inflation lately in 2022. The broad pattern reflects the ebb and flow of the wider economy, but you can see that rates move around a bit beyond this general tendency. The point to see is that rates are not static, they change all the time.

The Purchase Price of the Home

Perhaps no other factor will have greater influence on the size of your mortgage payment than the purchase price, naturally. But by now you have seen that mortgage payments are also significantly influenced by the size of the down payment and the interest rate. To drive home the relationships among these three factors, let's look at homes at three different common "starter home" price points in table 5.2, depending on where you live. For simplicity's sake, these payments are all calculated for a thirty-year mortgage term, the most typical arrangement.

TABLE 5.2 Payments, Interest Rates, and Down Payments

Interest Rate	3 Percent		4.5 Percent		6 Percent	
Purchase Price/Down Payment	5 Percent	20 Percent	5 Percent	20 Percent	5 Percent	20 Percent
$150,000	$ 600	$ 505	$ 722	$ 608	$ 854	$ 719
$275,000	$1,348	$1,174	$1,570	$1,361	$1,813	$1,556
$400,000	$1,931	$1,678	$2,254	$1,950	$2,607	$2,247

A few things might stand out to you. First of all, the range of possible payments is quite large, even for a house that costs the same amount. For instance, depending on the interest rate and the size of the down payment, a house at $275,000 could cost you anywhere between $1,174 and $1,813 per month or more, if interests rates went higher than 6 percent. This is about a $550 difference!

Second, you might notice that the interest rate has nearly as big of an impact on the monthly payment as the down payment does. For the $150,000 house, for instance, a larger down payment makes a difference of about $100 at a 3 percent interest rate, but a difference of about $135 at a 6 percent interest rate. More strikingly, the difference in payment with 20 percent down at a 3 percent rate vs. a 6 percent rate is over $200 per month. And for the $400,000 house, the difference is nearly $600 per month.

Because of these differences, the size of your down payment and the interest rate can have a big impact on how much house you can afford to buy. For instance, someone with a monthly budget of $1,200 who has poor credit and has only saved $7,500 will only be able to afford a $150,000 house ($1,019 per month, with a 5 percent down payment). That same individual with strong credit and larger savings could afford a $275,000 house, if they were able to obtain a 3 percent interest rate and make a down payment of $55,000.

Similarly, and perhaps even more strikingly, the highest monthly payment on a $275,000 house is almost $150 more than the lowest possible payment on a $400,000 house (at least, in the hypothetical examples used here).

And, in fact, these examples significantly understate the difference in monthly payments between 5 percent down and 20 percent down. The reason is that most loans require that you carry mortgage insurance if the amount you have invested in your home is less than 20 percent of the original purchase price. Mortgage insurance rates can range significantly depending on the type of loan you have, but a typical rate on a conventional loan might be around 1 percent of the mortgage. If you were to add mortgage insurance to the payment on a $150,000 house, you would pay about $120 more per month—that is, 1 percent of $142,500, or the sale price minus a 5 percent down payment of $7,500, divided over twelve months. Typically, insurance payments are made out of an escrow account, as part of the monthly mortgage payment. The text box below will help you dig a bit deeper into the idea of an escrow account.

WHAT IS AN ESCROW ACCOUNT?

If you pay your insurance policies and taxes out of an *escrow account*, three additional costs will likely factor into your monthly payment. In this case, the lender collects your annual insurance premiums and taxes from you monthly, by averaging the annual expenses on a monthly basis, and adds this amount into the monthly payment you make toward principal and interest on the loan.

- **Private mortgage insurance (PMI).** PMI protects your *lender* from the possibility that you will walk away from your loan. Yes, you are paying for insurance to protect the mortgager against the chance that you will renege on your obligation. You are likely to pay somewhere around 1 percent of the home value in PMI each year until you "own" 20 percent of the house.
- **Home insurance policy.** You will also have a home insurance policy when you take out a mortgage. Home insurance protects you, your house, and your stuff. The average home insurance policy is around $1,300 per year at the start of 2021.[18] To learn more about the extent of this insurance, review chapter 4, "The Decision to Spend," where the parameters of homeowner's insurance are discussed more fully.
- **Property taxes**. In every state, local governments collect property taxes on homes, but as with insurance policies, the rates can vary quite drastically. On average, as of 2019, the lowest property tax rates were in Hawaii, at .28 percent, and the highest were in New Jersey, at 2.49 percent.[19] On a $250,000 house, then, the annual liability could range anywhere from $700 per year to $6,225 per year! Like insurance policies, property taxes are also deductible, as they count toward your overall tax liability.

The insurance and property tax bills are then sent to the lender, who pays them on your behalf out of the escrow account. The budgeting happens for you. With an escrow account, your payment will more accurately reflect the costs of home ownership, and you won't be surprised by these large expenses (home insurance, property taxes, and in some cases PMI) every six months or so.

All the pieces in the payment make it complicated, so consider the following breakdown of the monthly expenses on a $250,000 house. Assume you only make a 10 percent down payment, which means you have $25,000 in equity and will assume a mortgage of $225,000. You will pay PMI in your escrow. For simplicity's

18. Cate Deventer, "Average Cost of Homeowners Insurance for 2021," Bankrate, June 11, 2021, https://www.bankrate.com/insurance/homeowners-insurance/homeowners-insurance-cost/.
19. John S. Kiernan, "Property Taxes by State," WalletHub, February 23, 2021, https://wallethub.com/edu/states-with-the-highest-and-lowest-property-taxes/11585.

sake, assume a PMI rate of 1 percent, and property tax and insurance rates at the 2019 national average. Assume a 4.5 percent annual percentage rate for the mortgage, the middle case in the previous example. The resulting payments are shown in table 5.3.

TABLE 5.3 Monthly Mortgage Payment Breakdown

Principal and Interest	$1,140.00
Principal ($296)	
Interest ($894)	
Private Mortgage Insurance (PMI)	$ 187.50
Home Insurance	$ 117.00
Property Taxes	$ 206.00
Total Monthly Payment	**$1,650.00**

The huge difference between the house payment and the bill you pay to escrow should make it very clear that you can't decide to buy the house simply based on the purchase price of the home alone. You will need to budget monthly for $500 more than what you are paying toward the mortgage itself! Of course, you will save $187.50 per month on PMI if you are able to make a full 20 percent down payment; you will also pay a little less in principal and interest if you are only mortgaging $200,000 instead of $225,000. In that case, your principal and interest payment will be $1,013, so your total monthly bill will be only $1,336—over $300 less.

Notice that the payment was broken down by the amount paid toward interest and the amount paid toward principal. You may have further noticed that a whole lot more is going toward interest—three times as much, in fact—than is going toward principal! Finally, notice that the payment was specified as the first one. This is because the proportion of the payment that goes toward principal will gradually (very gradually) increase each month. This is called ***loan amortization***. You are encouraged to use mortgage calculators and explore amortization tables yourself. These will help you figure out exactly how much ***equity*** you have in the house at any specific point of time in the future, or how much of the house you actually "own." This will be very useful if you think you might sell the house at a predetermined date in the future. It will also be helpful for determining when you will reach 20 percent equity and can stop paying PMI, if you are unable to make a full 20 percent down payment at closing.

As you can clearly see, interest is front-loaded on a mortgage. In fact, in a typical amortization schedule, it will take over fourteen years—nearly half the term of a thirty-year loan—before your principal and interest payments are roughly equal (about $570 toward each, in the previous example). There are many reasons to think very carefully about the decision to buy a house, and this is one of the most important. When you sell, you will never get the interest back—only the principal, assuming you can sell the house for at least the price you paid for it.

Before you consider more practical matters—such as how to make the decision to buy, or to sell for that matter, and what kinds of additional expenses you will pay in each case—there is a fourth factor to address that will significantly affect your monthly payment: the length of the mortgage term. Every example discussed so far has been for a thirty-year mortgage, the most common type. But it is possible to get a twenty-year, fifteen-year, or even a ten-year mortgage.

How would a shorter mortgage term affect your payment? Imagine you took out a fifteen-year mortgage loan. In the previous example, the combined principal and interest payment on a $250,000 house with a 10 percent down payment was $1,140. If you were to take out a fifteen-year mortgage instead and pay back the loan twice as fast (essentially), this should double your payment, right? So, you would pay $2,280 per month?

Wrong. Being the astute and learned student of financial literacy that you are, you will immediately recognize that, because of the way interest is amortized on a mortgage—in which all the interest paid over the life of the loan is front-loaded—you will pay a great deal less in interest if you pay back the loan more quickly. After all, you are now paying only fifteen years of interest instead of thirty. The difference is stark. On a fifteen-year mortgage, the payment will be $1,720—only about 1.5 times what you would pay on a thirty-year mortgage, not double. In total, you will pay around $85,000 in interest over fifteen years, about $100,000 less than you would pay in interest over thirty years.

In short, it can be an incredibly beneficial financial decision to take on a shorter mortgage term, if you can afford to do so.

Accounting for the Full Cost of Ownership: The Rent vs. Buy Decision

As this chapter has shown, the decision to buy a home is a complicated one. You have already learned that your mortgage payment will be affected by a number of factors beyond the price of the house itself—the interest rate, the size of the down payment, the length of the mortgage term, whether or not you are paying mortgage interest, the property tax rate in the city or county in which you live, the type of home insurance policy you carry (for instance, whether you will be required to have supplemental flood or earthquake insurance)—and all of these things can add up to hundreds of dollars of difference in your monthly mortgage payment. In addition, there are a number of costs you will pay simply to buy the house in the first place! Finally, once you are a homeowner, you won't be able to call the landlord when the pipes burst or you need a window replaced; as a homeowner, you will need a much larger soft emergency fund for home repairs than you will need as a renter.

All of this might make you wonder whether home ownership is worth it. While this would have been largely beyond question at one point in recent history, it is an important consideration today. There are no universal rules that will help you make this decision, but the main considerations are:

- *Time in the home.* This is perhaps the most important consideration of all. Are you planning to stay put for a while? This makes buying more attractive, since some of your monthly payment will be going toward principal. The longer you are in the house, the more will go toward principal, based on your amortization schedule. This will help you build equity in the home and make it a lot more likely that you will get that equity back when you sell.

- *Closing costs.* Closing costs are up-front costs that are paid when the buying transaction takes place. They include the various fees that are paid to the bank and to the lawyers involved in drawing up the transaction. Average 2020 closing costs were between $3,000–$4,000, but these costs will vary depending on the price of the house and where you live.[20]
- *Selling costs.* The primary cost of *selling* is in real estate commissions and can be quite substantial if you use a real estate agent (as most sellers do). A typical realtor commission is 3 percent of the selling price of the house. Furthermore, it is typical for the seller to pay the commissions of the selling agent *as well as the buyer's real estate agent*—the person who helps the buyer find your home and make the decision to buy it. Consider the previous example, in which you purchased a $250,000 house with a 10 percent payment. If you can sell the home for $270,000—$20,000 more than you paid for it, about an 8 percent increase in value—you will probably just about break even. Real estate commissions will amount to around $16,200; adding in closing costs will bring you close to losing all your $20,000 "profit."
- *Tax consequences of home ownership.* Here is one very good piece of news for homeowners: mortgage interest and local property taxes are tax-deductible at the federal level. That is, they reduce your taxable amount of income dollar-for-dollar. Consider the same example used earlier, in which you purchase a $250,000 house with a 10 percent down payment. A quick calculation using the amortization table shows that you will pay around $9,220 in mortgage interest during the first year. If your taxable income is $100,000 and you are married, filing jointly, your mortgage interest payment will reduce your taxable income to $90,780. At this income, your marginal income tax bracket is 22 percent, so you will essentially "get back" 22 percent of $9,220, about $2,000. Add to this the deductions for your home insurance, property taxes, and mortgage insurance, and the total tax savings could be closer to $3,000.
- *The local real-estate market.* An obvious fact is that housing costs vary drastically from city to city. In 2021, median house prices in the 100 largest metro areas ranged from the $130,000s in cities like Cleveland and Toledo, to around $500,000 in Seattle and New York, all the way to around $1 million in the San Francisco Bay Area.[21] Buying is more accessible to some people than to others. Now, it is true that you will also pay higher rent in cities with higher housing prices. But the two factors are not perfectly correlated. In some cities average rent prices are lower than the average monthly mortgage payment, which might make renting more attractive in the short term; in other cities, it is the opposite.
- *The growth rate in the real estate market.* In cities such as Nashville, Tennessee, and Boise, Idaho, home prices have been on a strong upward trend for the last several years. On the one hand, this makes it a little more likely that prices will rise in the short term, which could make buying more attractive. On the other hand, places where growth is happening too fast can make buying quite risky, as happened when prices collapsed in Florida during the Great Recession.

20. Amy Fontinelle, "Average Closing Costs in 2020: What Will You Pay?" The Ascent, September 28, 2020, https://www.fool.com/the-ascent/research/average-closing-costs/.https://www.fool.com/the-ascent/research/average-closing-costs/.
21. Kiplinger's Personal Finance. "Home Prices in the 100 Largest Metro Areas." *Kiplinger*, January 23, 2021. https://www.kiplinger.com/article/real-estate/t010-c000-s002-home-price-changes-in-the-100-largest-metro-areas.html.

In sum, many factors influence the decision to buy a house. You must consider not only the monthly cost of a mortgage versus a rent payment, but also the additional costs you will pay to own a home as well as the benefits of ownership, including tax deductions and growth in the value of your home. Given the complexity of considering all of these factors, you can find "rent versus buy" calculators on the internet that allow you to make quick comparisons for various cities by taking into account average rent costs, property taxes, and home prices.

But in the final analysis, the decision should be made in accordance with the philosophy of this book. A home is an investment—and not just a financial one. An investment in the security of your family, the stability of your financial future, and your own well-being. This requires that you think long term, rather than being solely focused on short-term gain and rapidly rising home prices. Ideally, you will want to buy when you can afford to make a 20 percent down payment, giving you a big equity stake in the home right away and avoiding wasteful mortgage insurance payments. And you will want to buy when you have some certainty that you will stay in the house at least five years, to realize any appreciation in the value of the home and to cover your buying and selling costs. Hopefully, you will be buying a house that you can call home for a long time, to share with a partner, a spouse, family, perhaps children—a place to create memories that last a lifetime.

What About Car Loans and Other Debts?

This chapter has spent a great deal of time discussing mortgages. But if you understand how mortgages work, you can understand how any loan works. This may include things like car loans and student loans.

Car Loans

Car loans are paid off in a similar way to mortgages, with more of the interest and less of the principal paid up front. Typical car loan terms can range anywhere from three years to seven years and are often expressed in months—sixty months is quite common. Car loan rates are probably a little higher than mortgage loan rates but can vary widely according to credit scores. You can take out a car loan for a used car or for a new car; rates for used cars tend to be a little higher. Financing for car loans is typically provided by a dealer, who will work through a bank with which they have a pre-existing arrangement. That said, you can often find better rates by securing your own auto financing, especially through a credit union.

The decision to finance a car should be made with consideration of a couple of important factors. First, unlike houses, cars almost always depreciate. Buying a car might be a smart financial decision for lots of different reasons, but it may or may not make sense to think of it as an investment, the same way you would for an asset that will likely increase in value. Unless you are buying a restored vintage automobile that is rare or otherwise in high demand, chances are your car will only lose value. In fact, it is often said that a new car loses about 10 percent of its value the moment you drive it off the lot! Count on around 20 percent depreciation each year you own the automobile.

For this reason, you should consider buying a used car, provided you can buy one from a reputable dealer. Many new automobile dealerships also sell "certified" preowned vehicles, which means the manufacturer's reputation stands behind the quality of the vehicle. Companies like CarMax have their own methods of certifying vehicles and can provide a complete repair, damage, and collision report for any vehicle they sell. Gone are the days of being swindled by smooth-taking hucksters selling "lemons" for unrealistically low prices!

Some cars lose more value than others, however, so the benefits of buying used compared to new will depend to a large extent on the specific vehicle you are buying. Manufacturers like Toyota don't offer many discounts up front, and they have such a stellar reputation for high quality and durability that they will not depreciate as quickly. Luxury vehicles, on the other hand, may depreciate rather quickly, since a good bit of the price premium you pay is for the brand name, not for the quality or durability of the automobile. For this reason, you may not save much buying a Toyota used, whereas you will likely save a great deal buying a Mercedes used. It can be fun and enlightening to browse sites that sell used cars, such as CarMax and CARFAX, and compare brands like Toyota and Honda to brands like BMW and Infiniti.

If you do choose to buy a new car, see if you can wait for special-rate financing deals. Sometimes manufacturers will offer very low interest rates—occasionally even 0 percent. This may happen toward the end of the model year when inventory levels are being cleared for new models.

Because cars are typically not considered *investments*, you should think of buying a car as a ***spending*** decision. The Federal Trade Commission provides an excellent summary of the various costs and considerations that go into buying a car, which you should review before diving into the purchase.[22] If you want that decision to be financially wise, look for a car you can be happy with for a long time, say ten to fifteen years. *Consumer Reports* says that sticking with a car purchase this long could save you $30,000 or more.[23] This means not buying something to please others and being willing to stick with the car once you are a little bored with it.

Student Loans

Given that you are likely a college student, or perhaps a high school student getting ready for college, we could not close this chapter without discussing student loans. This topic is much bigger than we could give a full treatment here, but the good news is that unlike when it comes to things like credit cards and mortgages, you have dedicated professionals on your campus who can help you make good decisions about financial aid and student loans.

Like many of the topics in this chapter, student loans are complicated. The federal student loan program began with the Higher Education Act in 1965, which made guaranteed federal loans available to college students who demonstrated some degree of financial need. This essentially meant that the loans were backed by the government, eliminating the risk of default to banks that loaned the money. For many types of loans, interest rates were subsidized, meaning the government also took on the interest costs, reducing the cost of borrowing for the student to 0 percent.

22. Federal Trade Commission, "Consumer Information: Financing or Leasing a Car," August 2017, https://www.consumer.ftc.gov/articles/0056-financing-or-leasing-car.
23. Consumer Reports, "Make Your Car Last 200,000 Miles: How to Go the Distance and Save Tens of Thousands of Dollars," November 6, 2018, https://www.consumerreports.org/car-repair-maintenance/make-your-car-last-200-000-miles/.

Over the years, many changes drastically expanded various loan programs, making them available to all students regardless of financial need, and to students' parents (PLUS loans), increasing ability to graduate students, and raising the limits on borrowing. At the same time, throughout the 1990s and 2000s the costs of college crept upward, due to factors such as reduced state support at public institutions and increased demand for student services. While the federal student loan program has unquestionably increased college access for millions of students over the decades and changed countless lives in the process, it has not been without its difficulties. According to the Lumina Foundation,[24] there are forty-three million outstanding loans, and one in six Americans have student debt. The total bill for all outstanding debt tops $1.6 trillion, and average loan debt for college graduates has doubled from around $14,000 (in today's dollars) in 1990 to around $30,000 today.

All of this said, the cost of attending college may well be worth it. Though earnings vary significantly by major, college graduates earn, on average, $1.2 million more over the course of their careers relative to nongraduates.[25] It may be unfortunate that we finance higher education through debt in the United States (in many countries, higher education is free, much like secondary school), but for young people in the United States, taking on debt may simply be the only way to attend. Like everything in this book, you should think of higher education as an investment in your future, and you should think carefully about the costs you are willing to incur to realize the return that you desire.

Also think broadly about the investment returns. Attending college is not only about getting a better paying job. College provides a kind of learning and a set of experiences that are hard to capture solely in terms of dollars. Attending college to obtain a higher salary may be less of a reason than it used to be—there are many well-paying careers in fields like IT, advanced manufacturing, construction, and trade professions (electrician, plumbing, etc.) that pay surprisingly well. And as we've discussed in chapter 2, "The Decision to Earn," not all college degrees are a certain path to a high-paying job (though remember that there does not necessarily need to be a close relationship between your area of study and a career). The return on investment for college comes not only in terms of salary but also in terms of the quality of life and work-life balance you seek.

That said, there is no question that college is expensive, and you should borrow only what you can afford to repay. That means thinking carefully about what you can reasonably expect to earn in the career you would like to pursue. A good rule of thumb is that you should not carry more loan debt than your annual salary, in sum, and that you seek to keep any student loan payments to 10 percent of gross monthly income.[26]

You should also explore options to minimize the cost of attending college. In many cases, students are able to work on campus through a work study program that defrays costs. For instance, I briefly worked as a resident assistant in a dormitory, and in exchange received free room and board (unfortunately, this was a notoriously rowdy athletic dorm, and I didn't last long). Finally, there are many programs you can take

24. Lumina Foundation, "Growth of Federal Student Loans," https://www.luminafoundation.org/history-of-federal-student-aid/chapter-one/

25. Anthony P. Carnevale, Ban Cheah, and Emma Wenzinger. *The College Payoff: More Education Doesn't Always Mean More Earnings* (Washington, DC: Georgetown University Center on Education and the Workforce, 2021), 2. cew.georgetown.edu/collegepayoff2021.

26. Hanneh Bareham. "How Much Can You Borrow in Student Loans?" Bankrate. Accessed July 31, 2022. https://www.bankrate.com/loans/student-loans/student-loan-limits/.

advantage of to reduce the cost of your loan balance after you graduate. Federal student loan borrowers can use programs that cap repayment, such as income-based repayment (IBR). On an IBR plan, any remaining debt after twenty-five years is automatically forgiven, and anyone working in a nonprofit, government, or educational setting can apply to have their balance completely forgiven after just ten years. Other repayment programs exist for teachers, nurses, and medical workers, particularly those working in rural communities.

Identifying cost-saving programs ahead of time better informs the decisions you make about how much debt to take on. Most important, as suggested in chapter 2, "The Decision to Earn," do careful research on the typical pay and growth rate of various professions in which you are interested, and avoid borrowing more than you know you can reasonably pay back. Student loans can be an investment in your future, but they can also become a significant liability if decisions about them are not made carefully.

Because you have resources on campus to help you figure out financing for college, we strongly encourage you to take advantage of them.

Key Takeaways

Directions: Review the following list of key takeaways to help you remember what you learned in this chapter:

- Debt is a way to borrow from your future income stream to increase your standard of living today, and when used responsibly, it can be a good financial tool. However, credit cards can serve as a crushing blow to financial well-being when they are not used responsibly.
- Credit is for buying, not for borrowing. Use credit cards in conjunction with a budgeted spending plan. A general guideline is to not put things on credit that you can't pay off when you get the statement.
- Because *bad* credit has lasting repercussions, it is important for individuals to understand their spending habits before opening lines of credit.
- A good credit score, sometimes called a FICO score, provides several important benefits in terms of interest charged on mortgages, cars, or credit cards. Your credit score is also increasingly used for things you might not think about, like apartments and job opportunities, and more.
- Buying a home when you are just starting out may not be the best choice for everyone. The decision to rent or buy will depend to a large extent on how long you plan to be in the area, whether you want to assume the responsibility of home ownership, and whether your savings are established enough for you to handle the extra expenses of home ownership.
- Once you understand the way that a mortgage loan works, understanding car loans and student loans is easy. Because of the way the value of the car depreciates with time, it is financially prudent to consider a used car and to try to drive it for ten to fifteen years.

Application Opportunity: Do This Now!

Directions: Complete the activities below to apply what you have learned in this chapter.

Activity 1

Do you think that people are more likely to buy something they do not need when they use a credit card? Explain your answer. What doors does a good credit history open? What doors does a bad credit history close?

Activity 2

What can you do to improve your credit score? What financial practices should you have in place prior to getting a credit card?

Activity 3

Create a plan to help get Miriam out of debt. As her friend, you have offered to help her develop a plan to get back to some semblance of financial equilibrium. Below is a table of the debts Miriam faces:

Credit Card	Balance	Minimum PMT	Interest Rate APR
Chased	$11,000	$220	16.99%
Capital Two	$ 7,000	$ 70	22%
City Card	$ 5,000	$150	20%

Advise Miriam on reducing her **credit card** debt. You can assume she will not add to the debt at this point. Miriam says she can get a roommate (her parents pay the rent on her apartment) **and pay $500 a month** to get the credit card debt under control. Go to the Credit Card Payoff Calculator here: https://www.calculator.net/credit-card-payoff-calculator.html

What does the calculator advise her to do? How many months will it take for her to pay off her debt at this point? What will she pay in interest? Which card does she pay off first? Why that one?

The method used on the calculator is known as the *debt avalanche method*. What is that method (slide down the calculator page for an explanation)? Can you see this method in the plan? Another method is the *debt snowball method*. How is it different? Consider the type of person who might do better with the debt snowball method. Who is this method better for?

Activity 4

Visit *US News and World Report* (https://creditcards.usnews.com/student) to see their rankings for the best student credit cards. What kinds of options are currently available? What APR is currently being charged to students with limited credit experience?

Activity 5

Mortgage investigation. Using a reputable site (Yahoo! or MSN Finance, Lending Tree, Bankrate, any big bank), identify the rates on a:

Thirty-year fixed-rate mortgage ______

Fifteen-year fixed-rate mortgage ______

5/1 ARM _____

7/1 ARM _____

Now, using a mortgage calculator, calculate your monthly *principal and interest* payment for the thirty-year fixed-rate on houses that cost $125,000, $150,000, and $200,000, with 5 percent, 10 percent, and 20 percent down payments.

Purchase Price	5 Percent Down	10 Percent Down	20 Percent Down
$125,000	$	$	$
$150,000	$	$	$
$200,000	$	$	$

For the $150,000 house with 10 percent down,

1. How much do you pay in interest your first payment?
2. How many years and months will it take until you pay more in principal than in interest?
3. Assume interest rates climbed 1 percent. How much more would your monthly payment be?
4. What would your payment be at this rate if you put 20 percent down?
5. How much less would you pay in interest overall if you took out a fifteen-year mortgage?

Activity 6

Your housing strategy:

1. How much have you allotted for housing costs in your budget per month?_______
2. What is the median home price where you hope to live? ______
3. Can you determine from this how expensive of a home you can afford to buy (at today's interest rates)?
4. What is the median rent where you hope to live?
5. So, what is your housing strategy?

Bibliography

Bareham, Hanneh. "How Much Can You Borrow in Student Loans?" Bankrate. April 19, 2022. [accessed July 31, 2022]. https://www.bankrate.com/loans/student-loans/student-loan-limits/.

Bureau of the Census, "Tracking the American Dream—Fifty Years of Housing Changes," *Statistical Brief*, April 1994, https://www.census.gov/prod/1/statbrief/sb94_8.pdf.
Carnevale, Anthony P., Ban Cheah, and Emma Wenzinger. *The College Payoff: More Education Doesn't Always Mean More Earnings*. Washington, DC: Georgetown University Center on Education and the Workforce, 2021. cew.georgetown.edu/collegepayoff2021.
Chappell, Marisa. "The False Promise of Homeownership." *The Washington Post*, July 20, 2017. https://www.washingtonpost.com/news/made-by-history/wp/2017/07/20/the-false-promise-of-homeownership.
Consumer Reports. "Make Your Car Last 200,000 Miles: How to Go the Distance and Save Tens of Thousands of Dollars." November 6, 2018. https://www.consumerreports.org/car-repair-maintenance/make-your-car-last-200-000-miles/.
DeNicola, Louis. "What Is a Good Credit Score?" Experian. February 11, 2021. https://www.experian.com/blogs/ask-experian/credit-education/score-basics/what-is-a-good-credit-score/.
Detweiler, Gerri. "Tips for Improving Your Credit: The Types of Accounts in Your Credit Report." Credit.com. October 27, 2020. https://www.credit.com/credit-reports/tips-for-improving-your-credit-types-of-accounts/.
Deventer, Cate. "Average Cost of Homeowners Insurance for 2021," Bankrate, June 11, 2021, https://www.bankrate.com/insurance/homeowners-insurance/homeowners-insurance-cost/.
Federal Reserve. "Report on the Economic Well-Being of U.S. Households in 2016–May 2017." Board of Governors of the Federal Reserve System. June 2017. https://www.federalreserve.gov/publications/2017-economic-well-being-of-us-households-in-2016-education-debt-loans.htm.
Federal Trade Commission. "Consumer Information: Financing or Leasing a Car." August 2017. https://www.consumer.ftc.gov/articles/0056-financing-or-leasing-car.
Fontinelle, Amy. "Average Closing Costs in 2020: What Will You Pay?" The Ascent. September 28, 2020. https://www.fool.com/the-ascent/research/average-closing-costs/.
Freddie Mac, 30-Year Fixed Rate Mortgage Average in the United States [MORTGAGE30US], retrieved from FRED, Federal Reserve Bank of St. Louis; https://fred.stlouisfed.org/series/MORTGAGE30US
Harzog, Beverly. "Best Credit Cards for Students." *US News and World Report*, March 26, 2021. https://creditcards.usnews.com/student.
Kiernan, John S. "Property Taxes by State." WalletHub. February 23, 2021. https://wallethub.com/edu/states-with-the-highest-and-lowest-property-taxes/11585.
Kiplinger's Personal Finance. "Home Prices in the 100 Largest Metro Areas." *Kiplinger*, January 23, 2021. https://www.kiplinger.com/article/real-estate/t010-c000-s002-home-price-changes-in-the-100-largest-metro-areas.html.
Lin, Judy T., Christopher Bumcrot, Tippy Ulicny, Gary Mottola, Gerri Walsh, Robert Ganem, Christine Kieffer, and Annamaria Lusardi. *The State of U.S. Financial Capability: The 2018 National Financial Capability Study*. FINRA Investor Education Foundation, June 2019. https://www.usfinancialcapability.org/downloads/NFCS_2018_Report_Natl_Findings.pdf.
Lumina Foundation. *Growth of Federal Student Loans*. https://www.luminafoundation.org/history-of-federal-student-aid/chapter-one/ n.d.
myFico. "What Is a FICO® Score?" Accessed April 2, 2021. https://www.myfico.com/credit-education/what-is-a-fico-score.
Shalby, Colleen. "The Financial Crisis Hit 10 Years Ago. For Some, It Feels Like Yesterday." *Los Angeles Times*, September 18, 2018. https://www.latimes.com/business/la-fi-financial-crisis-experiences-20180915-htmlstory.html.
Sweet, Joni. "Timeline: History of the Housing Market over the Last 50 Years." The Simple Dollar. October 6, 2020. https://www.thesimpledollar.com/mortgage/history-of-the-housing-market-over-the-last-50-years/.
Tretina, Kat. "Is It Worth Using Bankruptcy to Free Yourself from Student Loans?" Credit Karma. November 18, 2020. https://www.creditkarma.com/advice/i/student-loans-in-bankruptcy.
US Bureau of Labor Statistics. "Learn More, Earn More: Education Leads to Higher Wages, Lower Unemployment." Career Outlook. May 2020. https://www.bls.gov/careeroutlook/2020/data-on-display/education-pays.htm.
US News Staff. "Average Credit Card APR." *US News and World Report*, March 15, 2021. https://creditcards.usnews.com/articles/average-apr.

Figure Credits

Fig. 5.2: Source: Data from www.savvymoney.com.
Fig. 5.3: Source: https://fred.stlouisfed.org/series/MORTGAGE30US.

CHAPTER 6

The Decision to Own Shares

Invest in the Stock Market

Imagine...

OK, you are on your way! You have a job that you like: check. Emergency savings, both soft and hard, are ready and in place: check. Student loans and credit card debt are under control: check. You are happily situated in living circumstances as preferred: check. Things are going well in terms of utilizing the retirement plan from work. You are making the match from your employer, but maybe you are looking for other ways to invest and save. Perhaps this is an opportune time to learn more about the stock market. Is this a source of easy money? Your cousin's wife's brother always talks about making big bucks on the stock market. He doesn't seem any smarter than you, but he was a business major. Still, how difficult could it be?

Introduction

This chapter seeks to demystify the stock market. Wall Street is the "place" where buyers and sellers meet to trade their ownership claims in companies. It is that simple, but it seems complicated because the actual place is often not a specific location and is more likely to be a trading platform. In 1792, stockbrokers congregated under a buttonwood tree on Wall Street in New York City to trade securities.[1] It was there that they signed what came to be known as the Buttonwood Agreement to trade with each other. Today, the New York Stock Exchange (NYSE) is vast, listing 82 percent of the largest publicly traded US companies (from the S&P 500). Large means market value, measured by the firm's market capitalization of stock price times the number of shares outstanding. Today, there is no longer a tree where the trades occur, but a trading platform branches out to handle trading for over 8,000 securities.[2] The NYSE

1. NYSE Euronext, "History," 2010, https://web.archive.org/web/20100309083240/http:/www.nyse.com/about/history/1089312755484.html.
2. New York Stock Exchange, "The World's Leading Markets," NYSE, 2020, https://www.nyse.com/trade.

has grown to include four different equity (which is just a fancier name for stock) exchanges and three additional markets in bonds, exchange-traded funds, and options. This does sound complicated, granted, but the truth is that technology today is evolving and competitive. This democratization of financial services makes it reasonably easy to start small and engage in the process of investment.

Chapter Objectives

After reading this chapter, you will be able to:

- Understand what it means to own a share of stock, what the market mechanics of buying and selling in the stock market are, and how the process of submitting a trade works.
- Explore the ways that investors categorize general approaches to investing, distinguish between investing and trading, and investigate the ways that the stock of companies is classified.
- Consider classic stock-picking strategies that would be good for a beginning investor.

Who Needs the Stock Market?

Most of us will need the stock market to help us accumulate wealth for retirement. Gone are the days (the 1980s) when CDs offered 8 percent interest for merely parking your money in the bank for six months.[3] Your emergency savings account is likely offering less than 1.5 percent right now, even with inflation in 2022. Still, the idea of putting money into the stock market is, frankly, scary, and there are just too many choices; that decision is something that can easily be put off until tomorrow, right?

If you have made it to this chapter, you know that it is vital to invest earlier in your career instead of later. You will have to contribute less, and the sooner you begin, the more your money will grow. But what is new here is this idea: **you are your own best financial advisor**. Anyone can invest their money nowadays, starting small and in a personalized way that respects individual willingness and tolerance for risk. How does the stock market work?

For many young adults, the stock market is a place of mystery. Surely it would help if you had specific classes or a particular degree, to understand how it operates or what to expect to benefit from it. The financial industry feeds this belief to the public, mainly because they have every incentive to make us believe that we will lose hard-earned savings without their help. And the industry has done such an excellent job of convincing the public it has the secret recipe to financial success that they are laughing all the way to the bank. You can pay for financial expertise, and the better an advisor has performed in the past, the more they will charge you for the privilege. Still, no one knows the future, and timing the turns in the stock market is exceedingly difficult for anyone to do. Indeed, studies show that most financial advisors don't beat the

3. Board of Governors of the Federal Reserve System (US), "6-Month Certificate of Deposit: Secondary Market Rate." (DISCONTINUED) [DCD6M], FRED, Federal Reserve Bank of St. Louis. July 1, 2013. https://fred.stlouisfed.org/series/DCD6M, June 26, 2021.

market for you, after you subtract the fees they charge.[4] Other studies show that financial experts don't make better-than-average stock picks for their own portfolios, much less for those of their clients.[5] Knowing this may provide some relief. With a few common-sense guidelines, anyone who wishes to do so can manage their investments at a minimal cost and do as well as the market experts do.

What follows is a beginner's breakdown of how the stock market works. It will progressively introduce you to market vocabulary to help you think about what it means to own shares in a company, what trading in the market means for investors and companies, and what happens when an investor buys or sells a stock.

Stockholders Are Owners

When you buy shares in a company, you purchase shares of stock, and you become an owner, albeit a small one, with a stake in its future. To put this in perspective, the number of shares outstanding for Apple is $16.19 ***billion***. Owning 100 shares or even 1,000 shares is barely a blip percentage of the shares floating among the public. Still, you are a stakeholder, an equity owner, a shareholder, a residual claimant; all these terms apply to you. In the market's language, you are *long,* which means that you believe the company's share price will rise. Effectively, you have bought *low,* intending to sell *high* at some point.[6] In exchange for your purchase, you expect a return on your money that comes either directly through a dividend or indirectly through a rise in the stock's price. In return jargon, you get a dividend yield and a capital gains yield, where yield is a fancy term for return.

A CLOSER LOOK AT STOCK RETURNS

An investor makes money on a stock investment when the company pays dividends, or when the price of the stock rises higher than it was when it was purchased. As an equation, return can be captured by the following:

$$\text{Dollar Return} = \text{Dividends} + \text{PriceToday} - \text{PricePaid}$$

The rate of return is found by dividing this equation through, using the price the investor paid for each share of stock:

4. Burton G. Malkiel, *A Random Walk down Wall Street: The Best Investment Advice for the New Century* (New York: W. W. Norton & Company, Inc., 1999).
5. Andriy Bodnaruk and Andrei Simonov, "Do Financial Experts Make Better Investment Decisions?" *Journal of Financial Intermediation* 24, no. 4 (2015): 514–36.
6. If investors believe the stock price will fall soon, they can *short* the stock. This is a slightly more complicated transaction because it involves borrowing another investor's shares and selling them. Ideally, the price does drop, and the short transaction closes when the shares are repurchased and returned to the original owner. The short makes money on the difference between the sell and the buy prices. Because responsible financial literacy does not advise shorting, the transaction is a footnote in the way the stock market works. Shorting is not the best idea for beginners or for those looking to save for retirement.

Percentage Return = Dividends/PricePaid + (PriceToday − PricePaid)/PricePaid

The first term in the equation is called the ***dividend yield***, and it reflects an income return for the investor. The second term is the percentage by which the stock value rises relative to what was paid for it, and it is called the ***capital gains yield***. This return reflects the amount the investor makes by buying low and selling high.

New investors sometimes believe that the heart of the return on the stock comes from the dividend, but nowadays a good portion of the return in a strong company will come from the capital gain. If you can sell the stock for more than you paid for it, then you have a capital gain return. It does not matter that you have not realized that return yet. You may be holding onto the stock because you believe it will go even higher. You have an *unrealized return* if you have not sold the stock yet. Just because a company does not pay a dividend does not mean that the company is a bad investment. It may mean that the company is reinvesting the cash from would-be dividends back into growing the firm.

American companies pay regular dividends four times a year, or quarterly. The amount of the dividend can vary by company and by economic conditions, but a high dividend yield is probably between 4–6 percent of the original price you paid when you bought the stock. Imagine that you purchased ten shares of a company's stock for $100, and the dividend yield is 4 percent. You will receive a payout of $40 per year at that particular stock price: 4 percent of your $1,000 worth of equity (10 shares × $100). Of course, the share price could increase or decrease, which will have an impact on the capital gains part of the return.

Firms that pay dividends set them at a level they know they can pay because firms that suddenly stop paying dividends send the market a signal of financial trouble. In such circumstances, investors rush to sell the shares, causing the share price to drop very quickly. Thus, many firms work very hard not to make sudden, unexpected changes to dividends. Stability is a crucial attribute of the firm's dividend policy in most circumstances. Table 6.1 shows you ten well-known firms with high dividend yields for common equity in 2020.

TABLE 6.1 Companies with High Dividend Yields in 2020

Company	Price per Share	Div. Yield
Sunoco LP	$ 36.16	10.33%
Altria Group Inc.	$ 47.85	7.16%
Philip Morris	$ 94.91	5.02%
Chevron Corp.	$106.11	5.01%
Progressive	$103.13	4.86%
H&R Block	$ 22.68	4.67%
Stanley Black & Decker	$124.61	4.61%
IBM	$145.75	4.60%
Dow Inc.	$ 66.22	4.48%
Phillips 66	$ 83.03	4.45%

Typically, older investors who want to live on the income that dividends provide will be attracted to companies that pay regular and high dividends. Know that dividends may not be the ideal choice for younger investors because they are taxable. If a younger investor wishes to keep those resources in the market, realizing the dividend and reinvesting it after taxes is inconvenient and costly. One popular strategy is dividend reinvestment, though you will still have to pay the taxes. Most online brokerages make this a simple setting to select, and some even use it as a default. If you use this strategy, the brokerage will simply use the dividend payout to buy more of the stock, usually in partial, or fractional, shares. To return to the previous example, if you own $1,000 worth of equity and receive an annual dividend of $40, then over the course of the year, the brokerage will buy $40-worth more of the stock for you (in reality, this will amount to a .10-share purchase every three months, since dividends are typically paid quarterly). At a stock price of $100—the original price you paid—you will own an additional .4 shares of the stock. After 2.5 years, you will own an entire extra share, simply from reinvesting dividends! Now you will realize a 4 percent return on eleven shares of stock, or $1,100 of total equity, assuming a $100 share price, for an annual dividend of $44. Dividend reinvestment is a simple way to realize compound returns, as discussed in the chapter on the time value of money, "The Decision to Be Financially Literate."

Many firms do not pay dividends, but this does not mean the company is unworthy of investment. These firms want to take any of their extra cash (known as free cash flow) and reinvest it in their growth—for instance, by developing new products or building new manufacturing facilities. The company managers believe that this investment will provide a higher return than the owner would get by investing those dividends in another opportunity. An investor who disagrees can always sell the shares and invest those funds in another place that may be better. In the past, dividends served as a signal that the company was doing well. Today, in a world where information on how the company is doing is readily available, dividends may no longer serve the same purpose. As a young adult, you may not even want the dividends because they create a taxable event. Unrealized returns in the form of higher stock prices are not taxable.

Instead of paying dividends, a firm may repurchase its own shares on the stock market. By removing shares from circulation, they ensure that the value of the remaining shares goes up. The shareholders who did not sell their shares will see a rise in stock price, which is an unrealized capital gain. Those who sold their shares back to the company have a realized gain. A share repurchase will have the same total return impact on the investor as a dividend, and these have become very popular in the last thirty years or so.

As an investor, you can *realize* returns on a stock investment at any time by selling it back on the market. When you sell the shares for a higher price than you bought them for, you earn a capital gain. The investor chooses stocks based on expectations of future performance. When a company announces that it has a contract to sell its products or services to others in the future, the stock price goes up. The sooner those sales are expected, and the more certain the cash flows are, the bigger the rise in the current price will be.

Ownership does not mean that you will get the firm's product for free, or that your office is waiting for you if you ever get to visit the headquarters, or that you can catch a lift on the company jet if it happens to be going your way. Most of us will only be tiny owners in terms of our claim on the company's value.

In appreciating ownership, the potential investor can begin to understand how investing is different from day trading and/or gambling. Sometimes the language of investing may indeed use gambling terminology. For instance, when you buy a stock, some might say that you are "betting" on that company's future, and you risk losing money if your investment thesis is wrong. Investing is different because returns are not a function of luck, a card's turn in the river, or a faster horse. Better companies will tend to have higher valuations over time. Thus, knowing the companies you are investing in becomes a crucial mechanism for removing some of the uncertainty associated with not knowing what the general market will do. Good companies may see losses during a severe macroeconomic downturn, but these firms come back and regain their value once the economy improves. Any gamble is over quickly and is event dependent; investing occurs over your lifetime. Recognizing the implications of ownership gives the investor a different mindset towards the investing process. The ownership mindset is the foundation of long-term, grow-your-wealth philosophy.

The Share Price Is the Outcome of Buyer and Seller Beliefs

The stock market represents all the stock trading that occurs worldwide and is the generic term used to describe the general practice of investing in companies. Actual trading happens on stock exchanges, regional places, or trading platforms that operate much like a street market, where vendors sell their wares and buyers roam about the stalls looking for good bargains. Stock exchanges host the trading for member stocks and establish guidelines that the listed corporations must follow. Of course, the market's physical presence is becoming more a thing of the past because technological advancements in buy- and sell-order processing mean that transactions occur almost immediately during market hours. Figure 6.1 below shows the location of the world's most prominent stock exchanges (look for the black stars).

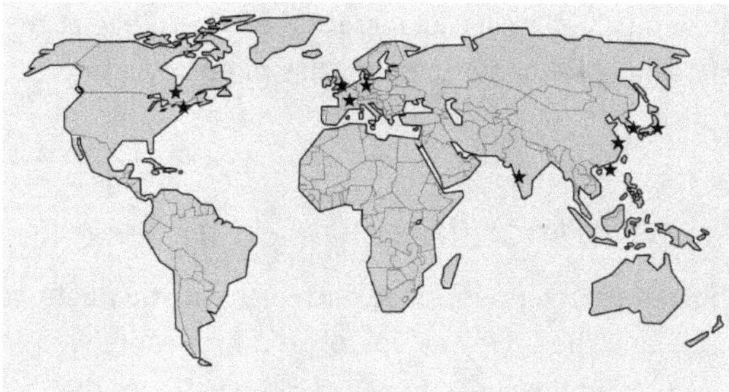

FIGURE 6.1 World's Prominent Stock Exchanges

The market mechanics we just discussed occur on an exchange—either a physical place or a trading platform—where registered companies' shares trade. We call this setup the ***secondary market*** because the company that initially issued the shares to the public is not one of the parties in the transactions. Shareowners are merely trading with each other. When a company initially decides to seek financing through the stock market, it is called the ***primary market***. There are different stock exchanges around the world, each specializing in the companies headquartered in their region. However, many international stocks register on US stock exchanges to access the large and liquid capital market.

The NYSE is a big platform for trading stocks and is notable because individual security "specialists" stand ready to deal with any buyer or seller who wants to trade at the going ***bids*** (what the investor can sell the stock for) and ***asks*** (what the investor can buy the stock at). Because someone is always willing to trade with you, the market is considered very *liquid*. Other exchanges may not have specialists or an actual trading floor. Still, they will have many *market makers* in their system, usually broker-dealer members of their exchange, who stand ready to buy and sell different stocks at the bid-ask spread. The more buyers and sellers in the market, the more liquid and competitive, the more efficiently news gets transmitted into the stock's price.

The price of a particular stock is established through shifts in supply of it and demand for it, just like with anything else in the market. As demand shifts up, price goes up; as demand shifts down, price goes down. Think about it: you want that pair of shoes, and many others in the store want them too ... would you pay a penny more if that meant you got to purchase the shoes? Or, more realistically, if you could get that big-screen TV for a great price by waking up at 4 a.m. and standing in line outside *Best Buy* the day after Thanksgiving, would you do that? Do you know someone who would? In that scenario, you would be using your time, which is another precious resource, to get the deal. But if you understand that transaction, the stock market transaction is not such a big jump. Bargain seekers offer more of their time by standing in line to get the deal. As the demand to own a particular stock increases, buyers become more willing to pay a higher price. The same logic works on the selling side, too. When there are lots of sellers, one will likely drop the price to get the transaction done. Prices frequently move to reflect the willingness to pay and the willingness to accept the deal.

On their stock order, buyers can specify a price, the maximum they are willing to pay for a certain amount of stock; sellers post the minimum price that they can accept for the same, again specifying the amount they will let go at that price. When those prices meet each other on the exchange, a deal is made.

Buyers and sellers can say how much of a particular stock they would like at the going market rate too, and those orders will execute immediately. When a company has more buyer interest, the competition to acquire the shares will push up the price.

Measure Market Performance through an Index

The nightly news tells you how the market performed each day, but you might not realize it. The newscaster can say, "The Dow was up 180, and the S&P was up 16," and for people who follow the stock market, this simple sentence tells them everything they need to know! But what does that sentence mean?

The Dow is short for the Dow Jones Industrial Average (DJIA), which tracks thirty of the largest, most well-known companies that trade on the NYSE. The companies chosen for this index are supposed to be a broad representation of the wider market. The idea is that if those companies are doing well, then the economy overall is also doing well. Or, more accurately, if investors think those companies will do well in the future, then investors believe that the economy is in good shape.

The companies in the DJIA change regularly over time as the composition of the market changes. Early in its creation, back in 1896, the DJIA included transportation and commodity stocks, which meant railroads and early manufacturing firms that processed commodities like sugar and cotton. The next text box shows you the companies included in the Dow when it was first created and those included in it in 2020.

TABLE 6.2 DJIA in 1896 and 2020[7]

DJIA 1896	DJIA 2020	
1. American Cotton Oil	1. Salesforce	16. Walmart
2. American Sugar	2. Procter & Gamble	17. Home Depot
3. American Tobacco	3. DowDuPont	18. Intel
4. Chicago Gas	4. Amgen	19. Microsoft
5. Distilling and Cattle Feeding	5. 3M	20. Honeywell
6. General Electric	6. IBM	21. Verizon
7. Laclede Gas	7. Merck	22. Chevron
8. National Lead	8. American Express	23. Cisco Systems
9. North American	9. McDonald's	24. Travelers Cos.
10. Tennessee Coal and Iron	10. Boeing	25. UnitedHealth Group
11. US Leather	11. Coca-Cola	26. Goldman Sachs

7. To find more information about the DJIA and its components, see S&P Global at: https://www.spglobal.com/spdji/en/search/?query=the+evolution+of+the+dow.

12. US Rubber	12. Caterpillar	27. Nike
	13. JPMorgan Chase	28. Visa
	14. Walt Disney	29. Apple
	15. Johnson & Johnson	30. Walgreens Boots Alliance

None of the companies in the DJIA in 2020 were included when it was first created. The last one from 1896 to leave the DJIA was General Electric. Today, the Dow includes technology, fast food, financial, and supercenter retail stocks. An investor's portfolio would perform like the DJIA by purchasing one share from each of the thirty companies comprising it. This index does not always tell us how the wider market did in a day because there are far more than thirty companies trading, but this is the oldest index, so people are used to judging how markets did on a day by translating what the DJIA did.

Another major index is known as the S&P 500. This is a shorthand reference to the Standard & Poor's 500 Index, representing, approximately, the 500 largest companies by market capitalization that trade in the United States. Market capitalization is equal to today's price of a stock times the number of shares outstanding and is the term the market uses to document the size and market value of a firm at any given time. For instance, a company with a stock price of $30 per share, which has one million shares of stock spread out among various stockholders, has a market capitalization of $30 million. This is a relatively small company compared to those that typically make up the S&P 500.

The S&P 500 is a better gauge for how the market performs in a given day because it captures more companies in its performance. When companies with a bigger market capitalization perform better, the index goes up by more. Because the S&P 500 represents the biggest publicly traded companies in the United States, it is a good approximation for market performance. The day's performance under this index is biased toward big market capitalization companies.

Knowing how these two market indexes move offers a snapshot of how the market performed over time. Consider the figure below to see the DJIA and the S&P 500 indexes for the last twenty years.

FIGURE 6.2 DJIA and S&P 500, 2000–2020

You can see that each index's pricing pattern is similar, though it is not precisely the same. It would not be uncommon for the two to move in opposite directions. Because the components are different, and the way they are weighted is different, the daily results may also be different. But the broader pattern is much the same.

Should I Trade with a Financial Advisor, a Discount Broker, or a Robo-Advisor?

Investors need a broker to process their trades for them on an exchange, and a brokerage account is used to house security vehicles, but the type of broker you choose differs widely from full service to online/discount to a mix of the two. Technology advancements and competition have democratized the financial industry, allowing anyone to participate in investing, even with small starting amounts of capital. One outcome is that there are lots of choices, and it has never been easier to join the market and become an investor. User-friendly apps make trading very easy, and a booming market cycle can make new investors feel invincible. Thus, it is vital to stress that the stock market is not a game but a place to grow wealth slowly and responsibly. Individuals will need to consider the level of service desired, their own confidence level for making financial decisions, and the level of expenses they want to pay when choosing the best type of broker for them.

The investor's choice of who to work with comes down to the level of service desired. Investors who don't know about the market and don't want to engage with their own financial choices regularly may want to hire a ***financial advisor***, who is sometimes called a ***full-service broker***. Full-service brokers can help you develop a retirement plan and choose your stock investments according to a pre-discussed investment strategy. It is generally smart to hire a *fiduciary*, which means the advisor must look out for your best interest. Still, the cost of this level of service can average 1 percent or higher of the assets under management, and many financial advisors will charge you more if you bring in fewer assets to manage. The advisor will take that 1 percent each quarter, at the start of the quarter. Obviously, advisors do better when investors do better. Advisors check in with their clients regularly, rebalance investment choices annually, and provide a level of confidence about how the assets are being managed. A Certified Financial Planner (CFP) or Chartered Financial Analyst (CFA) designation can signal that the advisor has taken the time and trouble to become professionally certified and has passed exams that qualify their training in the investment industry. Be wary: successful financial advisors tend to be very good with people and are really more like salespeople than analysts. If you want an advisor who knows a lot about the market, look for the CFP and CFA labels.

For young adults, who are just beginning their investment journey and may not have a large amount of assets to start with, a ***discount or online broker*** account may work well. Big banks and names like *Charles Schwab* or *Robinhood* offer online trading platforms and allow account holders to trade in the stock market. While it was once common to charge a commission for each trade—that is, a fee of $5–$10 or so for every transaction—most of these accounts now offer commission-free trades. However, investors may still pay commissions for fancier investment vehicles like options. Of course, discount and online trading means that account holders are making their own investment decisions to buy and sell securities. The trading platforms offer trading tools, access to research on stocks, and charting tools. There is usually a number to call if you have questions about your account, but these places will not help you make a financial plan or construct a portfolio of stocks for you. You choose your own financial direction, and only those who feel confident about their financial knowledge are likely to move in this direction.

This self-directed approach, using a discount or online broker, works well for an investor who wants to trade in the market actively and is comfortable conducting their own research for the companies they purchase. In some ways, though, a little knowledge can be dangerous when the market turns toward the downside. Every trader must understand that the stock market does not care if you make bad investment choices, and no one will console the investor who accepts unwise risks or tinkers with investment vehicles not fully understood.

Perhaps a better choice for the regular person who wishes to save for retirement and recognizes that beating the market is very difficult, even for the professionals, is a ***robo-advisor***. Over the last ten years, technology and the competition to attract investment dollars have led to the development and rise of the robo-advisor. In many ways, the robo-advisor combines the qualities of the first two types of broker services (a financial advisor or full-service broker, and a discount or online broker). Robo-advisors offer automated planning tools that can be personalized for different investors at a low cost, and the freedom to follow an automated process for determining what investment choices will work best in an individual's situation. You can start with a small amount of money, as low as $100, and develop a well-thought-out investing plan (driven by algorithms) that you can contribute to as time passes. You do not have the human connection and interaction that you would have with your financial advisor, but you also don't face the advisor's quarterly costs, which are charged whether their chosen stocks grew or fell over the quarter. Even if the costs *seem* small, they do add up, so it is worth thinking very carefully about the level of service you need in order to feel comfortable with your investment choices.

The robo-advisor works well for the young investor, starting small, who does not want to watch their finances every day. This path is for the investor who plans to contribute to their investment plan regularly and wants some guidance or wants a template that can be used for choosing investments. There is a lot of competition in the robo-advisor field, but examples of this type of broker platform in 2021 include names like *Betterment*, *M1 Finance*, and *Acorns*. Indeed, success in this new service has put some pressure on the online/discount brokers to adjust a bit. You may notice them providing services to purchase fractional shares, allowing self-starters to begin with only small amounts of committed capital. However, using a robo-advisor means being ready to operate without the human thumbprint on your choices, which can make some investors a little nervous.

What Kind of Investor Are You?

Most people don't want to stare at their financials every day. They have lives and careers that keep them busy, and their joy is not found in gamifying the stock market. The market risks are real, and while the stock market offers the prospects for growth needed for a comfortable standard of living later in life, any given period has the potential to be brutal on savings. It is essential to understand how the stock market classifies investment options and investor style so that you can follow your best pathway for growth.

What follows is a breakdown of how the finance industry classifies and defines different components of the stock market, investment style, and investor strategy. While this is not an exhaustive exploration of stock market terms by any means, its goal is to provide the beginning investor with the basic language needed for developing a long-run investment portfolio and a strategy for growing savings in the stock market. Responsible financial literacy education encourages the kind of investment that chooses blue-chip stocks, passive investment approaches, a diverse mix of value and growth companies across several different sectors, and an investor's mentality, not a trader's.

Blue-Chip or Penny Stocks: Thinking about Stocks and Risk

Market volatility, or the uncertainty associated with not knowing the future value of the stock investments you make, is a necessary evil of the activity. As a general rule, the greater the stock volatility, the more uncertain the investor will be as to its price at the end of some investment horizon. In turn, the greater the uncertainty, the riskier the investment. Investors do not like risk, but they may be willing to accept the risk if the expected promise of doing so is high enough. This is the origin of the phrase: the higher the risk, the higher the expected return must be. Risks do not always pay off, so having higher-quality, more stable stocks is financially smart.

The best-of-the-best companies within an industry that have operated for a long time get the label *blue chip*. In poker, the chips with the highest dollar value in the early 1900s were blue, and this is the blue-chip moniker's origin. Blue-chip companies tend to have large market capitalizations that average $10 billion, and they likely pay dividends very regularly. Although there is no set definition for a blue-chip company, the guiding factor is stability. Large, established firms with household names tend to be very stable investment choices with a lower but more reliable return. Think Coca-Cola, 3M, or Goldman Sachs. You can see that the firms in this category come from across the market, have very solid credit ratings and earnings, and tend to provide decent returns in both good and bad market cycles. Choosing a few blue chips for your portfolio offers some stability in the return.

At the other end of the spectrum are *penny stocks*. The Securities and Exchange Commission (SEC) defines a penny stock as any stock share that trades at $5 per share or below. Originally, penny stocks sold at a price below $1 per share, and there are still stocks today that trade in that range. Investment in these stocks is *speculative*; their value changes often and can move by a large percentage with good and bad news for the company's prospects. Traders like penny stocks because they can take a relatively large position in the company with less capital and capture big gains in a short period. Still, the typical investor should avoid penny stocks because they are generally considered low quality, and their low price reflects the fact that they are not worth very much. Many times, but not always, these companies are not listed on an exchange; instead, they trade over the counter (OTC) or through "pink sheets." The listing requirements are much lower, and financial oversight is not so complete, so investors can't always trust the financials or the promises of return for these companies.

In the movie *The Wolf of Wall Street*, Leonardo DiCaprio's character used penny stocks in a ***pump and dump scheme*** to push up these little companies' values by cold-calling people and promising big returns. He then sold his own shares of the company at their peak price, causing the stock price to collapse. Attempts to make money in penny stocks can lead to significant losses when trading rules stop working.

Value, Income, or Growth Companies: The Source of the Investment Return

A different categorization of stocks is into *value*, *income*, or *growth stocks*, where the categories are based on the origin for the stock's return. ***Value companies*** are those that, for whatever reason, are trading below their true *intrinsic value* at the moment. Warren Buffet is probably the most well-known value investor. The investor in these stocks believes that the stock is ***undervalued***—the share price is much lower than it should be, and market participants will soon recognize this and buy it in enough volume to drive its share price higher. Of course, there are many reasons why a stock might be trading below its intrinsic value; perhaps short-run business troubles have driven the price down, or the market overall is in a downturn, but the company is actually in a strong financial position. Know, however, that the value is neither the outcome of a hard-set formula nor a figure that is easy to determine. To invest this way means you are taking a position that is very different from the market attitude towards the stock. The market might label you a ***contrarian***; this is not a slur, just a note that you believe something the market does not.

Companies that pay their investors great returns through dividends earn the label ***income stock***. Companies from the utility sector, and the preferred stock from a range of companies, tend to be places where the dividend will be notable. Older investors use this type of stock to bolster the income component of their portfolios. Because they are in retirement, they live off their savings, and dividends offer a return on savings without selling any of the investment principal. During economic downturns, the dividend yield on income stocks can make a positive contribution to total returns. However, the dividend is taxed, so investors who simply wish to reinvest their dividends because they are not ready to live on their investments yet may face some penalty in realizing returns earlier than needed. Also, any cash flows to pay dividends cannot be used to help the firm grow, so firms that pay high dividends may not be growing very fast.

Growth stocks are those that are "the next big thing." These companies carry the expectation of strong performance in the future. Often, they are newer, smaller firms providing a product or service that is expected to be in high demand. The promise of future earnings has driven up the current stock price. If a company is still young, it may mean that the company is not profitable yet. The share price for growth companies may already be high, but investors buy the shares expecting the price to go even higher. Rarely do firms in the growth category pay dividends. The cash flows of the company are often reinvested into further growth. In 2020, a notable growth company was Tesla (TSLA), which grew over 600 percent in the last nine months of the year and was added to the S&P 500 in December (see figure 6.3).

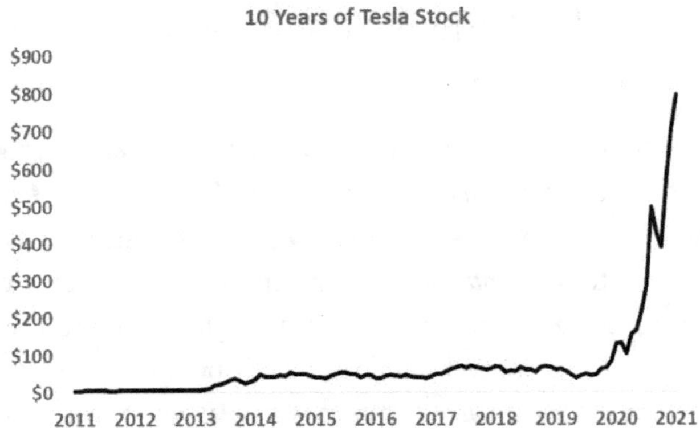

FIGURE 6.3 Tesla Stock Price 2015–2020

From 2015–2019, Tesla's average annual net income was negative, at just over –$1 billion.[8] The company's market capitalization jettisoned upward in 2020 to over $500 billion, making it more valuable than Ford, General Motors, Toyota, and six other carmakers *combined*. The fascinating aspect of this rise is that Tesla had only a 1 percent market share in the car market![9] Investors believed so strongly in the future of the firm that negatives in financial fundamentals were overlooked.

Such examples might lead beginning investors to believe that growth stocks are the investments to look for as they begin their investing journey. This would be a mistake. Academic research has generally found that value portfolios outperform growth portfolios, though the reasons why are more in dispute.[10] One good explanation is that value companies are better established, so they tend to be lower risk in the long run. More growth companies go bust or are victims of overspeculation. Thus, investors need to diversify their investments with both value and growth stocks. Young investors may avoid income stocks unless they are worried that a market downturn will erode capital gains too much.

Diversification across Industry Sectors

Another way to classify stocks is by industry sector. The Global Industry Classification Standard (GICS) provides a system for sorting companies between eleven sectors. Table 6.3 shows the eleven sectors in GICS and identifies one or two well-known companies that trade in each sector.

8. S&P Global Net Advantage.
9. Michael Wayland and Lora Kolodny, "Tesla's Market Cap Tops the 9 Largest Automakers Combined—Experts Disagree about If That Can Last," *CNBC*, December 14, 2020, https://www.cnbc.com/2020/12/14/tesla-valuation-more-than-nine-largest-carmakers-combined-why.html.
10. Louis K. C. Chan and Josef Lakonishok, "Value and Growth Investing: Review and Update," *Financial Analysts Journal* 60, no. 1 (2004): 71–86.

TABLE 6.3 GICS Sector Categories

Energy	Sunoco, Chevron
Materials	International Paper, Nucor
Industrials	Southwest, General Dynamics
Utilities	Next Era Energy
Healthcare	Intuitive Surgical, Teladoc, Pfizer
Financials	Goldman Sachs, Morgan Stanley
Consumer Discretionary	Marriott, TJX Industries
Consumer Staples	Walmart, Procter & Gamble
Information Technology	PayPal, Apple
Communication	Disney, Tencent
Real Estate	Keller Williams Realty, American Tower Corp.

Having investments across different industries means that a downturn in one sector will not decimate your entire portfolio. Chapter 3, "The Decision to Save," introduced diversification and applied it to the asset allocation decision. By segmenting your investments across different asset classes, the investor reduces the volatility of returns and adds greater certainty across time, which can leave savings in a better financial position. Even within asset classes, such as equities, diversification across industries is financially prudent. During a cyclical upturn in the market, technology's fast-paced growth might be quite appealing to investors. Still, you would not want all your retirement savings placed only in internet search engines because a market downturn might bring huge losses.

As figure 6.4 shows, it takes about fifteen stocks in a portfolio to rid it of any individual position's company-specific risks.

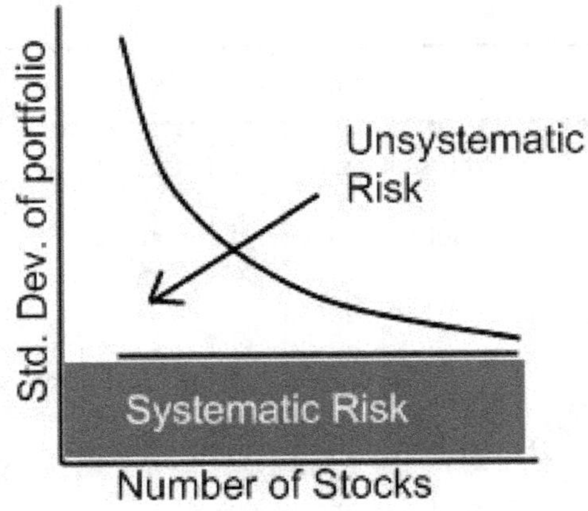

FIGURE 6.4 Diversification Visual: Risk and Number of Stocks

The total risk in the portfolio begins to fall as different stock positions are added. When a particular investment in the portfolio is doing well, something else may not be. Diversified portfolios will have lower returns in a year in which one particular industry leads market returns, but it is challenging to time the market, or to know when to jump into and out of the sector that will do well next. A lower, more stable return will leave your nest egg in a better position in the long run, over time. Investing only in banks, for instance, could have obliterated your portfolio in a financial crisis like the one the world experienced in 2008. Investing only in technology could have done the same in 2000, after the dot-com bubble burst in October of that year. No one knows the next source of disruption in the stock market, but most know that there will be one.

The other thing to notice in the diversification figure shown earlier is that no matter how many stocks the investor adds, there is still some amount of risk that will never go away. This risk is ***systematic***, and it does not diversify away. Systematic risk affects all companies to some extent. High unemployment, high interest rates, or global pandemics will affect markets worldwide, and financial crises can transmit quickly across geographical borders. Therefore, the lessons on asset allocation are worth repeating. The best safety net for growing and protecting your savings is the proper asset allocation. Stock picking is rarely a perfect substitute.

Investors will undoubtedly wish to pay attention to the principles of diversification. Some general heuristics include placing no more than 10 percent of investable assets in one position and no more than 20 percent in any single industry sector. The stock market will fall: 5–10 percent declines occur 1.5 times per year, 10–20 percent declines happen .5 times per year, and serious drops greater than 20 percent are experienced every seven years on average.[11] What this means is that price declines happen on a regular basis and that different stocks will decline on any given day, even if the company is a great investment. This should not stop you from investing, but it should encourage you to diversify your investment selections.

11. Logan Kane, "The Surprising Statistics of Stock Market Corrections," Seeking Alpha, October 17, 2018, https://seekingalpha.com/article/4212083-surprising-statistics-of-stock-market-corrections.

Should I Use Passive or Active Investment Styles?

So far, this discussion of the stock market has focused on how market participants classify and discuss individual stock positions. Investors whose strategy is to beat the market by finding stocks that will perform better than the market average will use these classifications. An investor trying to beat the market average is considered ***active***. Active investing assumes that the market is ***not efficient*** and that stocks regularly encounter short-term deviations from ***intrinsic value***, which is the fair value of the stock. When these deviations are identified, higher expected returns result. However, the stock universe is overflowing with choice. To suggest that the beginner investor should step into that world and pick the fifteen best companies sounds overly optimistic—OK, it sounds crazy. For active investing to work well, the investor needs to choose the correct stocks at the right time, but timing the market is quite tricky.

Nowadays, much of the money invested is put directly into ***passive funds***. This term refers to investment vehicles, not particular securities, which do not seek to beat the market's return; instead, they try to match the return of some portion of the market. Investment firms (known as sponsors) combine individual security positions in a pool of securities and sell shares in the grouping. If you own a fund share, you also own a fractional share of each security in the pool. The securities chosen match the performance of the market or sector or industry they mimic. A significant advantage of the passive investment style is that by mirroring market performance, the people managing the fund don't spend resources trying to find bargain companies or identify a growth stock before its meteoric rise, which is expensive. They buy the companies that make up the index such that the performance of the fund will match market performance. Investors in these funds get diversified market exposure, which means less risk, at a low cost.

This passive approach to investing is ideal for investors who want to invest money and forget it. This path has grown in popularity so much that in August 2019, the total amount of assets invested in passive funds was greater than that in active funds.[12] If the investment process is not one you enjoy, earning the market return is an excellent method for growing your savings. Especially for someone new to the process, this approach allows you to get started without requiring you to pick particular stocks that you don't have much experience with.

Are You an Investor or a Trader?

This book encourages you to be an investor, not a day trader. But it seems worthwhile to think about the differences for the trader in terms of attitude and results. Traders spend their days carefully watching stock positions, jumping in on a low, and jumping out again on the high. They seek regular small gains, and they interact with the stock market daily. The stock analysis they typically do involves watching the share price and discerning patterns that repeat.[13] There is more risk because trades happen without full information and get made quickly.

12. John Gittelsohn, "End of Era: Passive Equity Funds Surpass Active in Epic Shift," *Bloomberg*, September 11, 2019, https://www.bloomberg.com/news/articles/2019-09-11/passive-u-s-equity-funds-eclipse-active-in-epic-industry-shift.
13. This type of analysis is called *technical analysis*.

The day trader's job starts to look a lot like that of a professional gambler because you are not in the market as an owner and are playing in the market's "noise." ***Traders*** will lose a lot on trades, but the goal is to gain more than they lose. It is easy to feel invincible when things are going well and respond by increasing the stakes of the positions. Some traders are successful, certainly, but theirs is not easy money. Academic literature suggests that most traders do not do well over a long period,[14] but the financial industry teems with ex-traders ready to share their skills for only a small fee. Be wary of such offers. If the process is so easy to learn, why share it with the world?

Investors are trying to create wealth over the long haul. Daily noise or volatility is much less important to investors because the stock position is founded on the belief that the company has room to grow. The investor may not watch the market for weeks and certainly will not watch it every day. The key is to let the company do its thing over time and to benefit as the good results come to light on the market. There is a lot more patience required in this process. The gains are long-term gains and tend to be larger for a given position than the trader's day trade gains. Of course, investors can be wrong in their investment thesis, and time does not guarantee a return, but the emotions and attitudes towards the market are very different.

Be a long-term investor. Choose stocks from great companies that will transform consumer lives. Make stock purchases with the intent to hold them for three to five years, and don't sell the stock unless something changes its financial fundamentals or its demand prospects. The following sections lay out some starter principles.

How Do I Pick a Winning Stock?

This is THE question. Keep in mind that if there were a definitive answer or a detailed process, like a recipe that anyone could follow, no one would share it publicly because that would be like giving away a money machine. Remember that stock prices result from what buyers and sellers currently believe about the company's value. If most investors believe a company's stock is undervalued, they buy it, which forces the price upwards until the company is no longer a bargain. Taking this one step further, once everyone followed the formula for what stocks to invest in, the process would not work anymore because the investor beliefs would have repriced the bargains upward.

The future is uncertain and noisy, but a few simple stock strategies that emphasize diversification and long-term investment horizons can get you started. Events happen; news that no one predicts ahead of time hits the market, and that has implications for companies' value. The economy can shift all at once, and even great companies can and will see their price valuations drop. Every investor needs to prepare for times when the broader market drops, and individual portfolios fall right along with it. The market has always come back, at least so far, and if it didn't, there would be other, more severe problems to contend with, like the world ending. Thus, the argument here is that, with a few guiding strategies, the beginner investor can make sound financial choices at a low cost without relying on anyone.

14. For instance, see Douglas J. Jordan and J. David Diltz, "The Profitability of Day Traders," *Financial Analysts Journal* 59, no. 6 (2003): 85–94, or Brad M. Barber, Yi-Tsung Lee, Yu-Jane Liu, and Terrance Odean, "The Cross-Section of Speculator Skill: Evidence from Day Trading," Journal of Financial Markets 18 (2014): 1–24.

Buy the Market but Watch the Expense Ratio!

One of the easiest ways to get started with investing is to "buy the market" through investment in *no-load index funds.*[15] Rather than trying to *beat* the market, your strategy is to achieve the same performance as the market. Once you recognize that most of us will never get rich by trading in the stock market, achieving an average market return between 8–10 percent seems like a reasonable return on your savings over time. Of course, you will do worse than that rate in some years and better than that rate in others, but a fund that is tracking the market index will help you stay in line with the market's performance without incurring the costs associated with funds trying to beat the market.

It would be preferable to beat the market, yes, if the costs were equal. Unfortunately, this event is quite unlikely on a consistent, risk-adjusted basis after costs.[16] The wording is important here. The word *consistently* is significant in this sentence. While many people can and do beat the market in any given period, it is much tougher to do this repeatedly. The next phrase, "on a risk-adjusted basis," is also an essential qualifier. An investor may achieve a higher return than the market average by taking greater risks, if those risks pay off. An illustration may help. The *Wall Street Journal* used to publish the results of a stock market contest between professional stock pickers and someone throwing a dart at all the listed stocks on an exchange. The stock picker would put forward their best companies, and someone would throw darts at the financial pages, and wherever the darts landed would determine the content of the random portfolio. Early on, it was shocking and funny to see how often the professionals got beat. Wow, talk about a crushing blow to your wealth management business. To be beaten by a dart thrown at the wall? By the 1990s, the professional stock picker rarely lost the dart game, however, because the stock market was climbing, and risky stocks were doing very well. The professional stock picker could pick stocks with many risk factors, and because the market was booming, these stocks did better than the market. The game was over when the dot-com bubble burst and the market fell by 30 percent. Riskier stock choices didn't pay off then, but no one was playing that game anymore.

So, how does an index fund work? The managers (the sponsors) of an index fund pool together investments in companies that make up the market or sector, whichever they are trying to copy. The fund holds the stock of those companies in proportion to each company's market value. So, if a company's market capitalization is 10 percent of the total market's capitalization, the fund holds enough of the company so that its position is 10 percent of the portfolio. Then the managers sell ownership shares for that fund. Each share represents a portion of the fund's performance. When you own index fund shares, your fund performance will match the market's performance because the fund positions mirror the components of the market.

Keep in mind that expense ratios matter a lot here. Index funds are less expensive because there is less to manage, and you should be looking for investment vehicles that have expense ratios well below .5 percent. This may not sound like a lot of money. But we are talking about retirement funds here—eventually, you

15. The no-load in this type of index fund means that there is not sales commission when you purchase this investment. The load is the sales commission that is retained by the financial advisor helping you facilitate the transaction. The fee comes off the top of the investment, so that you are actually putting less money into the investment than you think.
16. The SPIVA (S&P Indices Versus Active) Scorecard shows that US stock fund managers (the professionals) performed less well than the broader stock market between 2005–2020 (June). Murray Coleman, "SPIVA: 2020 Full-Year Active vs. Passive Scorecard," March 20, 2019, https://www.ifa.com/articles/despite_brief_reprieve_2018_spiva_report_reveals_active_funds_fail_dent_indexing_lead_-_works/.

will have a sizeable sum in your account. Imagine that you are forty and have the recommended $250,000 in your account by that time. A 1 percent expense ratio will amount to a fee of $2,500 per year, whereas a .5 percent expense ratio will amount to only $1,250. A .1 percent ratio, of course, will only cost you $250. These differences will add up significantly, considering that in a retirement account, these amounts represent money that is not earning additional compound returns over time. Remember that every dollar that goes toward expenses is not a dollar that is growing for you.

Even within the index fund category, you will have to decide whether you will purchase a mutual fund or an exchange-traded fund (ETF). The underlying index fund is the same in both investment vehicles, but the expense ratio is likely to be lower with an ETF that does not worry about redeeming shares at the close of the business day. No redemption of shares also means the tax implications are less for ETFs. Further, the minimum amount required for investment is the cost of a share for the ETF, but may be as high as $3,000 for a mutual fund. It is worth your time to find a no-commission broker to handle your trade for you, but this is standard nowadays, at least as far as buying and selling equities are concerned.

Look for High-Quality Companies, with Wide Economic Moats and Strong Balance Sheets, at Reasonable Prices

An alternative strategy for beginners is to buy stock in great companies. Every consumer knows the products and services on which they rely. New investors can begin a search by creating an inventory of the companies they know and regularly use. Do you love watching movies from home? Netflix or Disney might be excellent choices for you. Perhaps your best friend gifted you a beagle candle that has the sweet and cuddly warm scent of friendship. Etsy might be a stock worth evaluating. Once you develop a list of companies you use and know, you can begin your research process on each.

From this inventory or list, evaluate the ***economic moat*** of each company. An *economic moat* is a way to capture the competitive advantage a particular company might have. Economic moats arise when a company provides a service or product that is not easily copied by the competition, and when that advantage persists over time. Warren Buffett first coined the term when talking about his search for great companies; he likened a worthy investment to a castle surrounded by a moat for defense.[17] Just as the moat around the castle keeps invaders from hurting those within, an economic moat keeps competitors from taking company profits. Effective economic moats are *wide. Morningstar*, a financial services company, developed an "Economic Moat Rating" based on Buffett's illustration, using five sources of sustained competitive advantage that a company might possess.[18] These are shown in table 6.4.

17. Tae Kim, "Warren Buffett Believes This Is 'The Most Important Thing' to Find in a Business," May 7, 2018. https://www.cnbc.com/2018/05/07/warren-buffett-believes-this-is-the-most-important-thing-to-find-in-a-business.html.
18. Heather Brilliant and Elizabeth Collins, *Why Moats Matter: The Morningstar Approach to Stock Investing* (Hoboken: John Wiley & Sons, 2014).

TABLE 6.4 Company Experiences That Create Moats

Cost Advantage	Railroads
Efficient Scale	Pacific Gas and Electric
Intangible Assets	Disney
Network Effects	Zoom
High Switching Costs	Apple

By identifying firms with at least one of the sources for an economic moat, an investor may be one step closer to earning *alpha,* or excess returns. The idea is basically that the moat is a way for the firm to capture relatively higher cash flows in the future that the competition is unable to steal away. However, for this to work, other investors must not have bid up the company's price already.

Once you have identified a company with a lasting advantage against its competition, look for a strong balance sheet. A balance sheet is a snapshot of a firm's financial health that reflects its financial choices. Since the text advocates for buying long, the stock positions chosen will likely have to survive a market downturn. Some firms are more prepared than others to survive economic troughs. In an economic crisis, the demand for the product or service in a firm can change markedly, but the firm will not be relieved of making interest payments in any event. A firm with too much debt might find it difficult to be profitable during a downturn. Debt is a lever that magnifies the returns of the firm. When the returns are losses, this is problematic, and the stock price is likely to fall further to accommodate the financial risks inherent in the stock. Beyond how the firm has paid for its assets, it may be worthwhile to examine its working capital management choices. By weighing the firm's current assets against current liabilities and examining how those accounts are growing relative to each other over time, the potential investor may see the first signs of financial trouble. A *liquid* balance sheet where the current assets are more than the current liabilities can ease concerns that a short-term cash flow issue could ruin a great company's trajectory.

Having looked at the company from all these perspectives—great company, good future cash flows, impenetrable competitive advantage, and strong balance sheet—the last thing to consider is the price. The goal is to buy at a *reasonable* price. There the trick lies. What is reasonable? Financial professionals are geared toward solving complicated, quantitative models to determine the *intrinsic value*, which is what the stock price *should* be. When the current price is less than the intrinsic value, buy the stock because the actual worth is less than what it should be. Of course, confidence in the model and the assumptions made plays a big part in this decision. The larger issue is, what does the average investor do if they don't employ these fancy models that determine this reasonable price?

Two easy metrics you can use to check whether the price you are paying is a bargain or not are the PE (price-to-earnings) ratio and the PEG (price/earnings-to-growth) ratio. The PE ratio equals the stock market price per share divided by its earnings per share. Financial sites all report it. The number tells you what investors are willing to pay for each $1 of earnings. Investors compare the PE ratio to an industry average. A company PE lower than the average indicates either that the stock is undervalued or that the company is not as valuable. If you are still looking at the company at this point in your research (after the first five points), it is likely a good investment. It may still be a good company, but if the PE is higher than average, the market may have already bid up the share price. At this point, you will have to decide if the value you see has already been "baked into" the price. If so, the investment loses some allure.

The PEG ratio is a variation on the PE ratio. To find the PEG ratio, divide the firm's PE ratio by the growth percentage expected in the next period. This adjustment normalizes the market worth of each dollar of earnings around expected growth. If investors anticipate a large growth rate, the PEG is lower. A PEG less than 1 indicates a good buying opportunity but checking that a company's PEG is lower than the industry average may serve in robust market upturns. Note one caveat: earnings per share and expected growth must be positive for the PEG to make sense.

Ask yourself if you are buying because you think the stock will go higher, from other market participants pushing it higher, or if you believe the market has not fully recognized the extent of the firm's future cash flows. When you think the market is not fully incorporating its potential into the current stock price, you buy. If the market is moving upwards daily and the rise feels like "irrational exuberance,"[19] it might be worth looking for better investment alternatives. A fair price can be tough to judge clearly, especially when the market is already in a cyclical upturn and when financial commentary talks about stocks being rich or overpriced. The *Motley Fool Investment Guide* suggests that investors approach the purchase with a business focus rather than a stock focus.[20] They recommend stepping back to decide where the company will be in five years. Would you be glad you invested? That investment philosophy reminds investors to think like owners rather than traders.

This section provided a beginner's checklist of dos and don'ts when you are starting the research process for a potential investment. Greater particulars will vary, depending on strategy and risk tolerance. Always remember that no stock market strategy is foolproof. Investing still has risks.

Core and Satellite Strategy

If the thought of trying to find enough stocks to create a diversified portfolio all at once is a bit daunting, or if a portfolio with a little less return uncertainty is preferred, investors can consider a *core and satellite strategy*. The core of the investment portfolio comes from the asset allocation decisions made in chapter 3, "The *Decision to Save*." The average investor aligns return preference and risk tolerance and allocates savings to fund choices at work, making sure to make the match provided by the employer and seeking to save 15 percent of gross income each month automatically. The return on the core matches the weighted average of the asset allocation.

Beyond this core, some investors may want to select a few investments they feel confident about. These stock positions can form the portfolio's satellite portion, which tilts the return a little towards companies of real interest or meaning to the investor. If the investor believes that *Chipotle* or *Wingstop* or *Papa John's* has done a fantastic job of serving fresh food to customers using an innovative business model that is hard to

19. Alan Greenspan, chairman of the Federal Reserve in the 1990s, made the phrase famous, but this description of a stock market that was largely overvalued originated with Yale economist Robert Shiller in his book *Irrational Exuberance*, written in 2000 right before the dot-com bubble burst (Princeton: Princeton University Press, 2000).
20. David Gardner and Tom Gardner, *The Motley Fool Investment Guide: How the Fool Beats Wall Street's Wise Men and How You Can Too* (New York: Simon and Schuster, 2001, p. 98).

compete with, perhaps an investment in one of these will tilt the return of the portfolio above the market return. The goal is to seek higher returns, or *alpha*, in a few plays that the investor has the time to research, understand, and maintain.

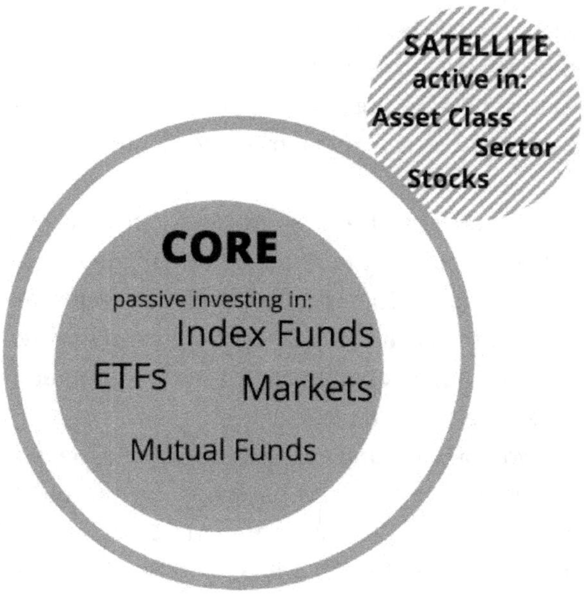

FIGURE 6.5 Hypothetical Core–Satellite Asset Allocation

With this strategy, the bulk of the portfolio return will come from the market's return, which is already diversified in an index fund or a target-date fund. The investor can also use a smaller portion of the funds to invest in growth, or in a particular sector where the investor sees a lot of promise. The core–satellite approach to investing might be a promising method for investors who are interested in investing but who have a career and life outside the finance industry. The system offers more stable returns but allows the owner to commit to an investment belief without risking everything.

Take Away the Emotion, Ignore the Noise, and Rebalance Annually!

One of the reasons that investing in the stock market is scary for people is that the risks are real; poor investing can cost you a lot of money. That concern is to be taken seriously, but hopefully, this chapter has alleviated some of that concern by demystifying the process for you and helping you understand that investing can be done relatively safely and wisely.

Investing is also scary, though, because we are not always particularly *good* at it. Some of the emotions we experience as investors can undermine our ability to invest safely and wisely.[21] Fear and greed, in

21. See Part IV of Michael M. Pompian, *Behavioral Finance and Wealth Management: How to Build Investment Strategies That Account for Investor Biases* (Hoboken: John Wiley & Sons, 2012).

particular, are worthy adversaries to success in investing. Much research in a field called *behavior finance* documents how emotions lead investors to make sizeable mistakes. The mistakes originate from fear or greed, which operate in all market cycles. When the stock market is on an upswing, the fear of missing out can push investors to purchase stocks at too-high prices. Greed operates here when investors don't take their profits and look for undervalued options. The belief that the stock price will go higher, and that you can get out before it drops, is folly. There is a rush from watching your money grow in the middle of a market cycle upturn. It is a little intoxicating to choose a company and see its value rise to a level higher than the original investment. However, success comes from having an investment thesis and holding onto it throughout the market cycle.

When the market is in a down cycle, fear and greed remain pivotal. The fear that the stock price will fall even lower can feed the desire to sell, but the result is buying high and selling low! The exact opposite of what sound investing principles suggest. The greed you feel—to make sure you capture some profit—can work against you if the market makes a small correction and bounces up after your trade. Investors are the most successful when they are aware that emotion can subvert the bigger return goals, though checking that emotional drive is sometimes easier said than done.

The greed for continued growth of a winning asset allocation, and the tendency to sell short-term losers too soon, can force investors to miss out on profitable growth in the portfolio. Rarely does the winning asset allocation from today remain so tomorrow. Likewise, the parts of the asset allocation that did not do as well in this period tend to perform better in the next. It is, therefore, very important to *rebalance* the entire portfolio annually. When you rebalance, you are taking some of the proceeds from the winning allocations and reinvesting them in the asset allocations that did not perform as well in the previous period. On a very simple level, say that you are invested in 80 percent stocks and 20 percent bonds. Say that bonds performed very well during the year and stocks did not perform as well, such that, your allocation ends the period with only 75 percent of your money in stocks and 30 percent of your money invested in bonds. It is prudent for you to take 5 percent of your allocation from the bonds which did so well this period and reinvest it in stocks to get back to your planned asset allocation. This process takes advantage of the notion that suitable investments will regress towards their mean returns with time. Something out of favor today will return to favor tomorrow. In contrast, it is hard for asset-class winners to stay winners period after period.

Consider a reproduction of the "Callan Periodic Table of Investment Returns" that uses publicly available data for a simpler asset class categorization in figure 6.6.[22]

22. This table looks like Mendeleev's periodic table in chemistry, but it focuses on the return of different asset classes across different years. It was created by Jay Kloepfer, an economist at Callan and Associates, in 1999. Callan is a financial consultant for institutional investors. See, Jay Kloepfer, "The Callan Periodic Table of Investment Returns: Year-End 2020." Callan. 2021. https://www.callan.com/research/2020-classic-periodic-table/.

2011	2012	2013	2014	2015	2016	2017	2018	2019	2020
BONDS 4.79%	VALUE 19.40%	GROWTH 23.67%	GROWTH 16.49%	GROWTH 1.60%	SMALL CAP 29.45%	GROWTH 32.65%	BONDS 2.17%	GROWTH 24.62%	GROWTH 29.65%
GROWTH 7.35%	ROW 17.02%	SMALL CAP 21.82%	LARGE CAP 11.92%	BONDS 0.16%	MID CAP 28.04%	BLUE CHIP 31.64%	GROWTH -0.02%	ROW 23.16%	SMALL CAP 26.55%
BLUE CHIP 6.23%	MID CAP 16.81%	ROW 21.57%	VALUE 11.83%	ROW -2.60%	VALUE 24.43%	ROW 24.81%	LARGE CAP -4.24%	LARGE CAP 19.28%	LARGE CAP 15.15%
SMALL CAP 2.52%	SMALL CAP 14.61%	MID CAP 20.03%	BLUE CHIP 9.34%	LARGE CAP -2.74%	BLUE CHIP 20.63%	LARGE CAP 23.91%	BLUE CHIP -4.40%	VALUE 18.23%	MID CAP 13.06%
LARGE CAP 2.04%	LARGE CAP 14.15%	LARGE CAP 18.99%	MID CAP 9.29%	VALUE -3.98%	LARGE CAP 17.45%	VALUE 19.15%	VALUE -5.24%	BLUE CHIP 13.03%	ROW 8.09%
MID CAP 1.27%	GROWTH 14.14%	VALUE 18.66%	BONDS 6.23%	BLUE CHIP -4.07%	GROWTH 15.79%	MID CAP 15.81%	MID CAP -6.07%	MID CAP 9.36%	BONDS 7.18%
VALUE 0.89%	BLUE CHIP 9.72%	BLUE CHIP 13.26%	SMALL CAP -0.10%	MID CAP -8.18%	ROW 3.29%	SMALL CAP 11.03%	SMALL CAP -13.19%	BONDS 8.67%	BLUE CHIP 6.11%
ROW -11.78%	BONDS 3.84%	BONDS -1.80%	ROW -3.88%	SMALL CAP -14.64%	BONDS 2.56%	BONDS 1.37%	ROW -13.64%	SMALL CAP 8.18%	VALUE 2.33%

KEY	
Blue Chip	Stocks in Dow Jones Industrial Average
Growth	S&P 500 Growth Stocks
Value	S&P 500 Value Stocks
Large	S&P 500 Lage Capitalization Stocks
Mid	S&P 500 Mid Capitalization Stocks
Small	S&P 500 Small Capitalization Stocks
ROW	Rest of the World Stocks (no USA)
Bonds	U.S. Bonds

FIGURE 6.6 Table of Investment Returns by Asset Class

The table in figure 6.6 ranks different asset classes by their return performance, from highest returns to lowest, for the last ten years. You can see that growth stocks have performed very well while bonds and the rest of the world have taken turns doing the worst over this particular time span. But don't think that you should put everything you have into growth stocks only! Over longer time periods, the same asset class rarely performs in the top two spots on a year-over-year basis and what does well can change from decade to decade. For instance, the Rest of the World (ROW), sometimes called Emerging Market Equity, was a strong performer from 2003–2009. No one would have guessed this at the beginning of 2003. After 2009, and especially in 2011, the investor who did not take profits in the emerging-markets asset class saw hefty losses that year. In 2018, when a massive market correction in the fourth quarter of the year rocked all asset classes, bonds did the best. The lesson from this version of a periodic table is: don't let the winners run forever, remember the investment plan, and realign your portfolio choices in alignment with that diverse allocation in stocks and bonds.

Last piece of beginner advice: rebalance, rebalance, rebalance! Once you have identified your investment/savings strategy and asset allocations, rebalance them annually. This practice will both help you maintain your investment thesis and protect you against fear and greed. Trust your long-term plan and stick to it.

Key Takeaways

Directions: Review the following list of key takeaways to help you remember what you learned in this chapter:

- Most of us cannot put enough in a savings account for retirement, and recent history shows us that the returns on this type of account are not enough to offset inflation, much less enough to grow to the levels required for retirement; the compounding of returns is a necessary component to successful saving strategies for retirement investments.
- The stock market is less complicated than it seems at first glance. Buyers and sellers move the market price by following their beliefs, buying where they see bargains, and selling when something is dear. The trick is to buy low and sell high; unfortunately, some investors do the opposite.
- Slow and steady wins the race. Remember that time is your most significant advantage for investing in your retirement. You are unlikely to get rich fast, so choosing investments that you plan to hold for at least five years is a good guideline.
- No one will look after your money like you do. The financial wealth industry has every incentive to convince you that you need its help when you are making investment decisions, but do not believe anyone who tells you that they know when the market will turn. They do not.

Application Opportunity: Do This Now!

Directions: Complete the activities below to apply what you have learned in this chapter.

Activity 1

Go to the Vanguard website below, and compare and contrast the following mutual funds:
https://personal.vanguard.com/us/faces/JSP/Funds/Compare/CompareEntryContent.jsp

Federal Money Market Fund

Total Bond Market Index Adm

Large-Cap Index Fund Adm

Growth Index Fund Inst

Intl Core Stock Investor

What do you notice about the asset classes? The risk potential? The expense ratios?

Slide down the page to consider the average annual performance. What patterns do you notice?

Now compare the expense ratios if you make the purchase as a mutual fund to the expense ratios if you make the purchase as an ETF. You will have to use the back arrow at the top left and then choose ETF for the same funds instead of mutual fund. Do you notice any difference? Which would be better to have?

Activity 2

Let's recreate the *Wall Street Journal Dart Game,* where you choose a five-stock portfolio of companies you use and love and test it against five high-beta stocks on the stock simulator on *Investopedia*. You will have to create an account, but it is free. https://www.investopedia.com/simulator/

The simulator will ask you to join a game. It does not really matter which game you pick, but if you choose "beginners" you will get a simulated $10,000 to invest in the stock market. Choose "Trade Stock" in the upper right and buy the five stocks for the companies of your choice (you can use symbol lookup to find the tickers). An example selection might be:

Starbucks SBUX

Spotify SPOT

Lululemon LULU

Tractor Supply TSCO

Coca-Cola KO

Spend $1,000 on each at the market price (you will buy the number of shares that gets you closest to $1,000). Now buy these five high-beta companies:

Office Depot ODP

Rockwood Holdings ROC

Shift4 Payments Inc FOUR

Lightspeed POS Inc LSPD

Magnetek Inc MAG

Spend $1,000 on each of these. Now watch the portfolio for a couple of weeks to see what happens. If the market is strong, the high-beta stocks may do better, but if the economy is weak, your stocks may do better. What do you notice?

Activity 3

Identify a great company that you know and use today. Work through the research process described in the chapter to see whether that company would make a good investment opportunity today.

Bibliography

American Century Mid Cap Growth Impact ETF (MID). *Yahoo Finance*. https://finance.yahoo.com/quote/MID?p=MID&.tsrc=fin-srch

Barber, Brad M., Yi-Tsung Lee, Yu-Jane Liu, and Terrance Odean. "The Cross-Section of Speculator Skill: Evidence from Day Trading." *Journal of Financial Markets* 18 (2014): 1–24.

Board of Governors of the Federal Reserve System (US), "6-Month Certificate of Deposit: Secondary Market Rate." (DISCONTINUED) [DCD6M], FRED, Federal Reserve Bank of St. Louis. July 1, 2013. https://fred.stlouisfed.org/series/DCD6M.

Bodnaruk, Andriy, and Andrei Simonov. "Do Financial Experts Make Better Investment Decisions?" *Journal of Financial Intermediation* 24, no. 4 (2015): 514–36.

Brilliant, Heather, and Elizabeth Collins. *Why Moats Matter: The Morningstar Approach to Stock Investing*. Hoboken: John Wiley & Sons, 2014.

Chan, Louis K. C., and Josef Lakonishok. "Value and Growth Investing: Review and Update." *Financial Analysts Journal* 60, no. 1 (2004): 71–86.

Coleman, Murray. "SPIVA: 2020 Full-Year Active vs. Passive Scorecard." March 20, 2019. https://www.ifa.com/articles/despite_brief_reprieve_2018_spiva_report_reveals_active_funds_fail_dent_indexing_lead_-_works/.

Dow Jones Industrial Average (^DJI). *Yahoo Finance*. https://finance.yahoo.com/quote/%5EDJI?p=%5EDJI.

Gardner, David, and Tom Gardner. *The Motley Fool Investment Guide: How the Fool Beats Wall Street's Wise Men and How You Can Too*. New York: Simon and Schuster, 2001.

Gittelsohn, John. "End of Era: Passive Equity Funds Surpass Active in Epic Shift." *Bloomberg*, September 11, 2019. https://www.bloomberg.com/news/articles/2019-09-11/passive-u-s-equity-funds-eclipse-active-in-epic-industry-shift.

iShares Core U.S. Aggregate Bond ETF (AGG). *Yahoo Finance*. https://finance.yahoo.com/quote/AGG?p=AGG&.tsrc=fin-srch

Jordan, Douglas J., and J. David Diltz. "The Profitability of Day Traders." *Financial Analysts Journal* 59, no. 6 (2003): 85–94.

Kane, Logan. "The Surprising Statistics of Stock Market Corrections." Seeking Alpha. October 17, 2018. https://seekingalpha.com/article/4212083-surprising-statistics-of-stock-market-corrections.

Kim, Tae. "Warren Buffett Believes This Is 'The Most Important Thing' to Find in a Business." CNBC. May 7, 2018. https://www.cnbc.com/2018/05/07/warren-buffett-believes-this-is-the-most-important-thing-to-find-in-a-business.html.

Kloepfer, Jay. "The Callan Periodic Table of Investment Returns: Year-End 2020." Callan. 2021. https://www.callan.com/research/2020-classic-periodic-table/.

Malkiel, Burton G. *A Random Walk down Wall Street: The Best Investment Advice for the New Century*. New York: W. W. Norton & Company, Inc., 1999.

MSCI World ex USA Index. MSCI.com. https://www.msci.com/documents/10199/99459e68-5e21-4888-ace6-72a3ffe9b1ab

Northern Small Cap Index Fd (NSIDX). *Yahoo Finance*. https://finance.yahoo.com/quote/NSIDX?p=NSIDX&.tsrc=fin-srch

New York Stock Exchange. "The World's Leading Markets." NYSE. 2020. https://www.nyse.com/trade.

NYSE Euronext. "History." 2010. https://web.archive.org/web/20100309083240/http:/www.nyse.com/about/history/1089312755484.html.

Pompian, Michael M. *Behavioral Finance and Wealth Management: How to Build Investment Strategies That Account for Investor Biases*. Hoboken: John Wiley & Sons, 2012.

Royal, James. "Best Index Funds in March 2021." Bankrate. March 1, 2021. https://www.bankrate.com/investing/best-index-funds/.

S&P 500 (^GSPC). *Yahoo Finance*. https://finance.yahoo.com/quote/%5EGSPC?p=%5EGSPC

Survey of Consumer Finances (SCF), 1989-2019. *Board of Governors of the Federal Reserve System*. https://www.federalreserve.gov/econres/scfindex.htm

Shiller, Robert. *Irrational Exuberance*. Princeton: Princeton University Press, 2000.

Wayland, Michael, and Lora Kolodny. "Tesla's Market Cap Tops the 9 Largest Automakers Combined—Experts Disagree about If That Can Last." *CNBC*, December 14, 2020. https://www.cnbc.com/2020/12/14/tesla-valuation-more-than-nine-largest-carmakers-combined-why.html.

Vanguard S&P 500 Value Index Fund (VOOV). *Yahoo Finance*. https://finance.yahoo.com/quote/VOOV?p=VOOV&.tsrc=fin-srch

Vanguard S&P 500 Growth Index Fund (VOOG). *Yahoo Finance*. https://finance.yahoo.com/quote/VOOG?p=VOOG&.tsrc=fin-srch

Figure Credits

Fig. 6.1: Source: https://commons.wikimedia.org/wiki/File:Simple_world_map.svg.

Fig. 6.2: Data source: https://finance.yahoo.com/quote/%5EGSPC?p=%5EGSPC and https://finance.yahoo.com/quote/%5EDJI?p=%5EDJI.

Fig. 6.3: Data source: https://finance.yahoo.com/quote/TSLA?p=TSLA&.tsrc=fin-srch.

Fig. 6.4: Source: https://commons.wikimedia.org/wiki/File:The_difference_between_systematic_and_unsystematic_risk.jpg.

CHAPTER 7

The Decision to Retire

Invest in Your Financial Independence

Imagine...

Bob was in his fifties with two kids in college when his Fortune 500 employer eliminated his research project, and his position, in a move to boost profitability for the year. Such thinking that harmed workers for the long-run with only short-term benefits for the firm was *en vogue*, and there were no hard feelings on the corporation's side of things. After all, the corporation allowed the newly available researchers the right to continue to work on their ethanol process, just not under the umbrella of the corporate structure. Bob had a choice: to put his retirement savings into a new start-up to see his research through, to retire early, or to seek employment elsewhere. Maybe he could teach high school chemistry? Bob knew that he wasn't ready to retire, though the savings were in place, and he knew that finding a job with seniority at his age was not going to be easy. Still, the idea of putting everything he had for retirement behind the strength of one idea felt risky.

What would you do if you were Bob?

Introduction

Retirement is a lifetime away for most of you. OK, forty-plus years may not be a lifetime, but it certainly might feel like one. It is more likely that you are only just figuring out what career would fit best or what internship is worth pursuing. Many of you are looking at your own parents and the adults around you and noticing that they have not yet started to save for retirement, so why would you even be thinking about it? The *Retirement Confidence Survey* shows that 70 percent of workers are confident they can retire comfortably, and the percentage of those who are feeling very confident is growing. That is good news!

Unfortunately, planning for the event is less universal. Only 40 percent have considered the annual income they will need, or considered the alternative funding possibilities that might be necessary in an emergency, medical or otherwise.[1] Thinking through the details of old age at this point in your life may not feel productive, as there are still too many unknowns about what you will need and where you will be. Knowing what to plan for and think about as a young person, however, is worthy of some thought because it provides a good foundation for the point in your life when the details will matter. A little thought now will allow you to reduce a lot of stress later.

This chapter focuses on the retirement planning process. What should you think about now so that when it becomes time to actually do the retirement planning, you are in a good position and don't have to experience the stress that many face in their forties and fifties? This chapter is meant to put you ahead of the curve for what many in the wealth advisory industry call the *retirement savings crisis.*

Chapter Objectives

After reading this chapter, you will be able to:

- Identify the steps required in retirement planning and know the choices available to individuals in terms of planning for the shortfall between spending and income.
- Consider general guidelines for retirement savings by age, learn about the 4 percent rule for distribution in retirement, and develop expectations for what living in retirement looks like when you plan for it.
- Calculate the amount needed for financial independence in retirement.
- Understand the benefits and limits of Social Security as a source of retirement income.
- Think critically about the opportunities and benefits of legacy and stewardship for living out what is important to you.

Aren't I Too Young to Think about Retirement?

It is really easy to avoid thinking about retirement. There are plenty of other things to worry about as you begin adulting, and since retirement is so far in the future, it seems reasonble to deal with other issues first, like spending, budgets, and credit scores! Luckily, this book has been arranged in such a way that you have thought about those things by now. And if you think about retirement when you are young, you can make great headway on the problem, such that it is not really a concern later on. The issue here is one of risk versus reward. While the time horizon of retirement extends far into the future, the risk of not having enough to be comfortable in retirement is great enough that it is worth beginning to think about now. You know that the saving you do in your twenties has the time and compounding value to greatly facilitate your financial goals. Still, thinking about how much will be needed, which issues are worth knowing about before earnest retirement planning begins, and the amount of Social Security funds to expect when you get there will greatly facilitate your financial journey.

1. Employee Benefit Research Institute and Greenwald & Associates, 2020 Retirement Confidence Survey Summary Report, April 23, 2020, https://www.ebri.org/docs/default-source/rcs/2020-rcs/2020-rcs-summary-report.pdf?sfvrsn=84bc3d2.

A little knowledge now about financial concerns in retirement can help you avoid the pitfalls that some fall into later in life. The earlier you begin thinking through the issues and making a plan, the more flexible you can be to handle whatever comes your way. Your plan for retirement is likely to change because few can predict all that life will give us, but an early plan is the key to landing on your feet, whatever happens.

Retirement Planning by Decade

Hopefully, I have convinced you to make the employer match within the retirement plan at work. If you don't do this, you will be leaving money on the table that you earned and that is rightfully yours to claim. You learned this back in chapter 3, "The Decision to Save," but it bears a little repetition. Of course, making the match means you have started to save for your retirement. This is the minimum, though, and seeking to do a bit more is a worthy goal if your financial situation will allow, as discussed in chapter 6, "The Decision to Own Shares."

Most of the information about retirement planning seems to be directed toward those who are just about to take the plunge. This may be because the audience members for such information want to retire now, but sadly, a little knowledge and thought ***earlier*** is the key to making good choices that allow you to personalize your retirement experience. How horrible to lose the chance to make the best choices because you did not realize you needed to think about it early! The good news is that the steps to retirement are straightforward. Breaking them down by decade might be helpful.

In Your Twenties—Set Up Your Savings Plan

Save through your employer-sponsored retirement plan. If you can save 15 percent of your gross paycheck, SUPER! If the budget does not support that yet, it is understandable. Make the employer match, for certain, and try to add 1 percent a year. Hopefully, annual raises will fully support this practice. If not, see if you can make it work anyway, but stand ready to adjust. If you cannot increase your contribution, seek options to stop from reducing it. This is your golden time to benefit from time and compounding. Recognize that. Do what you can to take advantage of it.

If you begin this savings and investment process in your twenties, early in your career, retirement planning can go on autopilot to a large degree. You really do not have to think about it much beyond the savings piece, when you are young, as long as you are putting enough back. As you get closer to the middle of your career, then you can think about all the major retirement planning questions a bit more thoroughly.

In Your Thirties—Own Your Savings Plan and Expand It

Look to maintain your savings plan from your twenties. If you can expand savings, consider savings/investment vehicles like the Roth IRA, which can be invested in any way that you desire. As you learned in chapter 3, the Roth IRA comes with significant tax advantages when you use the money, once you reach retirement. This is money that can be accessed early, but only under certain conditions (to buy a home, to pay for college expenses, or to use when you are having a child), much like your employer-sponsored retirement plans, so it is best and easiest if you don't need these funds before you are 59½. The contributions are made after tax, but withdrawals are not taxed; even the gains can be spent tax-free! There are limits to what you can save in a Roth IRA; for instance, the 2021 limit is $6,000. This limit goes up a bit over time and as you get closer to retirement.

If you can swing it in your budget, max out your Roth IRA contribution, because it will be very nice to have tax-free earnings as part of your regular retirement income.

Your thirties may also be a good time to make a will. This seems like a morose topic, for sure, but at this point in your financial journey, you have begun to build some wealth. Protecting what you have built provides clarity and peace of mind, should anything untoward occur. If you have a family, a will helps you be clear about your wishes and forces you to focus on what you want to see happen if you are not able to be there. State law will dictate the process for you if your will is not in place. This may not matter to you, but the people who love you will appreciate the preparations you made, because that will make things easier for them. Remember, they will just have lost you and will be dealing with that.

In Your Forties—Focus on Expenses and Debt

Now is the time to plan more specifically for the size of the retirement nest egg you want to have ready. Once you have reached your forties, you have a much clearer picture of the amount you will make each year. Indeed, peak earnings years look to be about mid-forties, once you have had your big promotions and are more centered on getting your kids through school.[2] This stability may allow you to dissect your expenses a bit and think through which expenses will still be present in retirement, which new expenses might be needed, and which expenses you will not face anymore. A second goal is to assess your savings accumulation so far and make necessary adjustments to insure you reach a much clearer target when it is time to retire.

The key input for the calculation of retirement savings is ***expenses***. Starting from your income in your forties, subtract the expenses you won't have once you are in retirement. Your kids will be out of the house and on their own. You will no longer need life insurance or long-term disability insurance, so those premiums will go away. Once you are living in retirement, all those savings expenses will also go away. You will likely spend less on housing,[3] as you may already have a big investment in a home. And when you retire, there is a good likelihood that the house will be paid off. Many retirees downsize in retirement because the house or the yard is too big. Grandparents may move closer to children, and older people may move to a place that is more suitable to the lifestyle they desire.

Add in expenses that increase a bit, too. For instance, traveling more during early retirement can create a very desirable lifestyle that is fulfilling and engaging. Just understand that early and sizeable withdrawals on retirement funds can be more difficult to recover from in terms of returns to the portfolio, so you may want to save a bit extra to accommodate for an expanded lifestyle. Dream big, but plan for it.

2. US Bureau of Labor Statistics, "Table 3. Median Usual Weekly Earnings of Full-Time Wage and Salary Workers by Age, Race, Hispanic or Latino Ethnicity, and Sex, Fourth Quarter 2020 Averages, Not Seasonally Adjusted," economics news release, January 21, 2021, https://www.bls.gov/news.release/wkyeng.t03.htm.
3. Fidelity Viewpoints, "How Much Will You Spend in Retirement?" April 9, 2019, https://www.fidelity.com/viewpoints/retirement/spending-in-retirement.

On the downside of getting older, medical expenses tend to rise in the golden years. One wealth advisory firm survey found that healthy sixty-five-year-olds expected to have medical expenses of around $2,700 per year. In fact, they were actually $11,400.[4] That is over 300 percent higher than the expectation! *CNBC* does nothing to assuage this anticipation, reporting that healthy couples will need a total of $387,644 to pay for their healthcare—and this amount is ***with*** health insurance in retirement.[5] Retirees may fail to factor in medical expenses not covered by Medicare, like long-term care, dentistry, and acupuncture. Also, health costs have historically risen faster than inflation. Older people tend to need more healthcare than they had in the past, so the anticipated cost is difficult to estimate. This is one reason why having a health savings account becomes even more valuable in later years. The savings continue to build in a tax-advantaged account that allows the owner to pay out-of-pocket medical expenses with tax-free income earned while working. The account stays with the owner and the funds are never lost for lack of use, as the funds in a flexible savings account are.

In your forties, you may have a better idea of the age at which you want to retire. Or you may not! If you are still unsure, plan your savings goals around the full retirement age, which stands at sixty-seven in 2021. You can always delay when the time is near, and that can give you a few more years to accumulate funding. Be aware that most retirement calculators will tell you that you need more money to retire if you plan to retire later. This may go against common sense, because from the individual perspective, that is one less year in retirement. But most calculators are increasing each year's needs with respect to ***inflation*** and are not decreasing the number of ***years spent*** in retirement.

This decade is also a great time to tackle your debt and get that under control. The goal is to pay off any high-interest debt you face while you are still working. Seek to pay off credit card balances, any old student debt, and any outstanding car loans. You may not completely finish paying off the house at this point, and the kids may face college expenses that you want to help with, but look for ways to reduce the debt you are currently using in order to consume. I found a good goal for me at this point was to not carry a balance on my credit cards anymore. I was amazed that once I made this a primary goal, I stopped having to use my credit as a loan mechanism. I become much more careful when I purchased big items and I planned better for them. Of course, having a bit more resources at this point really helped, but much of the shift was a mental one as well. The more you can remove debt before you retire, the less of a drag it will be on your retirement savings. If you can devote your retirement income to current retirement consumption, living on your savings will feel much easier.

As you move toward your fifties, you want to develop a better sense of the funds you will need to start your retirement. You will want an amount that allows you to maintain your standard of living now and accommodate the lifestyle you expect in retirement. This decade will help you better understand your expenses and should put you in a better financial position to control your debt choices.

4. RBC Wealth Management, "Health Care: The Real Cost of Health Care in Retirement," accessed March 15, 2021, https://www.rbcwealthmanagement.com/us/en/research-insights/the-real-cost-of-health-care-in-retirement/detail/.
5. Darla Mercado, "Retiring This Year? How Much You'll Need for Health-Care Costs," CNBC, July 18, 2019, https://www.cnbc.com/2019/07/18/retiring-this-year-how-much-youll-need-for-health-care-costs.html.

In Your Fifties—Visualize and Personalize Your Retirement Lifestyle

The decade of your fifties is the time to envision broadly the lifestyle you want in retirement. Is it active, with travel or volunteering or part-time work? Is it more quiet, with reading, gardening, and golfing? All choices are valid nowadays, and one type of retirement will not fit all personalities. You can start to think more about the classic retirement questions at this point. It is likely that you now have much firmer answers to many of the following lifestyle questions, discussed in the text box below.

LIFESTYLE QUESTIONS FOR RETIREMENT

Retire sooner or later? When you retire is not set in stone. If you want to retire sooner, make sure your savings can last for longer. That may seem obvious, but retirement models need to know how long you live in retirement. Recognize that you can't apply for Medicare Health Insurance until the age of sixty-five, so retirement before that is likely to mean that you will be covering your own health insurance for a few years. Given your age, this is likely to be expensive, and it will require some extra planning.

Live simple or big? Some folks really just want to stop when they retire. They enjoy relatively inexpensive hobbies and like to eat at home. Others want to travel and see the world or participate in boating or golf. Eating out in good restaurants is on the bucket list. The replacement rate for your income is likely to be higher than the 70 percent often used in retirement models. If you live bigger than you did when you worked, you may want to replace 100 percent of your income in retirement. Your fifties is the decade to see what is really possible for spending. Understand that living big early in retirement can place a significant drag on your savings, much like a big market correction right when you retire. You no longer have time for the market to recover. The desire to live big means saving more.

Work for fun or for a cause? Many people find it hard to imagine not working. They love what they do, and stopping is not appealing. That is OK, too. Just because the normal retirement age has been in the sixties does not mean it has to be there for you. People are living longer, and it may make sense to work longer if you love it. Others may wish to work part time because suddenly stopping what you have done for forty years feels like too much. A partial exit may make sense. An alternative to this is to look for ways you can volunteer, supporting a cause that is important to you. Now is the time to think this through a bit because you still have some flexibility to plan.

Establish home base or seek new horizons? Where you will live is a fundamental question. Your kids are grown, and you may be done with the big house and all the yard work! You may want to downsize. It is likely that your kids will want you to visit on holidays because it is more difficult for them to visit you with small children. Or you may want to move closer to family. My partner is really pushing for the classic retirement plan of spending the winter in a warm place like Florida and the summer in a place like Michigan or Wisconsin where you can swim or fish. We are figuring out how to accomplish that dream now. Is it a fancy mobile home or two condos?

The key is that you want to ***live well,*** but that goal looks different for different people. The reason you will take a hard look at these choices in your fifties is that your answers may impact your savings choices. If you realize you want to upsize your lifestyle after retirement, you may want to save more in this last decade to support that choice. Today, we live a long time in retirement, and your fifties is the decade to safeguard your nest egg from too much depletion early in your retirement period. Big withdrawals for travel or other expensive lifestyle choices, when you are still relatively young and eager to pursue all that work has kept you from in life, can zap retirement funds if returns are particularly bad when you first stop working. You don't have the time to wait for the money to build back up anymore, so having an extra buffer for that situation may be wise, and you may want to focus on saving more to accommodate this. Early in your fifties you still have some time for growth and compounding to help you save.

Beyond the dreaming you can do about how and where you will spend your time, you may want to revisit a few of the financial decisions you made earlier in your working career. A few ***financial*** questions to consider are listed below.

Does life insurance still make sense for your family and in your situation? Remember that the general purpose of life insurance is to make sure that loved ones are taken care of if you leave this world too soon. You may have enough in your savings at this point to stop paying for life insurance and start putting those resources back into more savings to enjoy in retirement.

Are your investments positioned for tax efficiency in retirement? In other words, do you have some income that will not be taxed when you use it? If you have not had the opportunity to set up a Roth IRA, your fifties might be the perfect time to do so. Remember that the Roth allows you to invest after-tax income in whatever you wish. When you use the investment proceeds, there are no taxes. In your fifties there is usually a catch-up provision that allows you to save $1,000 more per year. There are no required minimum disbursements because the IRS has already taken its slice of the money, but it can be nice to pull some of your income from places that are tax exempt to lower your tax expectations in retirement.

Be aware also that states tax their citizens differently, so moving to a state with rates for income, property, estate, and even sales taxes that suit your lifestyle choice makes some sense! Lots of people focus on climate or family locale when they make their living choice in retirement, but financially savvy retirees will also look at tax burden. Some states do not tax Social Security benefits at all, and some states offer nice exemptions for at least some other retirement income. Have you ever considered Delaware? No sales tax, low-income tax rates, low property taxes, and no estate taxes.

Should you annuitize? Insurance companies, and more and more employers through their retirement plans, sell annuities that offer the purchaser the hallmarks of a defined benefit pension plan if the annuity is ***annuitized.*** But what does it mean to annuitize your annuity? That sounds crazy. Basically, an annuity is an insurance product that you buy. Say you purchase an annuity for $100,000, and it grows in value, usually at a low rate of 2–3 percent per year. The period of growth is called the accumulation phase. After a period of time, maybe as low as five years or as late as age ninety-five, you can convert the annuity into a monthly stream of payments called annuitization, say $475 a month for as long as you live. $5,700 a year is not a great return on your money, but if you live longer than twenty-four years in which the money is earning 2.5 percent, that starts to become a pretty good deal!

On the positive side, this can be a way to convert some of your retirement savings into regular monthly income that will continue to pay you even if you effectively draw down all the money by living longer than anyone expected. This product provides some protection for the dreaded "outliving your money" scenario. The downside is that if you die sooner than expected, your heirs will not get what is left over from the original assets used to make the annuity purchase, or the return those assets created once they were invested by the insurance company. The money you did not access before your untimely death will be used to pay a stranger who is outliving *her* annuity. Plus, the fees and the lingo in the annuity can be quite large and very confusing, respectively.

These annuity products can get quite fancy, with different riders or contract clauses that allow you to pay two people for as long as one of them lives, or that pay you some excess amount of the original investment to your heirs if you die early. The decision is a very personal one that rides on your risk tolerance, your need for some safety in the form of guaranteed income, and your expectation that you will live longer than the insurance life model predicts. You sacrifice liquidity for safety and growth for longevity. Looking at this option in your fifties will allow you to have some accumulation before you decide about annuitization in the payout phase.

In Your Sixties—Practical Steps and Planning your Legacy

It is finally time to retire. There are a number of practical steps to take. In terms of your retirement savings, it is time to adjust your portfolio to move from accumulation to preservation. This will mean adjusting your asset allocation so that market corrections do not weigh as heavily as you begin your drawdown of assets; that typically means moving out of higher-risk stocks into lower-risk, fixed-income investments such as bonds. When you are young, you have a long time to recover when stock prices fall—indeed, as you've learned, this can make for great buying opportunities. Unfortunately, when you are older, you might need that income, and you definitely don't want to have to sell stock when your investments have lost money. Bad timing, which is completely beyond your control in this case, can undo a decade worth of saving, especially given how volatile the market has become in the last two decades. Still, you don't want to completely shift into bonds even as you get ready to retire, because some market growth will still be required to get you through the thirty years you are likely to spend in retirement. You will still need higher returns to keep up with inflation and stop withdrawal depletion. Depending on your risk tolerance, you will likely want to keep 50–60 percent in the stock market as you get ready to use your funds.

The decade of your sixties is also when you will claim Social Security and choose your Medicare plan. You want to take care of these tasks at the proper time and in the proper way. You have a lot of choice for when to collect Social Security (see the section "Will Social Security Save Me?" below). Also, there are a number of different Medicare plans, each designed for certain retirees. Determining the best plan is a project; you might be thankful for all those class projects you completed in college when you begin to research which medical plan fits your needs best!

Intention and Action Don't Always Match!

You may know some people who don't think it is normal to start saving for retirement at an early age. Before reading this book, you may have thought the same! We all know someone who hasn't saved enough, perhaps because they didn't start soon enough. One study shows that 40 percent of American workers have less than $10,000 saved for retirement.[6] If you have heard of the *retirement savings crisis,*[7] now you know what that means! Individually, we do not do a good job of matching the savings targets that prudent financial management suggests we need. Too many retirees count on Social Security as a primary source of income in retirement. One consequence is that some of us will end up working longer than planned, or working part time, in order to make ends meet during retirement. Finally, many of us will be trying to save a big chunk of money in midcareer, trying to catch up to the amount desired in retirement. As you've learned, though, this is an inefficient strategy. Without the benefits of longer-term compounding, you may end up having to save five to seven times more than you otherwise would if you had not waited until you were mid-career!

What You "Should" Save versus What Americans "Do" Save

The truth is, the amount of money that people think they need to save and the amount they actually do save still differ from the targets recommended by financial professionals. Even though American workers suggest that they are confident about retirement, other survey questions reveal they don't have the resources to make true retirement a real possibility without a lot of late saving and stress. Much of this disconnect occurs because folks don't really realize the targets for saving that they are shooting toward. Though never a perfect measure for everyone, a few aspirational guidelines, based on income level and age, can at least give you a sense of where the retirement savings targets lie.

The following figure is an average for how much *should* be saved, by age, according to several different financial wealth firms. Notice that as a person ages, the benchmark is to save total current salary times a certain number. So, at the age of thirty, a person should have two years' worth of their current salary (2x, with the x standing for times) saved for retirement. Note that this representation is just a benchmark and not a guarantee, so individuals must think through their own individual positions to accommodate for life circumstances or market conditions. Each wealth management firm provides this average guidance under the caveat that the models used do not guarantee investment results and are based on various assumptions a person might make in terms of what to invest in, how much to draw down once retired, and how long the money must last. The information is an average of the targets provided by several firms in the wealth management industry.

6. Ellen Stark, *Expanding Retirement Security through Public and Private Innovation*, Aspen Institute Financial Security Program, September 2018, https://assets.aspeninstitute.org/content/uploads/2018/08/2018_RetirementSavingsReport.pdf.
7. Diane Oakley and Kelly Kenneally, "Retirement Security 2017: A Roadmap for Policy Makers: Americans' Views of the Retirement Crisis and Solutions," National Institute on Retirement Security, February 2017, https://www.nirsonline.org/wp-content/uploads/2017/06/2017_opinion_nirs_final_web.pdf.

FIGURE 7.1 Retirement Savings Target Averages by Age

It is worthwhile to think a bit about why there are ranges for suggested retirement savings at each age. Most of the models employed in the wealth advisory industry assume that your salary is increasing over time, but the percentage of salary growth often ends up being different across different models. Each advisory firm also makes different assumptions about risk tolerance, or about the average return on investment before and after retirement. It is best to use the target as just that—a target to shoot toward—because your choices may be different from the wealth firm's assumptions.

One thing that is true across any of the models is that the higher your salary, the more you will need in retirement to maintain your standard of living. Your retirement savings is expressed as some multiple of your current income, before savings and before taxes. No one wants to stop working only to find that they can't live to the standard that they are used to. Typically, the models assume that ***retirees seek to replace 70–90*** percent ***of preretirement income*** and intend to ***withdraw approximately 4*** percent ***from savings each year in retirement.*** On the brink of retirement, most people wish they had started to save sooner. Does it help to tell you that, later on, you are going to wish you had started to save for this sooner?

You see, many Americans may not be saving as much for retirement as is recommended by financial planners, and many start the saving and investing process quite late. Even though the United States has seen considerable improvement in income since the Great Recession in 2008, the percentage of workers planning and saving for retirement is relatively unchanged over the last ten years, especially for women.[8] When you look at retirement preparation from the perspective of income level, the results are not surprising: those with more income think more about retirement and are more likely to have retirement accounts through their employers. Further, the trends within income levels have not changed significantly over time.[9]

The data for savings by age is interesting. Figure 7.2 shows retirement savings over time for ten-year cohort groups. The amount of savings before the age thirty is low and flat, showing that young adults don't have the means to save or have much interest in saving, though there is some. Starting with 2010 right after

8. Judy T. Lin, Christopher Bumcrot, Tippy Ulicny, Gary Mottola, Gerri Walsh, Robert Ganem, Christine Kieffer, and Annamaria Lusardi, "The State of U.S. Financial Capability: The 2018 National Financial Capability Study," FINRA Investor Education Foundation, June 2019, p. 17, https://www.usfinancialcapability.org/downloads/NFCS.

9. Lin et al., "National Financial Capability Study."

the Great Recession, the other age cohorts do look like they are saving a bit more, and as expected, each cohort has more savings as they age. From the late thirties through the early fifties, the savings pattern is similar for the last ten years, but the fifty-five-plus group has really picked up their savings.

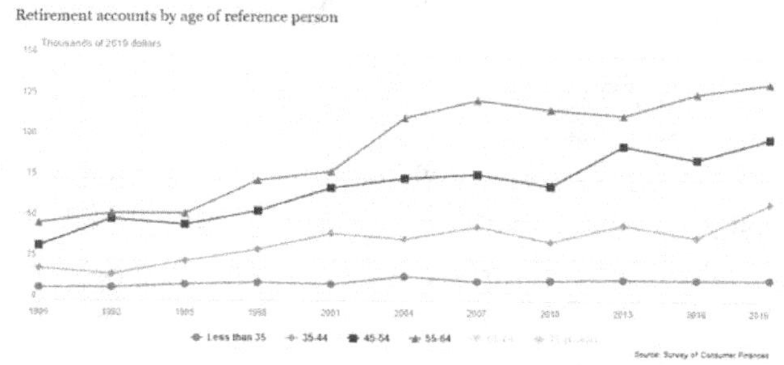

FIGURE 7.2 Average Actually Saved by Age

What is more surprising, a 2014 study of households around the world found that as many as one-third of American households live without savings or other liquid assets. Liquid assets are basically cash, or savings and investments that can easily be turned into cash. This one-third of American households, by the way, ***includes two-thirds of wealthy households***. These Americans spend their entire paycheck every month and possess only nonliquid assets, like homes and retirement accounts.[10] Americans tend to consume their income immediately, whether or not they are wealthy. Not saving well happens across class, income level, and gender in the United States.

Over the last half-century, the trend has been toward lower and lower rates of saving, though the trend has recently reversed. Before the pandemic, the personal savings rate in the United States over the last fifty years fell from above 12 percent in the '70s to a paltry 3.8 percent in 2008. The pandemic during 2020 has encouraged a much higher rate of savings, though—as high as 33 percent! This was a drastic move upward from the relatively flat and somber 7 percent between 2013 and 2019.[11]

Given the way that compounding works, losing the time to save makes the process a lot more stressful. Also, as a young person, you have more ability to tolerate risk in the stock market because you have the time to rebound from market corrections, even large ones. This flexibility means you can allocate more of your assets to stocks early on in your career. While Social Security does still exist and is very likely to persist in some form by the time you retire, it will not provide all the income needed to prosper in the golden years.

Typical Pauses to the Best-Laid Plans

Many workers intend to save for retirement and set up the plan to do so, but life events can distract, and the best-laid plans can get bumped. The pull on the best intentions can be fierce. Unexpected job changes or

10. Greg Kaplan, Giovanni L. Violante, and Justin Weidner. "The Wealthy Hand-to-Mouth" [Working paper 20073], National Bureau of Economic Research, https://www.nber.org/system/files/working_papers/w20073/w20073.pdf.
11. JEC Republicans and Senator Mike Lee, "Saving and COVID-19," United States Congress Joint Economic Committee, September 30, 2020, https://www.jec.senate.gov/public/index.cfm/republicans/analysis?ID=754B52C6-04CD-458B-8755-98D1219398F1.

career shifts, additions to the family that come unexpectedly, the escalating cost of buying a home, or medical emergencies can require liquid resources fast, where the obvious solution might seem to be retirement savings. Resist the call of the funds if you can help it. Money that is meant for tomorrow should not be used today. Be on the lookout for the following retirement savings "absorbers."

Job Changes

Resist the urge to touch the retirement savings allocation if it is in a retirement plan at work and you are changing jobs. The US Bureau of Labor Statistics reported in January 2018 that the average number of job changes for an individual is twelve times! Gone are the days when a person worked for the same company for thirty-plus years. Typically, any retirement account invested under a defined contribution plan such as a 401(k) can be transferred to a new account with a new company. This is known as a ***rollover***. However, because job transitioning can be a financial stressor, and because your job retirement plan may offer the option to cash out your retirement savings when you leave, it can seem easy and tempting to do that.

For instance, you may change jobs quite a few times early in your career. My little brother is in sales and when he experienced a job shift early on, he would clean out the savings in his retirement plan as he walked out the door. He did not always need the funds, but the retirement resources never seemed to quite make it to the rollover. Once you see the money, it can be quite difficult not to spend it! While there are times when it does make sense to touch this money, it can be difficult to figure out which times those are.

You may have every intention of reinvesting the money into a new plan at a new job, but the cash out will come with taxes and penalties, and the intention to reinvest can get lost if a new position is not found immediately. This is what your emergency savings are for. If you have that fund in place first, you should not have to touch the retirement savings. Once you are in the new job, you can roll over your assets to an IRA without losing any of the funds to taxation or penalty.

Do the Most for Your Kids by Saving for Your Retirement

With the knowledge you have gained in this book, and with a good deal of careful planning, you should have no trouble saving the right amount for retirement. But be aware that as you get older, other financial priorities can seem to take precedence, because retirement seems so far away. One competing goal for your savings will be your kids' college education.

Retirement savings should happen before the college fund. It used to be the case that children moved up in the world to do better than their parents. In such a world, relying on your kids to support you in your old age did not seem to be such a burden. After all, your parents put a lot of time and energy into raising you so that you could be successful. The least you can do is return the favor to them later in life, right?

There are lots of ways to get to college and lots of funding opportunities for those who wish to go. Good students can earn college scholarships, even if they are not lucky enough to go to a school like Berea College, where there is a "no tuition guarantee" for all students. For instance, community colleges in Tennessee cut the price tag of a good education in half by providing two years of college to students. Private college price tags may look startling, but good students can get lots of financial help. Public universities also have residency guidelines that lower tuition. But even though you will want to help your kids pay for college, try to remember that ***there are no scholarships for retirement***, unless you count Social Security, and that is not really enough to support you.

Your greatest gift to your children is *not* to be a burden on them later in life, when they have their own families and are dealing with their own financial plans.

Of course, long before your kids go to college, they may go to daycare. When a good friend of mine had kids for the first time, he joked to me that everyone tells you to start saving for college right away, but no one tells you that you will face a college-savings-sized payment immediately if you use childcare while you are working. While costs differ greatly by location, and by the age of the child for whom you are seeking care, childcare cost between $450 (Mississippi) and $2,000 (Washington, DC) per month on average, depending on the state, in 2020.[12] If you are choosing to use childcare, the assumption is that you either have no choice or are better off financially for making this choice. Unfortunately, sometimes people—particularly women—have to make the choice that it makes better financial sense to leave the workforce for a few years when their children are young.

Finally, remember that both childcare and college savings can be paid for through tax-advantaged savings accounts and flexible spending accounts provided by employers. Childcare, by the way, can be defined quite broadly—for instance, I have recently learned that some summer camps can be paid for out of tax-free accounts, including the Cincinnati Reds summer baseball camp my son will be doing this year!

Bad Luck and Hardship

The National Financial Capability Study (NFCS) found that hardship withdrawals from 401(k) plans have been rising among eighteen- to thirty-four-year-olds since 2009.[13] Rarely does life offer us lemonade right away or all the time; unfortunately, the handout can sometimes be an armful of lemons.

If a catastrophe occurs, as a last resort, look into the option for a loan against your retirement savings. This way, you do not face the 10 percent penalties of early withdrawal on your retirement savings. You may also get a better interest rate because your loan is collateralized. But be clear: the decision to borrow means that the payback may subvert your savings goals somewhat.

This is all to say that a good financial plan will both anticipate these threats to retirement savings and plan accordingly for them. Remember, you have time on your side, and if you have to save less when the kids are young or divert some of your savings to a college fund when they are older, you should be fine, as long as you have accounted for these additional expenses.

If you are making the savings match at work and putting back the 10–15 percent for your retirement, *then* think about saving some for the kids' education—particularly if you have made it past the childcare stage! Like saving for retirement, saving for college might be accomplished with a little planning.

12. Economic Policy Institute, "The Cost of Child Care in ____," updated October 2020, https://www.epi.org/child-care-costs-in-the-united-states/#/WY.
13. Lin et al., "National Financial Capability Study," 9. *The National Financial Capability Study (NFCS) is a project of the FINRA Investor Education Foundation (FINRA Foundation).*

Different Financial Challenges for Young Adults Today

To be fair, the financial challenges faced by young people today are not the ones faced by their great-grandparents after World War I. An article in *The Wall Street Journal* says it well: "Your Parents' Financial Advice Is (Kind of) Wrong."[14] The article points out that certain items in our budgets, like student loan debt and rent or mortgage payments, have far outpaced inflation over the last twenty years. This means it takes a lot longer to pay down those student loans and to save for the down payment on the house. We are talking decades longer! In this environment, the inability to save and thrive is not a personal failing of the young, as some older generations might claim. The financial world is now fundamentally different for young adults, and this means that classic financial advice may no longer apply.

To make things even worse, the process of increased generational wealth may be breaking down in the new millennium. We seem to be moving into a time when the next generation will take a bit longer to get on its feet financially. Getting a career you want and getting established seems a lot more difficult today, and the longer this takes, the less able our young adults will be to take on the additional expenses of caring for their parents.

What Is My Financial Independence Number?

Several years ago, a financial advisory firm advertised their services by showing people walking around a city carrying a big number. The numbers were different, but the people shown were doing different things: painting, jumping in a pool, loading the number in an overhead bin of a plane, walking the dog. You get the idea. In the ad, an announcer tells viewers that everyone has their own number—the amount that person needs to retire comfortably. "Call us, we will help you find your number."[15] There is great peace of mind for the holders of the number, or so the commercial implies. The poor schlub who is working in his own yard with a "gazillion" sitting on his hedge is rumpled and confused. His neighbor, who lightly carries his $1,000,000 while walking his beagle, is neatly dressed, cool, and confident.

I don't know whether that advertising campaign was successful, but there is some evidence that many people do not know the number that signals their readiness to retire. Only about 40 percent of Americans have even tried to figure out how much income they will need for retirement.[16] Perhaps it all feels too complicated, too big, or too scary. How does anyone know what they will really need to live on in forty years? My students don't seem worried by this calculation. Usually, they are more focused on the million dollars the man is carrying around and see the expectation of needing a million dollars to retire comfortably as completely ludicrous. And scary! One perspective might be that there is no chance to reach that kind of number ever, so why bother?

14. Julia Carpenter, "Your Parents' Financial Advice Is (Kind of) Wrong," *The Wall Street Journal*, September 16, 2019, https://www.wsj.com/articles/your-parents-financial-advice-is-kind-of-wrong-11568367000.
15. ING marketing campaign from 2008–2011. See https://www.youtube.com/watch?v=gn1j13dn-ul for an example.
16. Lin et al., "National Financial Capability Study," 17.

A Million Dollars Is Not as Much as You Think It Is

The trick is to pick a retirement savings target that is specific to your needs and circumstances. This is sometimes called your financial independence number (FIN), or your ***number*** for short, and that is the number that people were carrying around in the commercial. Many specialists argue that your retirement savings should not be reduced to a single number like this, but having a goal in mind as you get started is helpful if it provides a target that keeps you motivated. A goal can be the thing that helps you stay focused and committed to an activity that seems like it will take way too long to achieve. But that goal can change.

There are many ways to calculate your FIN, but at the most basic level, it is the sum of your living expenses per year multiplied by twenty-five or thirty, which is a back-of-the-envelope way to capture your years in retirement. Fidelity Investments argues that your retirement income should be 50–80 percent of your final preretirement salary.[17] Thus, if you are making $100,000 just before you retire, you will want $50,000 to $80,000 a year to cover your expenses in retirement. Depending on the lifestyle you hope to have, annual expenses could be a little more or less. Remember the earlier "lifestyle in retirement" questions?

To get a little fancier and recognize the fact that most of your retirement savings will stay invested during your retirement so that it can continue to grow, and that prices may rise a bit throughout your time in retirement, your FIN at the start of retirement can be calculated to:

$968,153–$1,549,044 in total savings[18]

Suddenly, the $1 million carried around by the guy walking his dog in the commercial does not seem so unreasonable.

The challenge is that early in your career, it is difficult to even begin to answer the questions you need to answer in order to approximate your FIN. Life events categorically change your answers. Career shifts, whether good or bad, can completely upend entirely reasonable plans. That is OK. The key is to revisit your retirement plan every so often, to check in with your choices, so that if you wish to make changes you can do so with as little stress or loss of sleep as possible. It seems almost impossible to know what your income will be right before it is time to retire, but it is a good bet that you will need more than the average person today needs, if only because of inflation over forty years.

Do not get hung up on your FIN! This number gets you started on the path to having a plan. But you need to revisit it as life happens, most typically in your forties and fifties (see the section on "Retirement Planning by Decade" above). If you get to a place where you don't have enough, you can save more, work longer, or live more cheaply.

Finally, remember that million-dollar figure? As we showed you in chapter 1, figure 1.2, it's well within your reach. You can get there by saving $2,400 per year (which is just $200 per month) for forty years.

17. Fidelity Viewpoints, "How Much Will You Spend in Retirement?" April 9, 2019, https://www.fidelity.com/viewpoints/retirement/spending-in-retirement.
18. Authors' calculations assuming an inflation rate of 2 percent on average and a required return on investment of 5 percent in retirement. For those who want to do this calculation for their own expected amount: Savings Needed = [Income/(R – g)] * {1 – [(1+g)/(1+R)]^30}, where R=5 percent, g=2 percent, Income is $50,000 or $80,000, and thirty is the expected time in retirement.

Turning Savings into Income in Retirement

Making the shift from accumulating savings to drawing down savings requires a little thought and a big mental adjustment. Imagine how you will feel. You will have spent thirty to forty years putting these funds aside, never touching them, and now it will finally be time to spend! How does the typical retiree do that without accidentally spending too much?

Your biggest issue becomes how to live well without running out of money.

It will become much harder to replace your income once you stop working, and once you have retired, suddenly, time is no longer on your side in terms of compounding your money and riding out the rough times of price volatility in the market. How much of your nest egg should you spend in any given year?

The 70–90 percent ***replacement rate range*** for your income says that most of us won't need quite as much income to live on after retiring as we did when we were working. Besides the obvious fact that you are not saving 10–15 percent of your income anymore, it is also likely that some of your highest expenses, your mortgage and your kids, are in the rearview mirror by the time you retire. Also, the clothing budget and car needs may fall a bit, too. The range for the replacement rate is here, though, to allow you to consider whether you might spend a bit more in retirement, either through travel and fancy living or because of increased medical costs. The big unknown can be medical costs, especially in situations where a nursing home is needed. Being aware of these issues for your particular situation will tell you whether your target should be at a 70 percent or 90 percent replacement rate; if you want to travel, then use the higher percentage.

The ***4 percent withdrawal rate*** for how much to take from retirement each year comes from a relatively famous academic article, colloquially known as the ***Trinity Study***, named for the university where the authors worked.[19] In this study the authors used historical rates of return in stocks and bond indices to ask: if you had retired between 1926 and 1995, what withdrawal rate could you have employed over different payout periods without running out of savings? So, for instance, if you retired in 1926 and took 4 percent out of a 50 percent bonds/50 percent stock portfolio each year, did the money last for thirty years? What if you started that thirty-year retirement in 1965? The study looked at 200 different scenarios, considering different asset allocations between stock and bonds for payout periods from fifteen to thirty years, to examine withdrawal rates from 3 percent to 12 percent. Their findings showed that an allocation of 50 percent stocks/50 percent bonds outlasted withdrawal rates of 3–5 percent for each fifteen- to thirty-year payout period, *every time*, between 1926 and 1995. Thus, you could have retired at any thirty-year start date within their sample and had your money last for up to thirty years, if you drew down from your nest egg between 3–5 percent per year.

Since it is in the middle of the withdrawal range, the 4 percent rate specifically became the focus of a conservative spending rule for not outliving your money, even in historical periods of significant downturns, including the Great Depression. This is a guideline, though, and it may not hold true for every *future* scenario and its set of returns. If you happen to retire at a time in which returns are more negative than those during the Great Depression, for the first several years after you stop working, your retirement nest egg can take

19. Philip L. Cooley, Carl M. Hubbard, and Daniel T. Walz. "Retirement Savings: Choosing a Withdrawal Rate That Is Sustainable," *AAII Journal* 20, no. 2 (1998): 16–21.

such a hit that it will not recover, and your money won't last for the thirty years. There is a chance that this could happen.

Also, the model used by the authors did not account for management fees or taxes, which are items that can diminish your savings well beyond the 4 percent for any given year. In reality, it might be difficult to keep your rate of withdrawal level throughout your retirement time. You may want to travel early on, while you still can. Also, after age seventy-two, you will face required minimum distributions (RMDs), where the IRS ***requires*** seniors to withdraw funds in tax-advantaged accounts using a formula that is often a bit greater than 4 percent. The IRS is anxious to take their slice of the pie in taxes.

Given that individual circumstances and economic conditions in the market will require you to think more critically beyond any simple rate of withdrawal, however, this 4 percent guideline can still serve as an initial starting point for moving forward on your path to retirement. In a year when the portfolio falls, you can either consider limiting the withdrawal and tightening your belt a bit for that year or focus your withdrawal from your bond holdings, then allowing yourself to increase the withdrawal by inflation in solid-performing years. This adds some flexibility to your living-in-retirement plans. The text box below considers the withdrawal strategy in more detail.

WITHDRAWAL STRATEGIES

Fixed $ or %. Retirees can draw the same dollar or percentage amount each year. If you use a dollar amount, you will notice the crunch on your standard of living when inflation is high. This can be a simple rule to follow, and you have the benefit of knowing how to plan your expenses ahead of time. If you draw a fixed percentage from your nest egg, you will have a higher annual income when your investments do well and less when the market performs poorly. You may not know your income for the next year until the end of the year, and if the percentage you choose is too high, you may face running out of funds late in your retirement.

4% rule. This is the starting percentage you use in the first year of retirement. For each year going forward, you will increase the draw by the percentage rate of inflation. This rule can work well in most situations, unless there are very negative returns on your money, usually early in retirement. That can be difficult to come back from once you are in retirement.

Bucket. This strategy pulls money from the market during good times for the most profitable investments, such that you have liquid income for three to five years at any point in time in a good savings account or a money market fund, much like you do in your emergency savings. You only pull returns from the market when they are strong, so that you do not have to sell investments in a down year. If returns are not good one year, you can live on the liquid cash. Once returns rebound, then you can pour funds from the market bucket into the liquid, super-charged emergency savings bucket. Note the downside: a sizeable chunk of funds is not making a great return.

Flexible based on market return. You can customize your withdrawal strategy to reflect market return and the 4% percent rule. Take 4 percent in the first year of retirement. If the market performs well, adjust your draw for inflation, but if the market has a down year, only take the fixed 4 percent. Once the market returns become positive again, you can increase your drawdown by inflation once again. Allowing yourself to be flexible in what you take can help you extend the life of that nest egg without requiring that you cut your spending unreasonably.

The strategy you choose must ensure that you will not run out of money. This can be a stressor once you move into retirement. The flipside of avoiding not having enough resources is the job of planning your legacy. This is discussed in the last section of this chapter, "The Decision to Give Back."

Will Social Security Save Me?

Back in chapter 2, "The Decision to Earn," the focus on your paycheck taught you that we all contribute to the Social Security and Medicare programs throughout our working lives, with the expectation of full benefits when it is our turn to retire. Remember the 12.4 percent Social Security portion of the FICA tax that you and your employer split the payment for on every paycheck? That money goes into a trust fund to pay the retirement benefits of current retirees. Any extra money is invested by the government in a trust fund to be used to support future retirement or disability benefits for its citizens. So, the baby boomer generation that is living in retirement today contributed to this program throughout their working careers in order to support older generations back then, and now it is their turn to collect from the system, based on the contributions made by the Millennials working today. Someday, it will be your turn to move from contributing to Social Security to collecting from it. We all put money into this mandatory kitty and draw from it when it is our turn. It is not surprising that retirees feel entitled to their benefits in this system. The benefits are a promise from our government, and we have relied on them in planning our financial lives.

One perspective might be that the government requires us all to "save" for retirement through this system of taxation and that this entitles us to a worthy and comfortable retirement with good medical insurance once we stop working. Right? Well, sort of. The US government created this program as a way to ensure that its elderly and disabled citizens would have ***some*** financial security in retirement or in situations of disability, but it was never designed to provide all the income a retiree would need in retirement, only about 40 percent.[20] So, from the get-go, retirees faced a gap between the income they were used to and the benefits they were eligible to receive.

From our saving behavior, it looks like way too many of the older people in our lives are counting on Social Security to provide the bulk of their retirement income. Perhaps they don't recognize the inherent

20. Center on Budget and Policy Priorities, "Top Ten Facts about Social Security," August 30, 2020, https://www.cbpp.org/sites/default/files/atoms/files/8-8-16socsec.pdf.

limits of the system, because as the last sections made clear, they are not saving enough to make up the difference between income needs and Social Security benefits. Going forward, this may not be the best plan for anyone because beyond the limits of the plan for income replacement, it now looks like the system has been stretched a bit, with the trust fund of savings quickly depleting over time. Some may question whether they can count on Social Security benefits as their grandparents did.

Social Security Will Exist, but It Won't Be Enough to Live On

My best advice is that as you start your personal financial journey, plan your retirement so that you don't have to count on Social Security for retirement income. Prepare as if you can't count on it, because the best financial position is not to need it when you reach retirement. It would be very surprising if the Federal government eliminated the Social Security program entirely, but over the next forty years, it is likely to go through major changes. People may be nudged to retire later and, possibly, to accept less in benefits. However, assuming that you do get your share of Social Security, or at least something, this will be a nice bonus in addition to that which you have already saved.

The depletion of the Social Security trust fund is not a new idea, and academics have debated the implications of it for a long time. When I was in graduate school twenty years ago, a hot topic was the inevitable bankruptcy of the Social Security system. There was firm conviction that current workers would not be able to support the generation known as baby boomers in their retirement. The baby boomer generation is a BIG group of people, and the fear was that too many retirees would be making claims and that not as many workers would be paying the tax to fund the program.

The numbers made sense. Current workers fund the retirement benefits paid to current retirees. Actually, the system is one of the more efficient programs administered by the Federal government. For every dollar dedicated to the program, $.85 is allocated toward those receiving retirement benefits, and $.15 goes to those with disabilities. The cost of administering this is less than $.01 of every dollar contributed.[21] And, no doubt, the program provides benefits to a lot of people. The Social Security Administration reports that sixty-five million people earned monthly benefits in the program, based on contributions from 180 million workers, in 2020. That means that 2.76 workers contribute to the benefits for every retiree out there. That is just not enough! A little data will help to clarify the point.

TABLE 7.1 Ratio between Workers and Retirees in Social Security over Time[22]

Year	Workers (in millions)	Beneficiaries (in millions)	Ratio
1940	35.39	.222	159.4
1960	72.530	14.262	5.1
1980	113.656	35.118	3.2

21. Social Security Administration, *Understanding the Benefits*, May 2021, https://www.ssa.gov/pubs/EN-05-10024.pdf.
22. Social Security Administration, *Understanding the Benefits*, data as of June 2020.

2000	155.295	45.166	3.4
2010	156.725	53.398	2.9
2020	180	65	2.76

The number of people working and retiring has gone up over time, but the ratio between the two has diminished considerably. You can see in table 7.1 that the number of active workers per retiree has fallen from 159.4 to 2.76 workers per retiree since the program's inception. For the system to be stable, we need three workers per retiree to contribute to the system, and the actual number has crept below that threshold, beginning in 2010. This means that unless more money is put into Social Security, the program will only be able to pay 76 percent of the benefits that have been promised to workers when they retire after 2034.[23]

Congress may add resources to Social Security, but it is unknown when or by how much. It is probably a good bet that the bulk of Social Security will remain untouched because politicians cannot vote it down. Every voter is expecting to receive some benefits, and we are all related to someone who is currently receiving benefits. To change something that hurts everyone is political suicide. The likeliest outcome is that our politicians will reduce benefits at the upper end of the income distribution. Earners there only get a small percentage of their incomes replaced by Social Security anyway, which imposes less pain on them and saves the system a good bit because the payments going to the very wealthy are the biggest payments going out.

The baby boomers are well into their retirement today, and the program still stands, so my professors that argued that the sky would fall on retirees exaggerated a bit. To this crisis in funding, add that the benefits promised by Social Security only cover about 40 percent of the spending needs for retirees. Living on Social Security payments alone will be difficult in the future. Recognize these limits and plan around it.

How Social Security Benefits Are Determined

Anyone who earns forty credits in the Social Security system is eligible for benefits when they retire. Since you can earn up to four credits a year, it takes a minimum of ten years to qualify for the program. The credits are earned based on your wages, so in 2020, you could get four credits by earning $5,880 that year.

Your Social Security benefit is based on your highest thirty-five years of income while you are working. If you leave the workforce for a period of time, those years have zeroes, but the years do not have to be sequential to count, so working later or for more than thirty-five years can bump a zero year. Your benefits are adjusted for inflation over time.

As with any governmental program, the rules for claiming your Social Security benefits are pretty confusing, and that will probably not change. But some basic rules are reviewed in the next text box.

23. Social Security Administration, "Status of the Social Security and Medicare Programs: A Summary of the 2020 Annual Reports," accessed April 15, 2021, https://www.ssa.gov/oact/trsum/.

GENERAL RULES FOR THE SIZE AND TIMING OF SOCIAL SECURITY BENEFITS

Each person has to choose when to collect their Social Security. Individuals can start taking benefits as early as age sixty-two, but the benefit amount can be as much as 30 percent less than if you wait for full retirement to claim. No one knows what the gap will be by the time you are ready to retire, but hopefully, you won't have to work until you are ninety! You can even earn 8 percent more per year between sixty-five and seventy years of age by waiting to make that claim.

Most financial experts stress that waiting as long as you can in order to maximize the payout, if you are healthy, is the best plan. The thinking goes that individuals tend to live longer than they think they will (currently life expectancy runs into the nineties) and that having the additional benefit later in life tends to pay off. Of course, if you die early, you don't get anything. You may be tempted to take any amount allowed as soon as possible, thinking that having the funds now is preferable to later, because there is more to do when you are at the younger end of retirement. This seems reasonable if you are using the benefits as an extra cushion and not completely relying on them to make ends meet.

Partnership has its advantages when it comes to claiming benefits. You can claim half of your spouse's benefits, as long as they have entered the system to claim benefits. And you may want to do that if your partner makes a lot more money than you do, because your benefit allotment is bigger the more you made over your lifetime. So, if your benefit is $1,000 but your spouse's benefit is $3,000, as long as your spouse is making a claim for their own benefits, you are entitled to $1,500 per month, a $500 bonus for you both. If you are female and you have a husband who is older than you, and you are the big bread winner in your household, this benefit works against him. That scenario is much more likely today than it was fifty years ago, when the program was designed!

Even if you are now divorced from a partner, this spousal benefit may be open to you. If you were married for ten years, are still single, and are over sixty-two, you can make a claim based on your spouse's record to get up to 50 percent of the benefit the divorced spouse is eligible to claim.

Also, there is something called a "surviving spouse" benefit. If the partner has died, checking to see where your benefits are the highest is strategic and smart. If you are at full retirement age, you get 100 percent of the benefit your spouse was claiming. Or, if the spouse died before claiming benefits, you get 100 percent of what the spouse could have claimed.

Be aware, however, that some public employees will not have the option to claim benefits in the Social Security system. In some states, those who are employed by the state and enrolled in a state pension system are ineligible to receive Social Security benefits for themselves or for their spouse. Many public school teachers are limited in this way.

To summarize, Social Security benefits can add a nice monthly check to your income in retirement. The maximum benefit is a little over $3,400 per month,[24] but the average benefit check is $1,543 per month in 2021, according to the American Association of Retired Persons (AARP).[25] Whatever your benefit, it will be hard to live on Social Security alone, as it was never designed to be your only source of income in retirement. If you have a bigger benefit, it is because you made more in your working life and are used to a higher standard of living.

Because of the changes in the demographics of the American workforce, the best spot to be in is one where you do not need Social Security to support your retirement.

What Legacy Will I Leave? The Decision to Give Back

To conclude this chapter, consider the following thought experiment. Imagine that you've made it to retirement. Congratulations! If you have followed the advice in this book generally, and in this chapter specifically, you can count on steady, reliable income for many years to come. You may not be wealthy, but you are financially secure. Hopefully, you have a little extra to buy that vintage Corvette you've always wanted or to travel the world. Or perhaps you just want a nice RV to park at your children's house for an uncomfortably long time. Whatever it is you've always wanted but have never had the time for, or felt financially secure enough to buy before, now's the time. Enjoy it while you can! Because you can't take it with you. Perhaps you've seen the bumper sticker: "He Who Dies with the Most Toys Still Dies."

Though this discussion may have taken a bit of a somber turn, the point is this: there is a possibility that after doing everything financially "right," you may have to leave this world earlier than you wanted to, with extra funds still left to spend. This is a reasonably good problem to have, even though you are leaving money on the table, which I urged you never to do (if you could help it) in chapter 3, "The Decision to Save." One financial worry in this chapter has been outliving your money, but the question of what to do with leftover money after you are gone is also a worthy consideration. Think about your legacy and the stewardship of all your resources while you were here. What will you leave behind?

24. Social Security Administration, "Workers with Maximum-Taxable Earnings," accessed May 13, 2021, https://www.ssa.gov/oact/cola/examplemax.html.
25. American Association of Retired Persons, "How Much Social Security Will I Get?" Retirement: Social Security Resource Center, December 23, 2020, https://www.aarp.org/retirement/social-security/questions-answers/how-much-social-security-will-i-get.html.

Your Legacy Is Fundamental to How You Live Your Life

What you leave behind is as important a retirement consideration as the decision to save for retirement in the first place, especially if you are not just saving for yourself. Many of you will have children and grandchildren, and even if you don't, I hope that you may wish to leave something behind to support a cause that you believe in. If you don't have leftover resources, you will have put yourself in a much more tenuous financial situation than the lessons of this book have envisioned for you.

Legacy planning is the new estate planning. The idea of estate planning is a holdover from an era in which only the wealthy had anything to leave behind, and that came in the form of property in some way or another. All the Carnegie Libraries across the United States are testaments to the great philanthropy of the estate-planning era, as are Vanderbilt University and the National Forest lands around the Biltmore Estate in North Carolina and Bar Harbor, Maine. We have our national park system because Teddy Roosevelt saw the value in keeping that beauty available to all of us. Of course, he was our president, and that gift was very large; all of us paid for that gift then and now through our taxes. But none of this means that you have to be ***super rich*** to consider what you want to leave behind and how you want to target your resources to make a difference.

Nowadays, wealth does not take only the form of an estate, and it includes a great deal more than property. It is possible for nearly all of us to leave something behind, if we make good financial decisions, whether we leave property, investments, or savings. And all of us will leave a legacy, whether that comes in the form of the wealth we leave behind, the good works that we do, or the (hopefully) good things that people will remember and say about us after we are gone.

Thinking more about tomorrow and making decisions today with the long run in mind, has taken on new meaning in the last thirty years among modern corporations. Investors today will often look at a firm's environmental, social, and governance (ESG) score as a filter for whether management is situating the firm to be a force in its market for the long run. Because investors today care about what they are investing in, it has become important to understand what a firm is doing to protect the environment around them, to see how they treat their workers and the workers in their global supply chain, and to be clear about the institutions in place to insure that management is looking out for the long term health and wealth of the corporation.[26] At first, the finance industry viewed the companies that expended resources on the environment or offered generous benefits towards their workers as making wasteful uses of free cash flow. Only in the last thirty years did it became clear that the firms that addressed these issues in the short run actually positioned themselves to be more profitable over the long run.[27] Such thoughtful consideration of what is important in the long run also applies to your personal financial decisions! The findings about firms that stress ESG in their decisions were a result of investors looking for places to invest that synced with personal values, but

26. This might be something that is important to you too! If you are interested in looking at the ESG scores for different companies, you can look in three places for free: on Yahoo! Finance for any ticker under the "sustainability" tab, on S&P Global.com at https://www.spglobal.com/esg/scores/results?cid=4097175, or at Censible.co at https://esg.censible.co/companies. Search under the ticker for the company you are interested knowing more about in this regard.
27. There are many sources for this view of the corporation, but one newer source that tracks the way that returns on a firm are increased is: Guido Giese, Linda-Eling Lee, Dimitris Melas, Zoltán Nagy, and Laura Nishikawa, "Foundations of ESG Investing: How ESG Affects Equity Valuation, Risk, and Performance," *The Journal of Portfolio Management* 45, no. 5 (2019): 69–83.

the lesson for making choices today with ramifications that extend beyond our time here should apply to our personal lives as well.

If you start thinking about the legacy you want to leave now, you will make better financial decisions in the long run. I have a friend who has an amazing ability to calculate the time value of money for everything in his head nearly instantaneously. For instance, if you are contemplating buying a new home theater system, he would tell you that the $1,000 you are thinking about spending will be $10,000 in thirty years! While I don't necessarily recommend making' this calculation every time you are thinking about springing for dessert at dinner, I do think there is value in the mindset. Every time my friend contemplates an important purchase, he is basically asking, *is this consistent with the legacy I want to leave behind*? What could that $10,000 do for you in retirement, or for your grandchildren? What could it do for your favored charities, or for your alma mater?

The fact is, if you do save enough to have a comfortable, secure retirement, you will leave something behind, if for no other reason than that you don't know exactly how long you will spend in retirement. A good plan saves more than you think you will need.

Manage Your Resources through Planning and Stewardship

This book is about financial literacy, yes, and it offers you tools and techniques for planning a stable financial position. But the steps I have given you are really about ordering your life. The planning tools you now have will help you, whether you make a lot of money in your career or choose to dedicate your work to something that is really valuable to you, or both! Hopefully both. The mindset you assume, in thinking about your money and the resources you have, really matters. Because being financially responsible is not really about the stuff you will be able to acquire (though I joke about the classic Corvette that I *will* have one day); it is much more about how you lead your life and the ways in which you focus your time and money.

I encourage you to do more than be the owner of your wealth. Also be a manager of your resources, and use a ***stewardship mindset*** as you decide:

- Where you want to live and work
- How much to save
- What you allocate to spend
- Where you owe
- Why you invest
- When you retire

A steward is the person responsible for taking care of an organization or a property on behalf of others. Having the stewardship mindset empowers you to oversee and protect your resources and to be responsible for your choices, with preservation at the forefront. Rather than thinking only about yourself, you can think about the wider community in which you live, and which you value. You can look for ways to give back your time and money to things that are important to you.

Recognizing that you are the manager of all you possess can help you create your "identity." Your financial decisions are driven by your needs, and by some of your wants, but also by what you care about.

Remember the research on wants and needs and true happiness? People were happier when they spent their money in altruistic ways. This is particularly true later in life, when there is more time to volunteer. Research shows that retirees who have an altruistic attitude and find opportunities to make a difference experience greater satisfaction.[28]

Take a moment of introspection. Compile a list of priorities in your life. Once you rank this list, brainstorm some ways that you can offer your time, talent, or resources to the components of that list. For instance, if higher education is important to you and your college experience was special to you, giving back to your alma mater may be essential. Others may want to offer their resources to a cause that is important to them. If you value environmental sustainability, you will purchase sustainable products and avoid supporting companies that have a poor environmental record. You may even choose to make small donations to an environmental charity of your choice, while you are in your working career and have the financial means to do so. What do you want your legacy to be? If you can answer this question, then you have some very deep insight into your values, which ultimately will guide how you choose to make financial decisions.

The question about your legacy should perhaps have been asked at the outset of this book. If you can answer this question now, it will shape your career decisions, your saving and budgeting strategy, your decisions about mortgages and investments and retirement accounts, and every other financial decision you will make over the course of your life. If you can answer this question now, you will hopefully be able to look back and say that you lived your financial life in accordance with your values, and that doing so has provided the means for you to leave the legacy that you wish to leave. At the end of the day, that's all you will have—a legacy. But you can start living that legacy now through stewardship in your financial decision-making. Best of luck on your journey.

Key Takeaways

Directions: Review the following list of key takeaways to help you remember what you learned in this chapter:

- Saving for retirement is much easier when you are young. All you have to do in your twenties is start the savings process for retirement and resist the temptations to use those funds for other life events if you can.

28. Eva Kahana, Tirth Bhatta, Loren D. Lovegreen, Boaz Kahana, and Elizabeth Midlarsky, "Altruism, Helping, and Volunteering: Pathways to Well-Being in Late Life," *Journal of Aging and Health* 25, no. 1 (2013): 159–87.

- The reality is that most of us do not save enough for retirement. There are lots of reasons for this, but surprisingly, the lack of planning and commitment is not all based on income.
- Even if you are not ready to answer key retirement questions yet, having a sense of savings targets is important, to keep you headed in the right direction during your career. Knowing the questions that those who are closer to retirement need to think about may be enough as a young person beginning a career.
- For many Americans, Social Security has been left to close the gap in retirement savings for the baby boomers. Unfortunately, it is not the best idea for younger generations to count on that. Though the program is not likely to go away, it is likely that benefits will get pushed back and be made smaller over time.
- Your legacy is one of the most important decisions you can think about and plan for now because by determining what you want to leave behind, and by allocating resources in that direction, you can make purposeful decisions today that will help you stick to your financial plan over the long term.

Application Opportunity: Do This Now!

Directions: Complete the activities below to apply what you have learned in this chapter.

Activity 1

How much do you need to save for retirement? Pretend that you have just graduated and have just started your first job ...

Go to the retirement calculator at: http://www.calcxml.com/calculators/retirement-calculator?skn=606

1. Input the values provided below under Scenario #1 into the calculator and click Submit. Now report the Results you found in the three boxes below the inputs for the first Scenario #1 column.
2. Conduct a scenario analysis, where you look at a minimum of two additional scenarios for yourself. You can look at yourself at different stages in your life, give yourself a spouse, change your retirement age, change inflation or the returns you will get pre- and postretirement, or include Social Security benefits in the process. If you change only one thing at a time, you may be able to see a pattern for your retirement needs. Remember to **reset** the calculator each time you enter a different scenario. Fill in the rest of the table and report your results in the table below.

	Scenario #1	Scenario #2	Scenario #3
Income/Savings			
Current age	21		
Income	$50,000		
Retirement age	65		
Spouse's annual income ($)	$0		
Current retirement savings	$0		
Desired retirement age	65		
Number of years of retirement income	20		
Assumptions			
Expected inflation (%)	3%		
Income replacement at retirement (%)	75%		
Preretirement investment return (%)	8%		
Postretirement investment return (%)	8%		
Total retirement amount needed			
% of income that needs to be saved per year			
$ amount of income to save per year			
$ amount of income to save per month			

3. Write up to one page where you compare and contrast the results above. Can you see patterns in your calculations? Do you have weird results? Which factors in this decision are important to you? Can you do the saving you need to do?

Bibliography

American Association of Retired Persons. "AARP Retirement Calculator: Are You Saving Enough?" Updated July 1, 2019. https://www.aarp.org/work/retirement-planning/retirement_calculator.html.

———. "How Much Social Security Will I Get?" Retirement: Social Security Resource Center. December 23, 2020. https://www.aarp.org/retirement/social-security/questions-answers/how-much-social-security-will-i-get.html.

Carpenter, Julia. "Your Parents' Financial Advice Is (Kind of) Wrong." *The Wall Street Journal*, September 16, 2019. https://www.wsj.com/articles/your-parents-financial-advice-is-kind-of-wrong-11568367000.

Center on Budget and Policy Priorities. "Top Ten Facts about Social Security." August 30, 2020. https://www.cbpp.org/sites/default/files/atoms/files/8-8-16socsec.pdf.

Cooley, Phillip L., Carl M. Hubbard, and Daniel T. Walz. "Retirement Savings: Choosing a Withdrawal Rate That Is Sustainable." *AAII Journal* 20, no. 2 (1998): 16–21.

Economic Policy Institute. "The Cost of Child Care in ___." Updated October 2020. https://www.epi.org/child-care-costs-in-the-united-states/#/WY.

Employee Benefit Research Institute and Greenwald & Associates. *2020 Retirement Confidence Survey Summary Report.* April 23, 2020. https://www.ebri.org/docs/default-source/rcs/2020-rcs/2020-rcs-summary-report.pdf?sfvrsn=84bc3d2.

Fidelity Viewpoints. "How Much Will You Spend in Retirement?" April 9, 2019. https://www.fidelity.com/viewpoints/retirement/spending-in-retirement.

Fidelity Viewpoints. "How Much Will You Spend in Retirement?" August 27, 2021. https://www.fidelity.com/viewpoints/retirement/how-much-do-i-need-to-retire.

Giese, Guido, Linda-Eling Lee, Dimitris Melas, Zoltán Nagy, and Laura Nishikawa. "Foundations of ESG Investing: How ESG Affects Equity Valuation, Risk, and Performance." *The Journal of Portfolio Management* 45, no. 5 (2019): 69–83.

JEC Republicans and Senator Mike Lee. "Saving and COVID-19." United States Congress Joint Economic Committee. September 30, 2020. https://www.jec.senate.gov/public/index.cfm/republicans/analysis?ID=754B52C6-04CD-458B-8755-98D1219398F1.

J.P. Morgan. "Learn the Seven Principles for a Successful Retirement." *J.P Morgan: Asset Management.* https://am.jpmorgan.com/us/en/asset-management/adv/insights/retirement-insights/principles/

Kahana, Eva, Tirth Bhatta, Loren D. Lovegreen, Boaz Kahana, and Elizabeth Midlarsky. "Altruism, Helping, and Volunteering: Pathways to Well-Being in Late Life." *Journal of Aging and Health* 25, no. 1 (2013): 159–87.

Kaplan, Greg, Giovanni L. Violante, and Justin Weidner. "The Wealthy Hand-to-Mouth" [Working paper 20073]. National Bureau of Economic Research. https://www.nber.org/system/files/working_papers/w20073/w20073.pdf.

Lin, Judy T., Christopher Bumcrot, Tippy Ulicny, Gary Mottola, Gerri Walsh, Robert Ganem, Christine Kieffer, and Annamaria Lusardi. "The State of U.S. Financial Capability: The 2018 National Financial Capability Study." FINRA Investor Education Foundation. June 2019. https://www.usfinancialcapability.org/downloads/NFCS.

Mercado, Darla. "Retiring This Year? How Much You'll Need for Health-Care Costs." *CNBC*, July 18, 2019. https://www.cnbc.com/2019/07/18/retiring-this-year-how-much-youll-need-for-health-care-costs.html.

Oakley, Diane, and Kelly Kenneally. "Retirement Security 2017: A Roadmap for Policy Makers: Americans' Views of the Retirement Crisis and Solutions." National Institute on Retirement Security. February 2017. https://www.nirsonline.org/wp-content/uploads/2017/06/2017_opinion_nirs_final_web.pdf.

RBC Wealth Management. "Health Care: The Real Cost of Health Care in Retirement." Accessed March 15, 2021. https://www.rbcwealthmanagement.com/us/en/research-insights/the-real-cost-of-health-care-in-retirement/detail/.

Rhee, Nari, and Ilana Boivie. "The Continuing Retirement Savings Crisis." National Institute on Retirement Security. March 2015. https://www.nirsonline.org/wp-content/uploads/2017/07/final_rsc_2015.pdf.

Sallie Mae & Ipsos. *How America Saves for College 2018.* 2018. https://www.salliemae.com/assets/about/who_we_are/HAS2018_Full_Report.pdf.

Social Security Administration. "Status of the Social Security and Medicare Programs: A Summary of the 2020 Annual Reports." Accessed April 15, 2021. https://www.ssa.gov/oact/trsum/.

———. *Understanding the Benefits.* May 2021. https://www.ssa.gov/pubs/EN-05-10024.pdf.

———. "Workers with Maximum-Taxable Earnings." Accessed May 13, 2021. https://www.ssa.gov/oact/cola/examplemax.html.

Stark, Ellen. *Expanding Retirement Security through Public and Private Innovation.* Aspen Institute Financial Security Program. September 2018. https://assets.aspeninstitute.org/content/uploads/2018/08/2018_RetirementSavingsReport.pdf.

Survey of Consumer Finances (SCF), 1989-2019. *Board of Governors of the Federal Reserve System.* https://www.federalreserve.gov/econres/scf/dataviz/scf/chart/#series:Retirement_Accounts;demographic:agecl;population:1,2,3,4;units:median;range:1989,2019

TD Ameritrade. *Road to Retirement Survey: Evolving Timelines, Expectations and Investments.* January 2020. https://s2.q4cdn.com/437609071/files/doc_news/research/2020/road-to-retirement-survey.pdf.

T.Rowe Price. "You're Age 35, 50, or 60: How Much Should You have Saved for Retirement by Now?" May 2022. https://www.troweprice.com/personal-investing/resources/insights/youre-age-35-50-or-60-how-much-should-you-have-by-now.html

US Bureau of Economic Analysis. "Personal Saving Rate (PSAVERT) 1970–2020." FRED, Federal Reserve Bank of St. Louis. June 17, 2021. https://fred.stlouisfed.org/series/PSAVERT.

US Bureau of Labor Statistics. "Table 3. Median Usual Weekly Earnings of Full-Time Wage and Salary Workers by Age, Race, Hispanic or Latino Ethnicity, and Sex, Fourth Quarter 2020 Averages, Not Seasonally Adjusted." Economics news release. January 21, 2021. https://www.bls.gov/news.release/wkyeng.t03.htm.

Figure Credits

Fig. 7.1: Source: Data from https://www.troweprice.com/personal-investing/resources/insights/youre-age-35-50-or-60-how-much-should-you-have-by-now.html, https://am.jpmorgan.com/us/en/asset-management/adv/insights/retirement-insights/principles/, and https://www.fidelit.

Fig. 7.2: Source: https://www.federalreserve.gov/econres/scf/dataviz/scf/chart/#series:Retirement_Accounts;demographic:agecl;population:1,2,3,4;units:median;range:1989,2019"; https://www.federalreserve.gov/econres/scf/dataviz/scf/chart/#series:Retirement_Accounts;demographic:agecl;population:1,2,3,4;units:median;range:1989,2019.

AFTERWORD

Financial Literacy Education Efficacy

There is a lot to learn before you become financially literate. When I was in college thirty years ago, no one worried about whether students had instruction in the content of this book. It was assumed that a good liberal arts education would provide all those students needed in the way of critical thinking skills to tackle little financial decisions. The fact is that Americans are not saving what they need for an easy retirement. Booming technology advances mean that good people can get themselves into dangerous investing choices very easily nowadays. Student loan debt and skyrocketing housing bubbles mean that the path to the American Dream remains obscured from view for the young. And the Great Recession of 2008 and the COVID-19 pandemic of 2020 have shown that all we work toward can be taken away in the blink of an eye, in an increasingly volatile market. Suddenly, a little focused education on the best practices for financial stability is not only a decent idea, but also increasingly essential.

It may surprise you to learn that the research on financial literacy education largely shows that students don't learn very much in the typical financial literacy course.[1] This is especially true when the financial decisions being discussed will be made far in the future. Further, the content that was learned degrades over the next two years following completion of the course. For me, this news is disheartening, but for our nation, this evidence is devastating because US citizens have demonstrated that they need the skills and knowledge found in this book to enhance their own well-being.

This means that you have the best shot of remembering what you learned if you put the principles into practice right away, as you need them. Don't wait to do the

1. For particularly good examples of the issues, see: Daniel Fernandes, John G. Lynch, Jr., and Richard G. Netemeyer, "Financial Literacy, Financial Education, and Downstream Financial Behaviors," *Management Science* 60, no. 8 (2014): 1861–83; and Pamela M. LaBorde, Sandra Mottner, and Pamela Whalley, "Personal Financial Literacy: Perceptions of Knowledge, Actual Knowledge and Behavior of College Students," *Journal of Financial Education* 39, no. 3/4 (2013): 1–30.

budgeting. Try to budget on your student salary. Save 10 percent of whatever income you have at this point so that you are practicing good saving principles. As you move into your career, make the match from your employer, and choose your retirement savings allocation thoughtfully.

The Department of the Treasury has been tasked with solving the puzzle of what financial literacy education needs to look like so that the ideas and the skills developed stick with students after they are exposed to them. A 2019 report from the US Financial Literacy and Education Commission addresses the best practices for educating the future workforce at the college level. They present the following as "Best Practices:"[2]

- Know the individuals and families to be served
- Provide actionable, relevant, and timely information
- Improve key financial skills
- Build on motivations
- Make it easy to make good decisions and follow through

Your college or university will have to work together across departments to achieve these best practices. The academic piece—the content of this book—is one important part, but having financial aid, student life, and labor on board (if the school has a Labor Department) to address individual student situations and provide financial coaching throughout the four years will help solidify the knowledge and skill set in this book. Making best practices easy to follow while you are young will likely build good practices as you get older.

This book has addressed that knowledge and skill development in the following ways.

Financial Decisions as Investments

Every financial decision you make is an investment in something. The chapter titles in this book have tried to show you that all the decisions you will make—the decisions to be financially literate, to save, to spend, to owe, and so on—are all investments with *choices*. They are choices you make to invest in your future, your vocation, yourself, your well-being now, the market, or your financial independence. If you *choose* to live in New York City after your graduation, you get a package of opportunities that includes vibrant energy, restaurants, and culture, but you will

2. U.S. Financial Literacy and Education Commission, *Best Practices for Financial Literacy and Education at Institutions of Higher Education*, U.S. Department of the Treasury, 2019, https://home.treasury.gov/system/files/136/Best-Practices-for-Financial-Literacy-and-Education-at-Institutions-of-Higher-Education2019.pdf?utm_content=&utm_medium=email&utm_name=&utm_source=govdeliver.

find certain costs too, like congestion, crowds, and rental costs. If you actively save for retirement as soon as you begin your career, you will set yourself up for the retirement you want tomorrow, but you may have to forego a few wants today. The popular financial coach Dave Ramsey might say, "Live today like no one else, so that you can live tomorrow like no one else." I think he means that resources are limited, that we all make choices, and that while many people choose to spend their resources now, you can make the choice to use your resources in such a way that they will give you a life well-lived. A life that is consistently stable across all stages, from career to retirement. The book is designed around making the choices that are best in your circumstances.

The financial decisions discussed in this book are the ones most relevant to you as a young adult in college. The chapters in the book are structured around questions that students before you have raised. There is other financial information that may not seem applicable to you yet. Textbooks tend to be very "listy," full of checklists and choices, delivered in a formal, dry way. In regard to retirement, for example, they might dive right into the different types of retirement plans available: employer-sponsored plans, the Keogh plan, a Roth IRA— an overwhelming amount of information, little details, and facts. But you, and students before you, have asked a much more important question: how is all of this relevant to me? A memorable student once asked, "Ain't I too young to think about retirement?" Yes, but you are not too young to think about saving for it. This book has attempted to step back and think about the issues from your perspective, to fill in some of the details, but to deliver the necessary information ***as a starting point***. I wanted to open up a conversation with you.

The approach in this book recognizes that the material you are learning is more about process and general guidelines than about specific information. I want you to know what to look for on Google as you become ready to make a big decision. Things change, and what works today may be different in even five years, so I apply the ideas in this book to imaginary people in typical situations, showing you how their decisions could play out later. There are many free resources out there, for those that know what to look for. Hopefully, now you have a better idea of where to look for information when you need it. You are at the start of your financial journey, and you will learn more and more as you work your way through the opportunities that naturally arise for all of us.

The Cycle of Living Paycheck to Paycheck

One best practice for teachers of financial literacy is to know you, the student, and be able to talk specifically to the financial issues you are facing.

Some of you have been taught very different financial lessons, growing up, from the ones taught in this book. The lessons on responsible credit card use and on development of a good credit score are immediate examples of ideas that could go against the grain of everything you know to be true from personal experience. The extreme response to never use credit, to go off the grid and pay for everything with cash, is a reasonable response if your experience has shown you many people who fell into bad credit card experiences. That is a choice, and it emphasizes safety. You cannot get into trouble with your credit cards if you don't have any!

The ingrained nature of what some of you have been taught, and what you have seen, can leave you in a cycle of financial decisions that may make it more difficult for you to thrive. Students will often remark, "How can I make a budget, when I can't even cover my bills?" The idea of saving anything can seem impossible. But you are not stuck here.

If you are in college or have graduated from college, that education gives you the greatest chance to break the chain of living paycheck to paycheck. You can choose your career and develop the skills you need to succeed in the labor market. Use college as a fabulous opportunity to develop the skills that employers want. Put yourself in a good place for employment. That means not treating your education like a checklist to be ticked off. That means engaging with the development of your brain and actively seeking to build it, as it is the engine that will make you valuable in the workforce. What you construct in college are the tools for financial stability; try not to take this for granted by settling for "just getting by" in the classes you choose.

In all of this, you get to ***choose***. You get to make decisions. If you want to change some of the things that you experienced or saw others experience, you can. This does not have to be a statement about the important people in your life, either. They can still be the ones you look up to and seek to care for as they age. It may be part of your culture to take on the debts of your parents and to care for them as they get older. You can still do this and be financially literate at the same time. The key is to know and understand your choices and to plan.

Knowledge Is Power, Time Is Money, and Planning Is Everything

This little book is only the beginning. and what I have really sought to do is provide you with some places to go to research the financial choices that are right for you when you are ready to make the actual choices. Sometimes it can be difficult to see how some of these choices will apply to you. Even though the book was designed in a wholly practical way, for many of you, the idea of figuring out how to buy a house might still seem like a very faraway thing. In today's housing market, this is very likely the case because housing prices have shot through the roof! The point is that the actual decision you make is less important than the three big takeaways from the book.

First: ***knowledge is power***. If you can understand the trade-offs of the choices you make, you can make the decisions that are right for you and your circumstances. So, if you have a hard time saving, be sure to save before the money ever hits your checking account. This is the principle *pay yourself first*. If you plan to help your kids with college bills, you may plan to stay in the workforce a few extra years, or maybe decide that you don't need a pool with your house. This is the principle behind "The Decision to Spend."

Second: ***time is money***. Time is your best asset as a young person. Use it while it can do the most for you. This means you skip something you want to spend money on if it allows you to make the employer match in the retirement plan. This means you commit to building your emergency savings first, so that when the time comes, you are not placed in a financially distressed situation that can set all your plans back.

Third: ***planning is everything***. You can accommodate almost any individual circumstance if you plan for it. After spending four years of your life, maybe five or six, to obtain your education, you have worked and studied too hard to take a job that does not feed your vocational aspirations. Plan for what that career looks like. Give yourself the gift of the retirement you want after you finish your career. It will take a little planning. Take the time to do that.

Give yourself the gift and practice of financial literacy. You deserve it.

Bibliography

Fernandes, Daniel, John G. Lynch, Jr., and Richard G. Netemeyer. "Financial Literacy, Financial Education, and Downstream Financial Behaviors." *Management Science* 60, no. 8 (2014): 1861–83.

Fox, Jonathan, Suzanne Bartholomae, and Jinkook Lee. "Building the Case for Financial Education." *Journal of Consumer Affairs* 39, no. 1 (2005): 195–214.

Huston, Sandra J. "Measuring Financial Literacy." *Journal of Consumer Affairs* 44, no. 2 (2010): 296–316.

Jacobsen, Christopher, and Joao Correia. "Analysis of Financial Literacy in a College Population." *Journal of Higher Education Theory & Practice* 19, no. 4 (2019). https://doi.org/10.33423/jhetp.v19i4.2197.

LaBorde, Pamela M., Sandra Mottner, and Pamela Whalley. "Personal Financial Literacy: Perceptions of Knowledge, Actual Knowledge and Behavior of College Students." *Journal of Financial Education* 39, no. 3/4 (2013): 1–30.

U.S. Financial Literacy and Education Commission. *Best Practices for Financial Literacy and Education at Institutions of Higher Education*. U.S. Department of the Treasury. 2019. https://home.treasury.gov/system/files/136/Best-Practices-for-Financial-Literacy-and-Education-at-Institutions-of-Higher-Education2019.pdf?utm_content=&utm_medium=email&utm_name=&utm_source=govdeliver

www.ingramcontent.com/pod-product-compliance
Lightning Source LLC
LaVergne TN
LVHW080050210926
848481LV00011B/3322